RESOURCE CENTRE

From Prejudice to Genocide

From Prejudice to Genocide

Genocide

Learning about the Holocaust

Carrie Supple

tb

Trentham Books

First published in 1993 by Trentham Books Limited

Trentham Books Limited
Westview House
734 London Road
Oakhill
Stoke-on-Trent
Staffordshire
England ST4 5NP

British Library Cataloguing Publication Data
A catalogue record for this book is available from the British Library.

ISBN: 0 948080 60 4

Designed and typeset by Trentham Print Design Limited and printed in Great Britain by Bemrose Shafron Limited, Chester

Contents

Acknowledgements

My thanks go first to Nick Hudson, the father of this book and to my own father for his advice and inspiration.

I want to thank Sharon Gerwirtz, who spent hours scrutinising the text and became resident consultant.

Gillian Klein was my trusting editor. She eased the path to publication, giving her time and expertise and saying all the soothing things a first-time author needs to hear.

I am indebted to Martin Gilbert for his generosity and for guiding me with invaluable references, information and encouragement.

Rabbi Douglas Charing, Chris Culpin, Ronnie Landau, Ralph Levinson and Barry Troyna all helped me transform the idea of a book into practice and I am very grateful to them.

Then there are the institutions whose resources and staff were crucial to the project. In particular: Jan-Eric Dubbelmann, Dienke Hondius and Cornelius Suijk and the Anne Frank Centre (Amsterdam), Marc Skvirsky and *Facing History and Ourselves* (USA); Gerry Gable and Tony Robson of *Searchlight* (London); Trudy Gold and the Spiro Institute for the Study of Jewish History and Culture (London); The Holocaust Education Trust; Elizabeth Boggis, David Cesarani and Tony Wells of the Wiener Library (London).

Special thanks must go to Steve Ayris, my head of Department. He has been helpful beyond the call of duty, or at least has bitten his tongue for four and a half years.

Gerry Miller and Colin Quigley read the whole manuscript and their unfailing support and feeling for the book has meant a lot to me.

For their help with translations, thinking of a title, reading specific chapters or advising on sources, I thank: Phil Andre, Gail Baker, Rabbi Tony Bayfield, Audrey Black, Deborah Burnstone, Vhairi Cardinal, Alan, Eric and Ian

Caller, Bruce Carrington, David Cebon, Bryan Cheyette, Duncan Churchill, Steve Cohen (USA), Roy Deane, Kenneth East, Len Edmondson, Tony Edwards, Sol Factor (USA), Peter Fisher, Jacob Gewirtz, Ofer Gidulter (Israel), Ela Ginalska, Gaby Glassman, Peter Gordon, Mark Graham, Jeremy Green, John Hajnal, Ben Helfgott, Alan Heinzman, Gordon Hogg, Nigel Hopper, Helen House, Diane Irving, June and Robin Jacobs, Marion Josephs, Doreen Joslin, Hugh Kelly, Donald Kenrick, Steve King, Reva Klein, Agnes Kohl (Germany), Tony Kushner, Jude Lancet, Ian Lister, Herbert Loebl, Ora Margoliot (Israel), Chris Mason, Ben and Vladka Meed (USA), Tony Moran, Shirley Murgraff, Tom Odley, Ken Oldfield, Des O'Reilly, Carol Pickard, Esther Polden, Joyce Purves, Lawrence Ranson, Mark Robinson, Dave Rosenberg, Laurie Rosenberg, Patrick Salmon, Don Salter, Ruth Schamroth, Viv Schwartzberg, Walter Sharman, Chris Skelton, Martin Smidman, Simcha Stein (Israel), Steve Sunderland (USA), Paul Vigveno (Holland), Ellen Weber (USA), Betty and Bob Weiner and Jay Winter.

The most formidable readers were probably my own students, current and former pupils of Seaton Burn Community High School, North Tyneside, in particular: David Felton, Kay Gibson, Joanne Grisdale, Garry Harbottle, Sarah Hasney, Steven Knaggs, Christine Smith, Craig Smith and Phil Tatham.

I also appreciate the contribution of staff and pupils who gave me their time during my research into the teaching of the Holocaust in autumn 1989 and everyone involved with making the video in 1990.

John Stipling and his son Shawn made it all look like a book, with infinite patience, and there are scores of people who have kindly responded to requests for information, contacts or finances.

In April 1992, I visited the village of Amstibava in Western Belorussia, where my mother's father was born. It was not an easy trip. I believe that all the Jews there, except for one man, were murdered in 1941. The effects of finding out about the Holocaust are profound and difficult to articulate. One of them, for me, was a need for love and warmth while I was exposed to such destruction and indifference. Thanks to everyone who, by their friendship or interest sustained me, above all to my parents and brothers Dave and Tim.

During my research I met and came to know some very special people. This book is dedicated to four of them: Esther, Harry, Liesl and Werner.

Foreword

This book examines the attempt by the Nazis to destroy all the Jews of Europe between 1941 and 1945. Considerable difficulty exists in explaining the origins and causes of this terrible crime. Other attempts at genocide, such as the slaughter of the Armenians at the time of the First World War, and the killing of Gypsies in the Second World War, are likewise on a scale of cruelty difficult to understand, even for adults.

Carrie Supple has sought in this book to make these terrifying aspects of recent history clear and explicable to students and teachers alike. She gives them a detailed account of the nature of what is now known as the Holocaust: the mass murder of six million people who were killed, for no other reason than because they were born Jewish.

The evidence that Carrie Supple presents, and the questions she poses, will provoke considerable thought and help students more easily understand what Churchill referred to as 'probably the greatest and most horrible crime in the whole history of the world'.

In raising wider issues such as racism and obedience, Carrie Supple has also brought the relevance of the events of half a century ago into the context of the contemporary world, and raises the issue of the involvement of people in the continuing human tragedies of our time in many parts of the globe.

Martin Gilbert
Merton College, Oxford
September 1992

Preface

- Who are the people being arrested?
- Which country are they in?
- When did this happen?
- Why are they being arrested?
- Who is arresting them?
- Where are they going?
- Why did it happen?

Are there any other questions you would ask about the picture?

There is a long tradition in world history of regarding certain groups of people as less than human. Racism*, prejudice and discrimination have led to persecution and murder, and sometimes even to attempts at genocide.

But never before has there been an attempt to kill every man, woman, child and baby of a particular group of people in this way — with factories built for the killing and plans to make use of the hair, skin and gold teeth of the dead. Never, until the Holocaust.

Today, most people define the Holocaust as the murder of six million Jews by the Nazis and their helpers during the Second World War (1939-1945). Death camps were specially built for the murder of Jews. But there were thousands of other people gassed and burned with them, including half a million Gypsies.

Millions of Soviet prisoners-of-war suffered on a terrible scale, most left to starve and freeze to death in vast barbed wire enclosures. Poles, communists, trade unionists, gays, disabled people, Jehovah's Witnesses, Catholics and anti-Nazis from all over Europe were also considered 'unworthy of life'.

The numbers are beyond comprehension. We can perhaps only begin to imagine something of what they experienced by hearing the voices of individuals who lived and died through those times.

From Prejudice to Genocide combines an historical account with themes and questions which encourage students to think about the events described in relation to their own lives and choices. It provides a wide range of written and visual sources, many of them original, such as translations of interviews with ex-SS men, applications for immigration to the UK and USA, and the memories of a British woman who was a guard at the Belsen trials. Every chapter contains the words and pictures of named individuals, including perpetrators, victims, collaborators, 'bystanders', resistance workers and rescuers. The stories of four survivors: Esther Brunstein, Werner Mayer, Harry Nagelsztajn and Liesl Silverstone are included in the book. They speak of their lives before, during and after the Holocaust in the video *Where Shall We Go?* (see p.307)

Research for this book began in January 1988 and involved consultation with educationalists in Britain, Germany, Austria, Holland, the USA and Israel.

The text and tasks have been written to fulfil the requirements of GCSE and the National Curriculum History attainment targets, with specific reference to Key Stage Three Core Study Unit, *The Era of the Second World War*. It includes sources and questions relating to the study of English, RE, Personal and Social Education and Social Studies. Guidelines on p.300-1 include

* Certain concepts are explained in the text, but a Glossary clarifies some of the terms relating specifically to the period.

suggestions for implementing key skills, dimensions and themes of the National Curriculum. Having been entirely left out of the original proposals, the Holocaust now forms a part of our secondary school curriculum. Despite its allocation as part of a larger topic, using the flexibility which will inevitably emerge, and with staff ingenuity, time can be made for in-depth and cross-curricular study.

The book is written for use in the classroom or for staff reference and has been widely tested by pupils in the 13-18 age range and staff of all the above disciplines. It is born out of frustration with the textbooks which cover the Holocaust in half a page accompanied by a photograph of corpses.

We cannot begin to understand the origins of the Holocaust without looking at the state of Europe at the turn of this century, in particular the position of Jewish people in European society. And to understand that, we need to look back at least four hundred years, if not three thousand. You can be sure about very few things in History. But you *can* be sure that the Holocaust did not happen simply because 'the Germans hated the Jews' or because 'Hitler was mad'. The story is much, much more complicated than that.

We need to know what motivated those who planned the Holocaust and those who carried it out. Although it was called the Nazi Holocaust, they could never have achieved it alone. Nazis were nowhere in the majority. So why did so many ordinary people, from France to Russia, make the Nazi's genocidal plans easier? What about those who knew what was happening, hated it, but did nothing to prevent it? What made their neighbour risk her or his own life by becoming a rescuer of victims of the Nazis? And how did the victims respond to being hunted, herded and wrenched from family and friends?

The Holocaust is part of the history of not just these people nor, as many think, of Jewish history. The Holocaust is part of the history of humankind. As such it should be part of the education of all children.

Note: The letters CE and BCE which appear after dates in this book denote Common Era and Before the Common Era. They refer to the period starting in AD1, as the Christian Era.

Chapter One

The Jews of Europe — from BCE to 1918

Europe, like every continent, is a huge mixture of ethnic, cultural, religious and national groups.

Think of as many of these groups as you can.

Europe will be the focus of this book, since the Holocaust happened there, but people and governments from every continent were involved.

There has been continuous migration within and between countries during the twentieth century. There are Turkish workers in Germany, Yugoslavs in Sweden and Algerians in France. In Inner London alone, almost 200 different languages are spoken.

Jewish people and Gypsies are two groups who first came from outside Europe but have settled throughout the Continent.

Although their lifestyles are very different, the treatment of the two groups has often been similar, varying between acceptance and persecution. Because they were singled out during the Holocaust, the following two chapters focus on their experience in European history.

There are many reasons why people migrate from one country to another and within a country. Think of as many as you can.

Jewish people, originally living in the area now known as Israel, began to arrive in Europe over two thousand years ago.

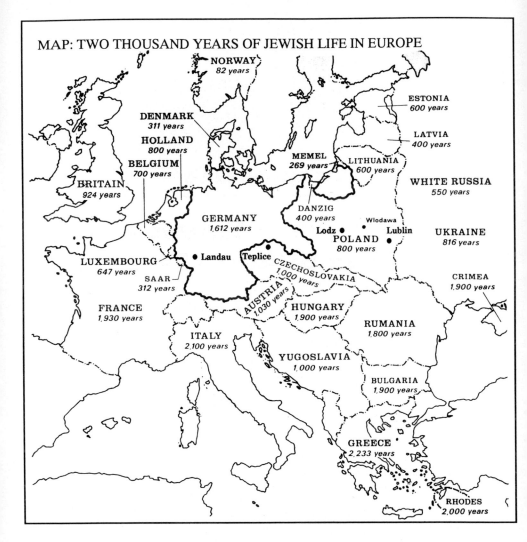

MAP: TWO THOUSAND YEARS OF JEWISH LIFE IN EUROPE

NORWAY
82 years

ESTONIA
600 years

DENMARK
311 years

LATVIA
400 years

HOLLAND
800 years

MEMEL
269 years

LITHUANIA
600 years

BELGIUM
700 years

WHITE RUSSIA
550 years

BRITAIN
924 years

DANZIG
400 years

Wlodawa

GERMANY
1,612 years

Lodz ●

Lublin ●

UKRAINE
816 years

POLAND
800 years

LUXEMBOURG
647 years

● Landau

Teplice

CZECHOSLOVAKIA
1,000 years

CRIMEA
1,900 years

SAAR
312 years

AUSTRIA
1,030 years

HUNGARY
1,900 years

FRANCE
1,930 years

RUMANIA
1,800 years

ITALY
2,100 years

YUGOSLAVIA
1,000 years

BULGARIA
1,900 years

GREECE
2,233 years

RHODES
2,000 years

By 1930, there were approximately thirteen million Jews living in Europe. Some were very religious, some lived in Jewish communities within towns or villages, others were totally assimilated (part of the society where they lived) and felt more French, Greek or German than Jewish. There were Jewish farmers, bankers, writers, shopkeepers, factory workers, teachers, singers and doctors. Divisions within Jewish communities have always existed, over religion, politics, how much they should assimilate and how to respond to antisemitism.

Top: Austrian Jewish athletes, Alfred König and Gerda Gottlieb, 1936.
Above: Tailors' workshop of Philip Weitz near Whitechapel Road, London. c. 1914.

Isaac Caller and Sons, cabinet makers, outside their workshop in Killingworth Place, Newcastle-upon-Tyne. c. 1910. The Caller family arrived in Newcastle in the late 19th century. They came from the village of Amstibava in Western Belorussia.

In Germany, Jews formed under one per cent of the population in 1933 (500,000 people in a total population of seventy million). Half were married to non-Jews, and they were to be found in virtually every section of society. For example, just over two per cent of professionals were Jewish and 31,000 Jews were receiving charity. Generally, German Jews felt a sense of belonging: they were a part of German life: its music, literature and art.

Werner Mayer

Werner was born on 27th December 1921 in Landau, South West Germany (see map p.2). His parents were Eugen and Mathilde. They owned a bakery and Eugen served in the German army in 1914-1918. Werner's sister Ilse was born in 1919.

Source 1

Life was very normal before the Nazis came to power. I lived the life of an ordinary schoolchild. I was a Mummy's boy. I took great pride in polishing and making myself useful in the kitchen. My favourite position was underneath a table, elbows dug in the floor and nose in a book. Ilse, on the other hand, enjoyed street games. Willi and Gerda (friends from a communist, Christian family) who lived across the street, were part of our club. At Chanukah, the Jewish Feast of Lights, they would come to our house for nuts and sweets. (Werner)

Look at the photographs of Jewish life and Werner's introduction (Source 1). Explain how some people in Europe were Jewish and at the same time a part of the society they lived in.

Left: Werner
Below: Werner, with his mother and sister.

Above left: Esther, aged 3, with her brothers David and Peretz.
Above right: Esther with her cousin Emmanuel and brother Peretz, March 1939.

In Poland, there were approximately three million Jewish people out of a total population of thirty-five million in 1930. Forty five per cent of them were craftworkers or industrial workers. Most Jews lived in urban areas. There was a thriving Jewish culture, with Yiddish and Hebrew literature, music, Jewish schools, charities, Zionist groups, athletic clubs, theatres and a strong socialist movement, dominated by the Bund (Jewish Socialists). As a result of years of violent attacks (*pogroms*) and antisemitic laws, some of the Jews of Poland had developed a tradition of armed self-defence.

Esther Brunstein (neé Zylberberg)

Esther was born on the 6th of May in 1928 in Lodz, Poland (see map p.2). Her parents were Philip and Sara, Philip was a foreman and trade union official in a weaving factory. She had two brothers, Peretz and David.

Source 2

I had a very happy home life, very secure. As a child, life was very interesting. I attended a Yiddish-speaking secular school. My parents were involved in a movement that was going to shape the world (the Bund) and I grew up with a strong sense of love for everybody. I lived in a block of flats which wasn't exclusively Jewish. I had a friend Halina, her family used to invite me in for the Christmas. She was nice, her brother was very nice, her mother was nice but her father was a vicious antisemite. (Esther)

Unlike Germany, in Poland there were very few mixed marriages and Jewish people were not so assimilated, though some were. Indeed Jews were among the leading Polish-language writers and journalists, fully participating in the life of the newly (since 1919) independent Poland.

1. What does Esther mean when she says Halina's father was 'a vicious antisemite'?

2. What similarities and differences are there between Esther and Werner's lives (Sources 1 and 2)? Think about their family, friends, attitude to religion etc.

A history of Antisemitism BCE — 1918

The history of antisemitism is very complicated. Its origins are religious, political, economic and social.

Hitler did not invent antisemitism nor the persecution of the Gypsies. He built on foundations which had existed for hundreds of years. It is impossible to understand how the Holocaust could have happened without knowing something about the long history of antisemitism. The way the Nazis described Jews, the way they made them look and the laws they passed against them, were all based on descriptions, pictures and laws which Europeans had seen and heard long before.

For nearly two thousand years, the Christian Church was hostile to Judaism and helped fan the flames of hatred.

The Gypsies have experienced a similar pattern of restriction, exclusion and extermination — though there are many differences between the two histories. Both Jews and Gypsies have settled throughout Europe, living amongst others without fully assimilating. Despite continuing persecution, both have kept their identity and exist in parts of Europe as distinct communities. Both their histories include periods of happiness and achievement. However, the focus of the following two chapters will be on their persecution.

Who are the Jews?

Today, Jewish people make up 0.27 per cent of the world's population. They are referred to as a nation, a religion, a People and a race. They live on every Continent and in virtually every country, there are Iranian, Ethiopian, Latin American, Indian and Swedish Jews. Anyone can convert to Judaism (although there is no proseletising) and many Jews marry non-Jews. The majority are not religious. Many identify with the history or culture of the Jews, whichever country they live in. They perhaps celebrate the main Jewish holy days of Rosh Hashana, Yom Kippur and Passover.

7

Above: Rabbi Jacobs, Harlem, New York, 1933

Left: Jewish girls. Morocco

1. Give two reasons why it is inaccurate to refer to Jews as a 'race'. Use the photographs to support your answer.

2. What do you understand by: 'Many identify with the history and culture of the Jews?'

Abraham, who lived 3500 years ago, is usually thought of as the first Jew. The Bible describes him as having been born in Mesopotamia (modern Iraq). The Jews were the first to believe in just one God instead of many. Religious Jews believe Abraham promised that he and his family would worship God and that all males would be circumcised as a mark of their faith. In return, they believe, God promised to look after Abraham and his descendants and give them the land now called Israel (then called Canaan).

On their way there, the Jews wandered into Egypt, where they were taken as slaves. In 1250 BCE Moses led them out of slavery towards the 'Promised Land'. Religious Jews believe that, while in the Sinai desert, God gave Moses the Torah (the Law, including the Ten Commandments, the five books of Moses from Genesis to Deuteronomy in the Bible). The Torah is the foundation of Jewish teaching and from it are derived the 613 rules about worship and daily life. Part of it is read every Saturday during the Sabbath service in synagogue.

Source 3

When Abram was ninety-nine years old, the LORD appeared to him and said... As an everlasting possession I will give you and your descendants after you the land in which you are now aliens, all the land of Canaan... For your part, you must keep my covenant, you and your descendants... circumcise yourselves, every male among you...and it shall be the sign of the covenant between us.... (Genesis 17)

After 40 years of wandering, the Jews reached Canaan where they fought tribes there, including the Philistines. When the Kingdom of Israel was divided, some of them formed the Kingdom of Judea in the southern part of Palestine. The Jews today are in the main descended from the Judeans, hence the word 'Jew'. Saul and David were the first Kings of Israel and the First Temple was dedicated in 953 BCE.

The Jews claimed that God had revealed himself to mankind through the Jews, who were chosen to spread His word and be 'a light unto the nations'. They believed that they were chosen for this responsibility, not that being 'chosen' made them somehow superior.

Because Jews had to obey the strict Law, which ruled their whole life (including diet and marriage), they usually lived apart from other groups and were often seen as strange and aloof.

---

1. What is the name of religions based on the belief in one god?

2. According to Source 3, what did the Jews have to do in return for the land of Canaan? Why?

3. How reliable is Source 3?

4. Find out about Jewish laws regarding diet and lifestyle. Why might they have led to the community living apart from non-Jews?

Pre-Christianity

Antisemitism is thought to date back to 586 BCE, when the armies of Babylon (now modern Iraq) attacked and destroyed the Temple in Jerusalem, captured Judea, taking 10,000 Jewish families to exile in Babylon. Many later returned to Israel, but some stayed — thus beginning the Jewish Diaspora (dispersion) which spread to Europe, China, India and Africa.

The Greeks

The Greeks conquered Israel in 320 BCE. Their rule and culture were not welcome by most Jews (though some were attracted to it) and many Jews left to travel as traders.

In 168 BCE the Greeks prohibited the observance of the Jewish Sabbath and circumcision. This led to Jewish revolts between 165 and 140 BCE. The most famous was led by Judah Maccabee whose army invaded Jerusalem and liberated the Temple which had been rebuilt after its destruction in 586 BCE but then ruined by the Greeks. The Jewish festival of Chanukah celebrates this victory of the Maccabeans over the Greeks.

The Romans

The Romans occupied Israel in 63 BCE (from that date until 1948 it was known as Palestine.) Life was very difficult under Roman rule. As a conquered nation, the Jews were subjected to heavy taxation. Many Jews longed for the coming of a messiah (saviour) promised by their holy prophets. The Jews refused to worship any Roman Emperor or god. This was seen as rebellion and the Romans worried in case some of their people might become Jews.

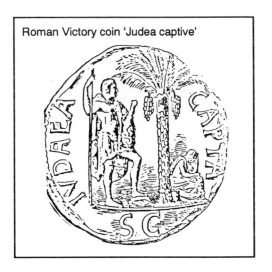

Roman Victory coin 'Judea captive'

---

1. What does Jewish Diaspora mean?

2. Find out about the Jewish festival of Chanukah. What is the connection between how it is celebrated today and the victory of the Maccabeans?

3. Which of the Ten Commandments were the Jews obeying when they refused to worship Roman Emperors or gods?

Christianity

Jesus was a Jew born in Nazareth, Palestine. Like other boys, at the age of 13 he had a barmitzvah. Some Jews, however, saw him as the Messiah, Son of God and he soon had a following of Jews and non-Jewish converts. Jesus was regarded as a rabbi (a teacher).

Christianity was born out of Judaism, a fact which Hitler found unacceptable and which partly explains his attack on the Christian Church. Today, religious Jews are still waiting for a Messiah.

In 30 CE, Jesus was crucified by the Romans, on the orders of Pontius Pilate (a Roman governor). They saw Jesus as a dangerous man, a powerful leader, capable of turning the population against Roman rule.

In 70 CE, the Romans, led by General Titus, destroyed the Second Temple of the Jews in Jerusalem. And in 73 CE, the Jews who were still under siege commited mass suicide at Massada, rather than be captured. Christians believed it was the end of Judaism. But in 132 CE, Simon Bar Cochba led a Jewish revolt against the Romans, driving them out of Jerusalem, where he ruled for three years. By 135 CE the Romans reasserted control and many Jews left for the Diaspora (Rome, Egypt, Persia, Babylon).

The Christian Church began to teach that the Jews were inferior, in order to make Christianity seem more attractive, and the gospels play down the responsibility of Pontius Pilate for the murder of Jesus. Written in order to win favour with the Romans, the gospels blame 'the Jews' for his death. In fact, Crucifixion was a Roman means of execution and Pilate a brutal tyrant, who was eventually recalled to Rome to face charges for his abuse of power. There were some Jewish Temple authorities who helped the Romans arrest Jesus, but they were neither supported by, nor represented, the Jews.

Nevertheless, the accusation of deicide (murder of a God) stuck, and from then on, as the gospels spread throughout the world, the myth of the Jew as Christ-killer and Devil remained.

In 1968, the Roman Catholic Church apologised, said it had been wrong and that the Jews did not actually kill Jesus. Despite this, the charge of deicide is still heard today.

With the growth of Christianity, antisemitism grew stronger within the Roman Empire. Tacitus, a Roman historian of the 1st century CE, referred to Jews as 'lepers and rabble'. Jews were such active missionaries that Emperor Tiberius expelled them from Rome in 19CE.

Christians wanted converts and resented those who had remained Jewish, and who did not recognise Christianity as 'the new, true religion'. So they did all they could to turn people against Judaism:

11

Source 4

The Jews are murderers of the Lord. Rebels and detesters of the mind, a race of vipers...enemies of all that is beautiful.
(St.Gregory 331-396)

'Christianity was taking on its parent religion in a war for pagan souls: it won, and spent the next 2,000 years writing the history books and exacting a brutal revenge'.
(Jonathan Freedland, *The Independent*, March 1992)

In 321 CE, Christianity became the official religion of the Roman Empire, under Emperor Constantine. Jewish men were forbidden to have sexual relations with Christian women and forbidden from holding high office in the government or military. Jews in Spain developed a tradition of Judaism called Sefardic Judaism (from the Hebrew word for Spain, SEFARD). Jews in the rest of Europe were known as Ashkenazi Jews (from the Hebrew word for Germany, ASHKENAZ).

---

1. What was the difference, in terms of belief, between those Jews who followed Jesus and those who did not?
2. Why were the Romans scared of Jesus?
3. What arguments could you use against the accusation that 'the Jews killed Jesus'?
4. Why did some of the gospel writers say that 'the Jews' killed him?
5. Using Source 4 and the information above, describe Christian antisemitism of the 4th century.

Jews and Islam

Islam, the religion of Muslims, was founded by Mohammed in the 7th century. Mohammed called himself a 'Jewish prophet' and the religion was born as an offshoot of Judaism.

Jews living in Muslim countries were criticised for not recognising Mohammed as a prophet, but Judaism was still seen as an official religion and Jews were often protected. Indeed, many of them prospered economically and in the atmosphere of learning in the Muslim world. Rabbis and scholars there studied and taught the Torah, attracting students from all over the Diaspora.

Later, when Christians in Muslim countries were forced to convert to Islam, Jews were often the only non-Muslims and many in North Africa and Spain were violently persecuted. In 638 CE Palestine was conquered by the Arab Muslims.

Jews in Germany

Until 1871, there was no one country called Germany. It consisted of scores of separate states, each with its own ruler and laws.

The first recorded appearance of the Jews in Germany is in the 4th century.

There is evidence of Jews working as merchants and traders (silk, glass, leather) by the 9th century. Because of the Jewish law commanding study (every Jewish boy had to study for his barmitzvah), Jews were literate and often spoke several languages. At first, they were free to practise Judaism and to buy, own and farm land. Jews were also tax collectors and doctors to to Emperors and princes. Kings, Emperors and bishops often protected them from attack.

Source 5

It is the duty of the Imperial Majesty...that we provide for the safety of the persons and the peaceful enjoyment of the possessions of all our faithful subjects, not only those of the Christian faith, but also those who differ from our own beliefs
(Emperor Frederic Barbarossa 1152–1190)

For some Church leaders, Jews were a threat. Archbishop Agobard wrote in the 9th century:

> Things have reached a stage where ignorant Christians claim that the Jews preach better than our priests...some Christians even celebrate the Sabbath with the Jews and violate the holy repose of Sunday...men of the people, peasants, allow themselves to be plunged into such a sea of errors that they regard the Jews as the only people of God.

Church Councils began to pass laws to prevent contact between Jews and Christians.

Read Source 5. Why did some German rulers protect Jews?

The Crusades

The three main Crusades (1096, 1147–72 and 1189), were an attempt by tens of thousands of European Christians to regain Palestine from Muslim control. On the way to Jerusalem, the Crusaders attacked any 'infidels' (non-Christians) using swords in the shape of a cross. Thousands of Jews and Muslims were massacred, some chose to save their lives by converting to Christianity, others commited suicide.

The Crusaders conquered Jerusalem in 1099 and ruled it until 1187. During the Third Crusade, led by the English King Richard I — 'Richard the Lionheart' — riots erupted in London, Norwich, Lincoln, Bury St.Edmunds

13

and other parts of Eastern England. Any Christian who offered a Jew hospitality for more than two days could be excommunicated.

In 1190, rioters attacked Jewish people in York. Leading members of the community were murdered and the Jewish quarter set on fire. Others, terrified, hid in the city castle Keep — known as Clifford's Tower. After days of siege, the rioters found the bodies of 150 Jews who had commited collective suicide.

1. Who in the opinion of the Crusaders were the 'infidels'?
2. What is the connection between the Crusades and the York Massacre of 1190?

Jews in England

Jewish bankers came to England with William the Conqueror in 1066.

There were approximately 6,000 Jewish people in England during the Middle Ages. Legally, they and their property and possessions were all owned by the King — he used them for his benefit. Jews were usually not allowed to work in trade, commerce or crafts — but were allowed to be money lenders for the government.

Source 6

All Jews over seven years of age had to wear a badge because they were officially Serfs of the Royal Chamber. In the late thirteenth century they had to pay the authorities whenever they changed their address, married, divorced, employed non-Jews, carried out a business transaction, went to law or died...In the end, perpetual government raids on Jewish financial resources destroyed the community. An Anglo-Jewry which was not wealthy was no use to the government and in 1290 the entire Jewish population, by then about 2,500 was expelled from England. (David Keys *The Times* 30/9/89)

King Edward I then took over their property and instead used the services of Italian bankers. Jews were not allowed back until invited by Oliver Cromwell in 1655.

1. Using Source 6 and information in the text, list the ways in which Jews in medieval Europe were discriminated against.
2. Why were they eventually excluded in 1290?

Medieval Europe

Because of its continued fear that Christians might be attracted to Judaism, the Church ordered:

- That Jews be forbidden to keep Christian servants.

- In 1215, Pope Innocent III instructed Jews to wear a distinctive badge, or special hat, to mark them out in society and to prevent sexual relations between Christians and Jews.

- In 1235, Jews were placed on a level with common criminals. Killing Jews was no longer a punishable offence.

Source 7   Middle Ages depiction of Jews, Frankfurt, Germany.

Even the word 'Jew' became an insult and Passion plays were performed all over Europe, re-enacting the Crucifixion of Jesus and blaming the Jews for his death. The Passion plays are still performed in Oberamagau in Germany every ten years.

By the end of the 19th century, 114 Popes and 96 Church Councils had passed decrees against the Jews, to degrade them and make them into pariahs (social outcasts). The Church was the most powerful influence on most peoples' lives at that time and centuries of anti-Jewish sermons and teaching was passed on to generations of German, French, Polish, Italian, Ukrainian, Russian, Romanian and Hungarian church-goers.

Source 8

'Without Christian antisemitism, the Holocaust would have been inconceivable.'

(D.Prager and J.Telushkin, 1983)

German Emperors put further restrictions on the Jews of Germany. Emperor Ludwig the Bavarian (1314 -47) taxed them, saying their bodies and property belonged to the State.

— every Jewish person needed a *'Certificate of Protection'*, without which they could not live anywhere. And in return, they had to give presents and taxes.

— if they wanted to move, they had to pay a 'Flight tax'.

Source 9

When Rabbi Meir of Rothenberg... set off for Jerusalem, he was arrested in Milan by the soldiers of Emperor Rudolf of Habsburg and thrown into prison for the rest of his life.

Rudolf was afraid that Rabbi Meir's example might be followed by other Jews and that he would lose the income from what must literally be translated as 'Jew Protection' (Judenschutz). In truth, it was the sort of protection the mafia offers its clients. (cited by Dr.H.Loebl, in 1989)

Other taxes included :

— *Death tax* — payable on the death of a Jewish person.

— *Horse tax* — Jews had to deliver two horses to the ruler's court every year.

— *Body Duty* — payable by all Jews when they passed the customs posts of the city, just as on cattle and sheep.

There were numerous additional special and occasional taxes demanded of the Jews. When the Swedes invaded Germany during the early 17th century, they found the vast majority of local Jews quite poor. Hundreds of years later, the Nazis introduced restrictions very like those imposed by the medieval Church and rulers. (see p.81-82)

1. Why is Source 7 antisemitic?

2. Explain what the quote in Source 8 means.

3. According to Source 9, what is the connection between the tactics of the German Emperors and the modern mafia?

Out of this degradation and separation came a distinctive culture and language. By the 12th century, the language of Yiddish was well established — a mixture of German and Hebrew, spoken only by Jews and a product of their treatment. Study and learning continued. Moses Maimonides was the most outstanding Jewish scholar (Law, Philosophy, Medicine) of the medieval period. Born in Cordova, Spain in 1135, he died in Cairo in 1204.

Synagogue, Grodno, Poland.

Medieval Myths

The lives and image of Jewish people were further damaged during the Middle Ages by :

1. The Blood Libel

The myth that Jews killed Christian children as a re-enactment of the Crucifixion and in order to get blood for Passover, to make their unleavened bread (made only from flour and water). Several Popes made pronouncements strongly condemning such unbelievable accusations. Pope Innocent IV said in 1253:

Source 10

Nobody shall accuse the Jews of using human blood in their rites, as their Bible forbids them to eat any blood, let alone human blood. Many Jews have been killed because of this libel, we strictly forbid similar occurences in the future (Pope Innocent IV).

But such decrees had little effect. At the end of the 13th century, massacres throughout Southern Germany were responsible for the death of 100,000 Jews.

The myth continued into the 20th century.

2. The Black Death

Twenty-five million Europeans, including one quarter of the German people, were killed by a terrible plague between 1347 and 1350. Caused by flea-infested rats arriving from the East, Pope Clement VI saw it as God's wrath against the wickedness of mankind. But others chose to blame the Jews — accusing them of poisoning the rivers and wells.

Source 11

A Christian doctor, Konrad of Regensburg, was one of the few Christians to recognise that it was totally wrong to blame Jews:

'But I know that there were more Jews in Vienna than in any other German city familiar to me, and so many of them died of the plague that they were obliged to enlarge their cemetery. To have brought this on themselves would have been folly on their part.'

But the Pope, Emperors and princes could not prevent the burning to death in 1349 of thousands of Jews, killed in revenge for the Black Death. Many of the survivors fled to Poland.

3. The Moneylender

Strict limits were imposed on the jobs permitted to Jews in virtually every part of Europe. Jews could not own land or join trade guilds. In order to pay all the special taxes and survive, many were forced into money-lending. Christians were not supposed to lend money after 1301 (although many did) and although the Hebrew Bible also disapproved of it, Jews had little choice.

Source 12

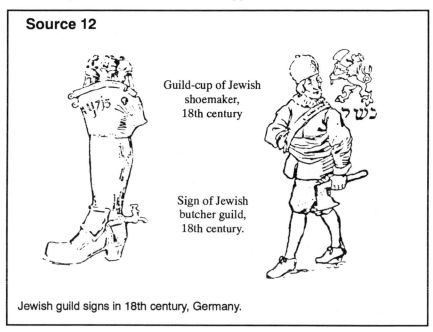

Guild-cup of Jewish shoemaker, 18th century

Sign of Jewish butcher guild, 18th century.

Jewish guild signs in 18th century, Germany.

Jews were then blamed and hated for being money-lenders and so was born the stereotype of 'the Jewish moneylender' and the association of Jews with money. In addition, some acted as middlemen or agents for landlords, collecting rents and taxes, so adding to their unpopularity.

These negative images have persisted right through to the 20th century. The literature of Geoffrey Chaucer, written in the 14th century, includes references to Jews as 'cursed' and as child-murderers and money-lenders.

> The charge is made more paradoxical by the fact that, whilst unfortunately, hundreds of thousands of cases are known of Jews being murdered by gentiles for their Jewish faith, there is virtually no example on record of a gentile being murdered by a Jew on account of his Christian faith (Harold Fisch, 1970).

In *The Merchant of Venice*, Shakespeare's Shylock portrays both the stereotype of the evil Jew and the Jew as a human being:

I am a Jew. Hath not a Jew eyes? hath not a Jew hands, organs, dimensions, senses, affections, passions? fed with the same food, hurt with the same weapons, subject to the same diseases, healed by the same means, warmed and cooled by the same winter and summer, as a Christian is? if you prick us, do we not bleed? if you tickle us, do we not laugh? if you poison us, do we not die? and if you wrong us, shall we not revenge?

---

1. Write a brief explanation of each of the medieval myths spread about Jews: The Blood Libel, the cause of Black Death and the Money-lender.
2. How do the authors of Source 10 and Source 11 add to your understanding of the views of the time?
3. Do you think that literature which portrays negative stereotypes of Jews (or any other groups) should be used in schools today?
4. How could Shylock's speech (above) be used as an example of a positive image of Jews?

Expulsion

When Jews were no longer useful to rulers or when hatred towards them became overwhelming, expulsion often followed.

In 1290 from England; 1306 from France; 1349 from Hungary; at different times during the 14th, 15th and 16th centuries from Germany; 1497 from Portugal; 1492 from Spain. Between the 15th century and 1722, the Jews were not allowed into Russia. The Ottoman Empire and Polish Galicia were two of the countries where Jews were allowed in after these expulsions. The Ottoman Empire, founded in the early 14th century, was Muslim and accepted Jews.

The Spanish Inquisition 1478

The 11th and 12th centuries witnessed what is known as *The Golden Age of Spanish Jewry*. In an atmosphere of toleration, Jewish communities flourished and contributed to Spanish society.

But by the 14th century, the religious and political climate had changed. The Spanish Inquisition was set up by Pope Sixtus IV in an attempt to force Spanish Jews, Muslims and Protestants to convert to Catholicism. Thousands and thousands of people were burnt alive in *Autos da Fe* (Acts of Faith).

Jews who converted were called Marranos. The rest were expelled in 1492. Some went to Holland, others to Italy, America, Greece, Bulgaria or the Ottoman Empire. By the 16th and 17th centuries, there were Jewish communities in South and North America and the Caribbean.

The Jews of Poland

Poland was to become the main country of refuge for Europe's Jews by the late 15th century. The Polish King Casimir the Great extended their rights in the 14th century and protected Jews for their commercial, administrative and craft skills. Jewish communities spread to the Ukraine and Lithuania, both ruled by Poland (see map p.2). Many were employed as traders in timber and hides. Others worked as tax collectors and ran estates, industries and mines owned by the nobility.

The fifteenth and sixteenth centuries were the *Golden Age of Polish Jewry*. The number of Polish Jews grew, until they represented a quarter of the population. There were Jewish glassmakers, furriers, painters, leadsmiths and goldsmiths. Antisemitism, however, was still strong, and some of their economic rivals and clergy forced rulers to restrict where Jews could live and work.

In the eighteenth century the Hasidic movement started in Poland. *Hasidism* was based on dance and song — Judaism through feeling rather than study. Today, the Hasidim are very orthodox in their dress and ritual. Communities still exist for example in Stamford Hill, London and Gateshead on Tyneside.

---

1. Why were the mass burnings of non-Catholics called *Autos da Fe* (Acts of Faith) during the Spanish Inquisition?

2. What and when was the *Golden Age of Polish Jewry*?

Ghettos

Although Jews had often lived in certain parts of towns, for safety and convenience, the word 'ghetto' was first used in 1516 in Venice, Italy, when Jews were forced to live in certain areas. These were nearly always gloomy, overcrowded areas with narrow streets. Surrounded by high walls and a gate which was bolted at night, no one was allowed to leave the ghetto from dusk to daybreak.

Neverthless, during the Renaissance (15th and 16th centuries) Jewish poets, like Sara Sullam, doctors, philosophers and musicians were popular and successful.

Right; Gate leading to the Jewish ghetto in Vienna.

21

The Reformation and Martin Luther

The fifteenth century saw serious conflict between Christians. It was the birth of Protestantism (led by those who protested about aspects of the Catholic Church). Protestants were persecuted in Catholic countries and some identified with Jews, but others were very antisemitic.

Martin Luther (1483–1546) led the Protestant Reformation in Germany and hoped that Jews would convert to Christianity. When they did not, he denounced them:

Source 13

'Know, Christian, that next to the Devil thou hast no enemy more cruel, more venomous (poisonous) and violent than a true Jew.' He urged Christians to destroy the houses of Jewish people and set fire to synagogues 'in honour of our Lord'.

Hitler praised Luther and his writings became popular again in the 1930s in Germany. In 1946, at the Nuremberg Trials, Julius Streicher (the Nazi propagandist and editor of the violently antisemitic *Der Stürmer*) argued that Luther should have been on trial with him.

1. Can you think of any reasons at the time to explain why some governments created Jewish ghettos?
2. Read Source 13. Is Luther expressing facts or opinion? Explain your answer.

Friends of the Jews

Jews were relatively free to settle in Holland, Belgium and Britain (after 1655). There, some prospered and developed a lively culture.

Individual Christians and Jews campaigned for the rights of Jews and occasionally improved their situation. *John Reuchlin*, for example, prevented the burning of the Talmud and other Jewish writings in sixteenth century Germany. *Josel of Rosheim*, Alsace (1480–1544) was a spokesperson for the Jews of Germany. He secured an agreement against forcing Jews to wear special badges and paying special taxes.

The Chmelnitzky Massacres 1648–9

Chmelnitzky was a Cossack leader who aimed for control of Poland and believed he had the Bible on his side. When he ordered the murder of thousands of Christian and Jewish Poles:

Some of them [the Jews] had their skins flayed off them and their flesh was flung to the dogs. The hands and feet of others were cut off and they were flung onto the roadway where carts ran over them and they were trodden underfoot by horses and many were buried alive. They ripped up the bellies of pregnant women, took out the unborn children and flung them in their faces (N.Hanover, *Yeven Mezulah*, cited in H.H.Ben-Sasson et al, (ed.) 1985).

Jewish Emancipation

In the mid-eighteenth century, followers of the *Enlightenment* began to challenge Christianity and argued that Christians and Jews were all humans, with the same rights. Based on tolerance and open-minded thought, Enlightenment writers said Jews were oppressed by Christianity.

The Jewish religion was changing too. *Reform Judaism* was started in 18th century Germany, by those who believed that the religion should adapt to the modern world, with services in German as well as Hebrew and men and women sitting together in synagogue. (Since the thirteenth century, men and women had sat separately in synagogue — so that they would not distract each other during prayer! Orthodox synagogues still have separate seating). Moses Mendelssohn, writer and philosopher, was associated with this Reform movement, to bring Jews out of the Ghetto and into the mainstream of German life.

In 1782, Joseph II of Austria granted the Patent of Toleration — making Jews eligible for military service (regarded as a great honour).

The French Revolution 1789

The French Revolution emphasised ideas of *Liberty, Equality and Fraternity* for all.

> Nobody shall be persecuted for his opinion, even religious opinion, provided their expression does not harm the public order established by law (Article 10 of the Declaration of Man and the Citizen).

In 1791, despite opposition, the National Assembly (Parliament) of France granted liberty to all the Jews of France. But they were to give up any commitment to a separate Jewish nation and declare that the only national identity of the Jews of France was French.

Isaak Berr of Nancy, France, said 'We are now recognised not just as human beings, not just as citizens, but as Frenchmen'.

In practice, antisemitism and prejudice continued; no law could banish years of hostility.

When the French General, Napoleon Bonaparte (later Emperor of France) and his armies conquered most of Europe between 1793 and 1815, he enforced these ideas of equality. In July 1797, twenty years after the Jews of Venice had been told they would never be allowed citizenship, Napoleon ordered that the ghetto gates should be removed and that all inhabitants of the city be free and equal.

When the French armies defeated Germany in 1806, the schools and army were opened to Jews. Certain states ended the special 'Jewish' taxes, and allowed Jews to own land and to become members of trade guilds. The great-great grandfather of Walter Sharman, now living in Newcastle-upon-Tyne, was a tailor in Zierenberg in Hesse-Kassel, and became one of the first Jewish apprentices allowed into the guild there.

However, the Germans, humiliated by defeat, particularly resented this enforced equailty and when Napoleon left in 1815, many of the rights were taken away. Ideas of Liberty and Equality were seen by many Germans as French and therefore un-German.

---

1. What does Emancipation mean?

2. What did Liberty, Equality and Fraternity mean in practice for the Jews?

3. Why was being eligible for military service a 'great honour' for some Jews?

4. Explain 'No law could banish years of hostility'.

The Hep Hep Riots

Anti-Jewish feeling always rose with German Nationalism and economic hardship. In 1819 there were violent attacks (pogroms) on Jewish communities in Germany. Calling for 'Revenge', the rioters shouted 'Hep! Hep! Hep! Death and destruction to all the Jews!'. Jewish organisations were formed, to deal with poverty in their communities, raise education and protect their rights, in the face of antisemitism.

At this time, the idea of VOLK was much heard among Germans — meaning the 'real German people'. Those who agreed with the idea argued that Jews were foreign and could only be granted rights if they became Christian. Many Jews were baptised to escape the restrictions.

In 1842 in Wittgenstein, a law of 1572 still operated, describing 'Heathens, gypsies and Jews' as outlaws.

In the 1840s, anti-religious socialist groups were formed. They were influenced by the writings of Karl Marx ('The Father of Communism'). Himself a Jew, he claimed that Jews were capitalists who worshipped money. Yet many Jews, both working and middle class, were attracted to Communism and Socialism.

Some Jews left Germany. Levi Strauss was among those who went to America. He founded the company whose denim jeans are so famous today.

In 1848 there were revolutions throughout Europe, including Germany. This secured certain improvements for Jews but they were not fully protected. The majority of Jews were still living in poverty — as traders and craft-workers in the Eastern part of Germany.

The Industrial Revolution

The Industrial Revolution of the 1850s brought complex changes to the country. Large numbers of workers concentrated in the towns; trade union membership grew from 300,000 in 1890 to 3 million by 1912 and there were demands for equality between men and women. For the old established ruling classes, these were days of insecurity. The landowners (Junkers) were used to sharing power with the Emperor (Kaiser) and they resented and feared the growing strength of the middle and working class. The Church was no longer as powerful as it had been.

The coming of factories, railways and increased trade brought many Jewish people into businesses such as brewing, silk, leather, cigars, spirits, metal, tools, chemicals, electrical goods, shipping and railways. An increasing proportion of businesses and banks were run by German Jews and many were workers, socialists and Liberals.

Those who disliked all the changes found scapegoats to blame for all of society's 'problems' — empty churches, feminism, trade unionism...: The main scapegoats were Jews and socialists.

---

1. Explain the term 'scapegoat'.

2. Find six causes of the German landowners fears in the mid 19th century.

3. Which groups are used as scapegoats today?

Equality and hostility

In 1871, after a victorious war against France, the separate German states united into one German Empire under the Chancellor Otto von Bismarck. In 1872, German Jews were granted full equality in law. Their legal equality was to last only 61 years, until 1933. But restrictions in education, the army and government remained.

Laws cannot eliminate antisemitism or racism and influential writers and politicians expressed their feelings loudly, sometimes inciting violent attacks and the burning of synagogues. *Paul de Lagarde* (1827-1891) a professor of the Bible, referred to Jews as vermin:

'One would need a heart as hard as crocodile hide not to feel sorry for the poor exploited Germans and — which is identical — not to hate the Jews and despise those who — out of humanity! — defend these Jews or who are too cowardly to trample this usurious vermin to death. With trichinae and bacilli [bacteria, disease] one does not negotiate...they are exterminated as quickly and thoroughly as possible.'
(Quoted in Alex Bein, 1959)

The musical composer *Richard Wagner* (1813-1883) wrote that Jews did not belong to any European community. He said they were not capable of true music, poetry or art (*Judaism in Music* 1850).

In 1879, *Adolf Stocker* of the Christian Social Workers Party, said Jews were 'a great danger to German national life...a people within a people, a state within a state...'. That same year, *Wilhelm Marr* founded the Anti-Semites League and was the first to use the term 'antisemitism'.

Hitler was to be profoundly influenced by these four men.

Racism and Social Darwinism

In a more secular world, anti-Jewishness became secular and antisemitism took a racial form. Once Jews were seen as a *race*, rather than as a *religion*, they could never be acceptable, even if they converted. The old anti-Judaism did not disappear, it continued alongside the new racial antisemitism.

This important change coincided with the spread of the ideas of Social Darwinism, taken from the ideas of Charles Darwin in his book *Origin of Species* (1859). He wrote about the evolution of humans from monkeys and described how the fittest and strongest of the species always survive. The inferior species degenerate and are not necessary. In fact they are a threat to the higher level of creation and can be destroyed.

Although Darwin had not intended his evolution principles to be applied to humans, it was soon extended by others to a notional 'ladder' of races with white, 'Aryan', Anglo-Saxons at the top and blacks, Slavs and Jews at the bottom. This fitted in well with Christian antisemitism and racism.

Since the 15th century, Europe had been colonising the land and peoples of Africa, the Americas, the West Indies and the Far East. As well as exploiting their raw materials (cotton, sugar, spices, silver etc), Europeans used the inhabitants as slaves and millions were captured, sold or murdered in the process. Blacks were stereotyped as lazy, uncivilised and cunning. This racism was perpetuated by certain scientists and by the Church.

Despite all the obstacles, Jews in Germany became doctors, dentists, lawyers and architects. Some, such as *Gabriel Riesser*, attacked the antisemitism they met with. Riesser had been challenged as a University teacher and lawyer, because he was a Jew. He refused to be baptised as a Christian and founded a newspaper *Der Jude* (The Jew) in which he spoke out against antisemitism and those who converted:

Source 14

'We have not emigrated to Germany. We were born here, and either we are German or we are men without a country'.

He became the first Jewish judge in Germany.

---

1. Read the views of Lagarde, Wagner and Stocker. In what ways do they express the same image of Jews?

2. How would a historian find out whether or not these views were typical of the time?

3. Explain the difference between racial and religious antisemitism.

4. How were Darwin's ideas used to support racism?

5. What would Gabriel Riesser (Source 14) have said in answer to the views of Adolf Stocker?

Most Jews hoped for more freedom and were optimistic about the future. They believed that antisemitism was part of the old order and would soon disappear. The majority of Jews felt they were German first and Jewish second. They tried to be 'good citizens' — patriotic and law-abiding. Many abandoned their religion and joined radical liberal/Left politics, seeking economic and social change as a way of achieving justice. The idea of a real attempt to exterminate them would have seemed completely incredible to the Jews of Germany during these years.

Zionism

Zionism is the belief that Jews have the right to self-determination in their own land. For nearly two thousand years, religious Jews prayed for their homeland in Israel to be restored. Zionist societies formed in Europe in the 1860s, training young Jews to settle and farm in Palestine.

When *Theodor Herzl* (a Hungarian Jew) advocated Zionism in the late 1890s, most German Jews rejected it. Many Jewish people felt, and still feel, that Jews should not live in a separate nation, but should be a part of whichever country they live in. Herzl argued that Jews could not assimilate into the European nations because of the deep-seated antisemitism. It was also a time of *nationalism*. There was more support for his ideas in Eastern Europe, Poland and Russia, where the Jews were poorer and less free than in the West.

Source 15

The saw-mill at Kibbutz-Hahshara in Klosawa, east Poland, 1935. Young Polish Jews training before emigration to Palestine. Kibbutz life was based on a collective, agricultural life-style.

The Bund

The Bund was a Jewish socialist organisation, started in Vilna, Poland in 1897 and active throughout Poland, Lithuania and Russia. Many Jews had experienced antisemitism in the existing socialist and communist groups, but wanted to be part of the movement for socialism. They were against Zionism.

The Bund had several functions. It:

- Supported and organised workers in their efforts to secure a decent standard of living and work.
- Formed self-defence squads against antisemites.
- Supported the cultural rights of Jewish people — their rights to speak Yiddish, run Yiddish libraries, schools and theatres.

1. Put the definition of Zionism into your own words.

2. What image of Polish Zionists do you get from the photograph, Source 15, in terms of class background, activities etc.?

3. In pairs, imagine one of you is a Polish Zionist and one a Polish Bundist. Write out the sort of arguments you might have about what the Jews of Poland should do about antisemitism.

Opposite: Mass meeting of Bundists in Warsaw.

Russia

Jews first settled in Russia in the 1st century CE, but were excluded from Little Russia (the heartland) in the 18th century. The ideas of the Enlightenment did not spread very far east in Europe and religious antisemitsm was still strong in 19th century Russia. Russia had annexed a huge part of Poland in the 18th century, including more than a million Jews who had lived under Polish rule for centuries. Most Jews lived in small towns and villages (shtetls), which many began to leave during the 19th century industrialisation of Russia.

But Jews were not allowed to settle wherever they chose. In 1835, they were restricted to the *Pale of Settlement*, including the Ukraine, White Russia, Lithuania and Poland (see map below). By the mid 19th century, three-quarters of the artisan class of the Pale were Jews.

Some Jews were compelled to serve 20 years in the army, in an attempt by the authorities to break up Jewish communities. The Russian Czar (Emperor) encouraged repression of the Jews. Many younger ones turned to revolutionary politics, seeing the overthrow of the Czar as their only hope. On March 13th 1881, Czar Alexander II was assassinated by revolutionaries, one of whom was a Jewish woman.

Below: After a *pogram* at Ekaterinoslav, 1905.

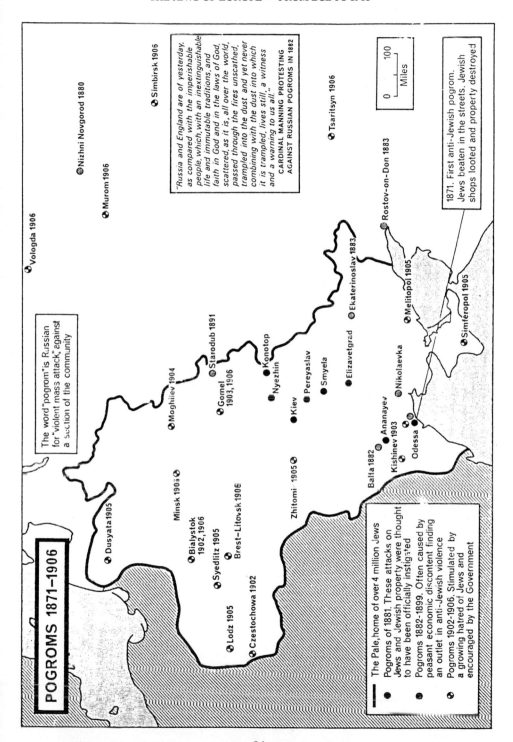

POGROMS 1871–1906

Vologda 1906

Nizhni Novgorod 1880

Murom 1906

Simbirsk 1906

Tsaritsyn 1906

"Russia and England are of yesterday, as compared with the imperishable people, which, with an inextinguishable life and immutable traditions, and faith in God and in the laws of God, scattered, as it is, all over the world, passed through the fires unscathed, trampled into the dust and yet never combining with the dust into which it is trampled, lives still, a witness and a warning to us all."

CARDINAL MANNING PROTESTING AGAINST RUSSIAN POGROMS IN 1882

0   100
Miles

1871. First anti-Jewish pogrom. Jews beaten in the streets. Jewish shops looted and property destroyed

Rostov-on-Don 1883

Ekaterinoslav 1883

Melitopol 1905

Simferopol 1905

The word "pogrom" is Russian for "violent mass attack", against a section of the community

Moghilev 1904

Starodub 1891

Gomel 1903, 1906

Konotop

Nyezhin

Kiev

Pereyaslav

Smyela

Elizavetgrad

Nikolaevka

Minsk 1905

Ananayev

Balta 1882

Kishinev 1903

Odessa

Dusyata 1905

Zhitomi 1905

Bialystok 1902, 1906

Syedlitz 1905

Brest-Litovsk 1906

Lodz 1905

Czestochowa 1902

The Pale, home of over 4 million Jews

● Pogroms of 1881. These attacks on Jews and Jewish property were thought to have been officially instigated

● Pogroms 1882-1899. Often caused by peasant economic discontent finding an outlet in anti-Jewish violence

◉ Pogroms 1902-1906. Stimulated by a growing hatred of Jews and encouraged by the Government

31

The result was an outbreak of violent physical attacks (*pogroms*) against the Jews all over Russia (mainly the Ukraine and White Russia). Thousands were left wounded and approximately one hundred dead. The new Czar, Nicholas II helped fund antisemitic organisations and encouraged the pogroms of 1903 and 1905, when eight hundred Jews were murdered in Odessa, Kiev, Gomel, Zhitomir and Bialystok. News of the pogroms shocked the world. Demonstrations against them were held in the East End of London and in New York. Some Russians protested too. The writer Leo Tolstoy wrote a furious letter attacking the pogromists and the government.

The 1880s, 1890s and early 20th century were times of mass emigration of Russian Jews. More than two million went west to Germany, Austria, France and Britain or even further, to the Americas, Australia and South Africa.

Jewish communities grew in the east end of London, Manchester, Tyneside, Glasgow and South Wales.

Below: Russian Jewish emigrants.

Source 16

Matters have been made much worse during the last few years by the arrival of an enormous number of poor foreigners from other European nations, chiefly Russian and German Jews. The previous conditions of life of the unhappy foreigners who are thus driven, or come here of their own accord, are such that they can live on much less than our English workers. They arrive here in a state of utter poverty, and are compelled to accept the work most easily obtained at the lowest rate of wages. In this way has grown up in our midst a system so bad in itself and so surrounded by evils, as to have caused, not only among the workers themselves, great suffering and misery, but in the minds of others grave thoughts of public danger (From an official report to Parliament on 'sweated labour' in 1888).

In 1905 the Czar's secret police published the *Protocols of the Learned Elders of Zion*. This document put forward a wholly false notion that an organisation of Jews existed who were planning to take over the world. It was a hoax, albeit a malicious one, but the publication was widely distributed in Europe and the United States, helping fuel Nazism in the 1930s. It is still used by antisemites today and new writings are based on it.

Source 17

Cover of the
French edition
of the *Protocols*,
c. 1934.

Many Jews took part in the Russian October revolution of 1917. Leon Trotsky, for example, was leader of the Red Army. In the Revolution, the Russian government was overthrown by workers and peasants. There followed a Civil War, during which thousands of people were murdered. By 1920 the Bolshevik Communists had secured themselves in power under Vladimir Lenin.

After the revolution, Jews were immediately given rights as equal citizens. But *pogroms* continued and Stalin's rule, from 1924, brought persecution for millions of Russians — including Jews. The Odessa Jewish Self-Defence Organisation, which *Solomon Yankelevich Jacobi* helped set up, was one of a number of Jewish defence organisations formed.

---

1. What is a pogrom?

2. Is Source 16 hostile or sympathetic towards Jewish immigrants? Quote from the Source to support your answer.

3. Suggest other reactions to the arrival of thousands of Jewish immigrants in Britain and America.

4. What was the aim behind the choice of the front cover of *The Protocols of the Learned Elders of Zion* (Source 17)?

5. Just because it was very biased and a hoax, does that make it useless as historical evidence?

France

The *Dreyfus Affair* of the 1890s brought French antisemitism into the open. Captain Alfred Dreyfus was the first Jew to become a member of the general staff of the French Army. He was wrongly accused of selling secrets to the Germans. He was imprisoned on Devil's Island, precipitating an outbreak of hysterical antisemitism. The authorities believed that a Jew was a natural traitor. The real criminal was very quickly discovered, but Dreyfus was not released immediately and it took twelve years to clear his name. He had allies in French society. One of them, the writer Emile Zola, wrote *J'Accuse*, in which he condemned the way Dreyfus was treated.

Germany

In Germany by the year 1900, twenty-five per cent of seats on boards of industrial and financial enterprises were occupied by Jews. Jews were also important in literature, art, music and science, in publishing and the press. Some were invited to Court balls and some, such as the scientist, industrialist and banker Walter Rathenau became friends of the Kaiser Wilhelm II.

The peak of Jewish Emancipation and integration was between the 1890s and 1914, when the German economy was strong. But antisemitism remained and in 1911, Walter Rathenau wrote :

Source 18

In the adolescent years of every German Jew occurs the painful moment which he remembers all his life... when he becomes fully conscious that he has entered the world as a second class citizen and no achievement and no service can liberate him from that world.

During the First World War (1914-1918), the vast majority of German Jews identified themselves with the cause of Germany. Several hundred thousand Jews fought and more than 12,000 were killed.

1. Why did the French authorities believe that Dreyfus would be a 'natural traitor'?
2. Despite the economic and social success of some Jews in the early 20th century, what can we learn from Source 18 about their position in German society, according to Rathenau?

Historian Raoul Hilberg has summed up the pattern of antisemitsm as follows:

1. 12th century Crusades: 'You have no right to live amongst us as Jews.'
2. 16th century Ghettos: 'You have no right to live amongst us.'
3. 20th century Nazis: 'You have no right to live.'

Source 19

On the 23rd of April 1939, the Reverend Richard Jones addressed his congregation in Pontypridd, Wales .

If a bad Englishman.... or a bad Irishman.... or a bad Welshman is in business in Pontypridd.... no one takes much notice.... But let a bad Jew be in business in Pontypridd.... and the name of the Jew — of the Jewish race — is dragged through every gutter and sewer from Treherbert to Cardiff. That is antisemitism, and we haven't got to go to Germany to discover that. That's why I say we can fight it here.

1. Discuss the meaning of the Raoul Hilberg summary.
2. Read Source 19. How does the Reverend Richard Jones express his opposition to antisemitism?
3. Can you think of how some people generalise about or stereotype minority ethnic or religious groups today?

Chapter Two

The Gypsies of Europe 1400-1928

As with 'The Jews' of Europe, it is impossible to generalise about 'The Gypsies'. Hungarian Gypsies differ from Swedish Gypsies, not only in looks, language and dress, but also in customs, beliefs and occupations. Neither is it possible to generalise about 'Hungarian Gypsies', since they differ from group to group and family to family. Gypsies came originally from Northern India. They left in three large groups — known as the Rom, the Sinti and the Kale. There is no clear evidence about their life in India or why they moved from there, first to the Middle East and then to Europe.

Much of what we know about Gypsies was written by non-Gypsies, since Gypsies maintain an oral tradition (stories, songs, customs etc). Most of the written evidence is found in government or local laws, court records or the writings of middle-class observers. So it is often difficult to find out the names and details of individual Gypsies and their families and opinions.

Origins

The first recorded descriptions of Gypsies in Europe date from 14th century Greece. There is a theory they were called 'Gypsies' because some groups said they had been expelled from Egypt and in several countries, Gypsies were referred to as 'Egyptians'.

They passed through numerous German states — Saxony, Bavaria and Hesse for example — in the early 1400s and on to France, Italy, the Netherlands, Portugal and Britain. They arrived in family groups: men, women and children with horses, each headed by a 'chieftain' or 'voivod'.

37

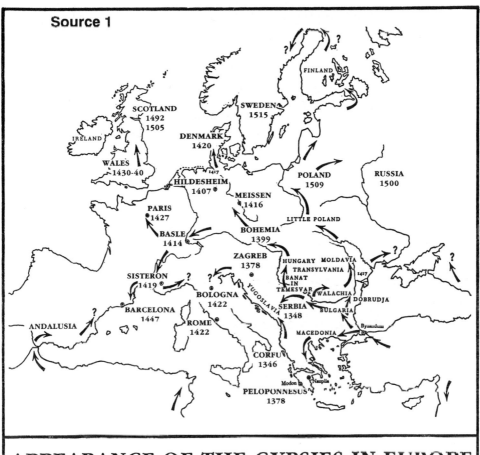

APPEARANCE OF THE GYPSIES IN EUROPE

Certain early German town accounts suggest that Gypsies received beer, bread, shelter and hay for their horses. Often they travelled with letters of protection written by European Kings or rulers. Some continued to move across the Continent, while others stopped and settled.

The lighter-skinned Sinti were usually tolerated as migratory workers in Western Europe, where they developed specific skilled crafts such as making baskets and jewellry, or working as tinsmiths, coppersmiths and blacksmiths. Others were travelling entertainers, fortune tellers, healers and horse dealers. In England, many Gypsies worked also as pedlars and farmers.

Gypsies brought their own music, dance and festivals, their own system of justice (the kriss), their own customs, myths and religious beliefs, most of which have survived, despite what was to follow.

39

Some married local people (although this was severely disapproved of by most Gypsies) and adopted family names — Berlingeri in Italy or Boswell in England. Certain aristocrats employed gypsies as dancers, labourers or soldiers. By 1500, there were several thousand Gypsies in Europe.

> In the course of history, some groups of people in rural areas, after a brief period of curiosity, have defended the Gypsies, urging that they be kept in the village, or return to it because of their economic value as blacksmiths or metal workers or sometimes as musicians. (Jean-Pierre Liégeois, 1987)

1. What is your image of Gypsies? Have you ever met any Gypsies?

2. Why is it misleading to talk about 'The Gypsies' or 'The Jews'?

3. What sort of problems might a historian have in finding accurate evidence about the Gypsies?

4. Look at the map (Source 1) can you think of a geographical reason why the first known Gypsy communities of Europe were to be found in Greece?

5. How do the various occupations of Gypsies fit in with their lifestyle?

6. How might their reputation as fortune-tellers have affected the way Gypsies were viewed?

Persecution

Gypsies have generally been treated very badly throughout Europe. Regarded as outsiders and non-citizens, their long hair, clothes, tents, caravans and lifestyle were viewed with suspicion and they were often accused of witchcraft. One of the myths which took root was that the Gypsy people were responsible for some ancient offence and carried a terrible curse and magical powers.

Reports and sayings of the Middle Ages refer negatively to their dark skins. In both Italian and Dutch, people used the phrase 'Black as a Gypsy'. The colour black was associated with evil and the Devil. Gypsies were generally condemned as 'racially impure'.

Churches called them 'heathens'. Anti-Gypsy laws were referred to as ' a service to God'. *Trade guilds* refused to allow them to practise their trades, thus forcing them to break the law or beg and steal. Folk sayings throughout Europe began to refer to Gypsy 'dishonesty'.

Source 2

Government laws made the same accusations. This, for example issued by King Henry VIII of England in 1530:

Diverse and many outlandish people calling themselves Egyptians....have gone from shire to shire....and used great and subtle means to deceive the people, bearing them in hand that they by palmistry could tell men's and women's fortunes ....and have deceived the people of their money and have also committed many heinous felonies and robberies. (D.Kenrick and G.Puxon, 1972)

Gypsies moved throughout Europe in order to trade, because they *wanted* to travel and be independent, but often because they had to migrate due to constant persecution: 'Surrounded by hostility, Gypsies had no alternative but to move on in the hope of a kinder reception elsewhere', (Jean-Pierre Liégeois).

In 1449, Gypsies were forced out of Frankfurt, Germany. The Parliaments of other German towns soon followed — accusing them of spying for the Turks, carrying the plague, being cannibals and stealing Christian children. The Church promoted myths that Gypsies were involved in the crucifixion of Jesus.

Source 3

A Spanish carol:

Into the porch at Bethlehem
have come the evil Gypsies.
From the newly born babe
they have robbed the coverings.

Rascally Gypsies with faces
like black olives.
The poor child they've left
of clothes bereft.
(From the Journal of the Gypsy Lore Society, cited in Kenrick and Puxon)

In 1500, the Emperor Maximillian I announced that Gypsies could be murdered without punishment and Gypsy women could be raped if found in Germany. Two hundred years later, Emperor Charles VI ordered their extermination, all the men to be executed and women and children to have one ear cut off.

In *France,* Gypsies were whipped, imprisoned and hanged. In 17th and 18th century *Netherlands,* organised *Heidenjachten* (heathen hunts) were held, when anyone could lawfully kill a Gypsy. Similar practices were carried out in *Switzerland, Sweden* and *Denmark.* As late as 1925, the Minister of Justice in Norway said: 'Should it transpire that Gypsies have Norwegian passports stating they are Norweigan citizens, those passports are not valid and should be withdrawn'.

Some leaders, including *Pope Pius V* in 1570, used Gypsies as galley slaves. Families were sold at auctions, wives and husbands separated and children given away as gifts. Townspeople in Germany were fined for doing business with Gypsies. Rewards were offered for the capture of Gypsies in 18th century France and Germany. In 18th century *Russia,* Gypsies had to pay extra taxes and were not allowed to enter St.Petersburg.

Source 4

In Frankfurt, 1722, Gypsy parents are branded and deported while their children are taken from them and placed permanently with non-Gypsy families. During this period, Friedrich Wilhelm makes it a hanging offence in Prussia (Germany) for all those over the age of eighteen merely to be born a Gypsy. A thousand armed Gypsies confront German soldiers in an organised fight for their freedom. Nineteen Gypsies arrested in Kaswasser are tortured to death: four broken on the wheel, three beheaded and the rest shot or stabbed to death. (*Gypsy history in Germany and neighbouring lands: A chronology leading to the Holocaust* by Ian Hancock)

In 1793, German minister Martinus Zippel wrote that: 'Gypsies in a well-ordered state... are like vermin on an animal's body'.

Throughout Europe, thousands of Gypsies were murdered, mutilated or banished. Hundreds were transported to the European colonies in North and South America.

1a. On arriving in 15th century European villages, Gypsies were often stared at and viewed with suspicion. List all the reasons you can think of to account for this hostile reception.

1b. Was the attitude of the villagers rational?

2. 'Lighter-skinned Gypsies were sometimes more tolerated'. What does this tell you about attitudes at the time?

3. What is the difference between 'tolerance' and 'acceptance'?

4. Why do you think that Gypsies and Jews sometimes had close links with each other?

5. Three of the most powerful groups in medieval society were the Church, the State and the trade guilds. Find evidence from the Sources and text to illustrate how they each helped to persecute Gypsies.

6. In what way did the Church, State and trade guilds play a similar role in the persecution of Jews in Europe? (see Chapter 1)

7a. What does the carol (Source 3) accuse the Gypsies of doing?

7b. What other negative images of the Gypsies does it use?

7c. Why are carols and folk sayings a particularly powerful form of continuing prejudice? Can you think of songs or sayings which stereotype any groups nowadays?

8. Read the above quote by Zippel. What evidence is there that Gypsies were treated like vermin?

When expulsion policies failed, laws were passed to control Gypsy customs, dress, food, language and marriage. Marriage between Gypsies was forbidden in Austria and anyone heard speaking the language of the Gypsies was given twenty four-strokes of the birch. In 16th century England, the Romany language of the Gypsies was forbidden by law. Anyone heard speaking it could be punished by death. And in Aylesbury, seven men and a woman were hanged in 1577 for 'keeping company with Egyptians'.

Such efforts at control spread from North to South Europe over the years. In the 19th and 20th centuries a special (inferior) legal status for Gypsies was created — they had to carry identification cards — and the discrimination continued.

Their very existence continued to be seen as an offence. A Strasbourg magistrate of the early 19th century said:

> I cannot accuse these persons of any crime, but their position is such that they must necessarily be tempted to commit crimes, should occasion arise...they cannot but be dangerous.

At the same time, the more liberal attitudes of the 19th century brought efforts by Quakers in England and Protestants in Germany to contact and convert Gypsies rather than exclude them. And writers began to portray them as romantic and beautiful rather than dirty and wicked.

Occasionally, Gypsies were protected by members of the local population. Some resisted the laws and it was impossible to imprison a whole people. The fact that orders were repeated suggests they were not always obeyed.

Gypsies in Eastern Europe

Persecution was less severe in parts of South-East Europe and Gypsies were freer to move around. This is largely due to the fact that the native inhabitants were also of Asiatic origin, but also because the Gypsies were a convenient source of cheap labour.

However, in 1758, Maria Teresa, Empress of Austria-Hungary, forced all Gypsies to sell their horses and waggons. Government-built huts replaced them and Gypsies became slaves, not allowed to move without permission. Objecting to the word 'Gypsy', she ordered them to be called 'new settlers'. The men were pressed into military service and the children had to attend school and Church.

> **Source 5**
>
> The results were described by a woman who travelled through Hungary in the 19th century: 'On one terrible day....handcarts escorted by soldiers appeared in all parts of Hungary where there were Gypsies and took away the children, including those just weaned and young married couples still wearing their wedding finery. The despair of these unfortunate people cannot be described: the parents dragged themselves on the ground before the soldiers, and clung to the vehicles which were carrying away their children...Beaten off with blows from batons and rifle-butts....some immediately commited suicide'. (cited in Jean-Paul Clébert, 1961)

There was open revolt and the policy of forcing Gypsies to change their lifestyle failed.

In Moldavia and Wallachia (modern Rumania), Gypsies were held as slaves from the 17th century and lived in inhuman conditions. Only after a huge revolt were they liberated, in 1855. Thousands then fled to Russia where they were allowed to live in relative peace, though in poverty.

1a. Why did certain governments (e.g. England, Austria) make the speaking of the Romany language a punishable offence?

1b. Some Gypsies call the laws against their language, dress, customs, marriage and migratory lifestyle, a form of genocide. What do they mean?

2a. There are two references to Gypsy revolts in this chapter. What difficulties would Gypsies face if they tried to oppose the laws passed against them?

3. How does Source 5 add to your understanding of the period?

4. What evidence is there that not all Europeans were hostile towards Gypsies?

The Twentieth Century

To improve surveillance, the German authorities set up an information office for Gypsy affairs in 1899. People were urged to contact the police with any information on Gypsies, who were referred to as a 'scourge'. Villages were instructed to ring their church bells on sighting a Gypsy.

This attitude continued into the 20th century and led to an influx of Gypsies to other European countries including Britain.

In 1926, the Swiss charity *Pro Juventate* took hundreds of Gypsy children from their parents and shut them up in homes, telling them their families were dead or did not want them. Some children were sterilised. This practice continued until the mid 1980s.

In Weimar Germany (1919–1933), it became compulsory to have a certificate of residence (proof of a permanent home) in order to get a trade license.

Source 6

Around big cities like Berlin, Frankfurt and Hamburg, there was a move to settle Gypsies in poor economic and insanitary conditions...In 1926, the Bavarian Parliament passed a law to 'combat Gypsies, nomads and idlers'. 'Hordes' or large groups, had to be split up and any individual unable to provide proof of regular employment could be placed in a 'House of Correction' and his children handed over....In 1928, Gypsies were put under constant police surveillance. (Jean-Pierre Liégeois, 1987)

Source 7

Police check on a gypsy camp, at Oberschwaben, 1925.

Before the second World War, there were about two million Gypsies in the world, including at least 850,000 in Europe. Some managed to maintain their traditional way of life, for example in Spain, Czechoslovakia and Hungary. In Germany many lived in flats with regular work and took part in the social and cultural life of the Gypsy community. Others had rejected their links with the community or were afraid to show them.

Between the two World Wars, in Poland, Rumania and the USSR, Gypsies set up organisations to oppose discrimination against them. They tried to win support from the League of Nations but time ran out in the face of growing European fascism.

1. Explain the meaning of the words 'nomad' and 'idler' (Source 6). Why do some people not accept those who choose to live as travellers?

2. What do Sources 6 and 7 tell you about the attitude of the German authorities towards Gypsies in the early 20th century?

3. What were the differences between the position of Jewish and Gypsy people in German society by the early 20th century (see Chapter 1)?

Chapter Three

Armenian Genocide 1915

At the beginning of the Second World War, before sending his troops to invade Poland, Hitler made the following statement about the attempted murder by the Turks of all Armenians living in Turkey, during the First World War.

Source 1

The destruction of Poland is our primary task...Be merciless! Be brutal! I have sent to the east only my 'Death Head Units', with the order to kill without mercy all men, women and children of Polish race or language. Only in such a way will we win the vital space that we now need.

Who still talks nowadays of the extermination of the Armenians?

Background

There are seven million Armenians living all over the world today. The year 700 BCE saw the beginning of an Armenian country. In 300 CE, they were the first people to adopt Christianity. From 400 CE Armenians came into conflict first with the Romans and later the Turks. In 1300 they were defeated by the Ottoman Turks and became a minority living in the Ottoman Empire.

The Armenians, always seen as inferior, had differing relations with their Turkish and Kurdish Muslim neighbours. Until the late 19th century, non-Muslims in Turkey (mainly Christians and Jews) were not allowed to join the military, hold government jobs, own guns or marry Muslim women. They also had to pay special taxes.

The Armenians were to be found in every social class — from the rich amiras (mainly business people), to the traders and peasants. They also contributed

Dikranagert, Armenia, Ottoman Empire, before 1915. The Garabed Deriklian family. They were all killed during the Genocide in 1915.

to architecture and theatre in the Ottoman Empire. *Krikor Balian (1764-1831)* was known as 'architect of the empire' and the Turkish theatre was started by an Armenian called *Hagop Vartovian.*

1. What is Hitler implying in his question at the end of Source 1 : 'Who still talks nowadays of the extermination of the Armenians?'

2. Do you notice any similarities between the position of Armenians in Turkish society and Jews in Germany and Poland in the 1930s? (see chapter 1)

The Genocide

Between 1894 and 1896, 200,000 Armenians were massacred in pogroms and many left Turkey for the USA at the same time as thousands of Jewish people were escaping pogroms in Eastern Europe.

During the First World War, the Turks claimed that the Armenians of the Ottoman Empire were not loyal to the Empire. The Turks, most of whom were Muslims, feared the Armenians, being Christians, would join with other Christians and fight against Turkey. (Turkey was on Germany's side in the war.) Pressure was put on Armenians to become Muslims.

In April 1915, Turkish officials began to round up Armenians, forcing them to abandon their homes. First the men were murdered — shot or bayoneted. Then the elderly, the women and children were marched into the Syrian desert (see map) where many were murdered, raped or starved.

Source 2

Aghavni Gulesserian survived the massacre, she remembers: 'It wasn't a fight for war ...it was just cutting up a nation into pieces...girls into pieces...killing them for nothing'.

And *John Bargamian*, aged 9 in 1915, witnessed the murder of his grandparents and 16 year-old aunt: 'Anyone who refused to go, they asked them : 'You believe in Christ?' and with a hatchet they put a cross on his head. They killed them... nobody could say No'. (Quotes taken from *The Armenian Question*, BBC TV, 1989).

There was armed resistance by Armenians, but most were killed fighting. Turkish officials, like Jelal Bey, who refused to co-operate with the executions, were dismissed.

The authorities tried to deceive Armenians into believing they were being relocated. Parents who feared the worst begged Turkish neighbours to take their children.

1,500,000 ARMENIANS WERE MURDERED BY 1920

1. Why were Armenian men the first target of the massacre?

2a. In Aghavni's opinion (Source 2), why did the massacre happen?

2b. The quotes by Aghavni and John were taken from a BBC TV documentary. Does this make them more or less reliable than if they had been quoted in a history book?

3. Are there any explanations for the massacre in this chapter?

4. Why was it so hard for the Armenians to resist effectively?

5. Can you think why the Turkish government carried out this massacre during the First World War?

The Turkish government tried to keep the massacre secret and pretended to foreigners that Armenians were 'only' being deported. They failed. When the German ambassador, Wolf-Metternich, wrote a report about the massacre, he was ordered home.

Henry Morgenthau, the American Ambassador to Turkey, sent telegrams and details of the slaughter to his government. The news was reported in hundreds of articles in American and European newspapers.

Governments condemned the murders, but the Turkish government denied it and the killing continued.

Source 3

According to Professor Frank Stone, although 'many Germans were in the Ottoman Empire at this time and had great influence over their Turkish collaborators, they failed to intervene. The French hardly lifted a finger. The British accepted Armenian volunteers but did nothing to stop the genocide. And as a matter of fact, at no point did the American government do anything substantial to halt the carnage in 1915 either, although Washington knew all about what was happening.' (F.Stone, *Armenian Genocide Studies*, quoted in M. Stern Strom and W.S. Parsons, 1982)

The American government did send financial aid and Armenian refugees fled to Europe, the Middle East and the USA. American, British and French forces managed to rescue a few thousand people from Turkey.

Armenian Refugee Camp, Aleppo, Syria, late 1920s photo by Vartan Derounian.

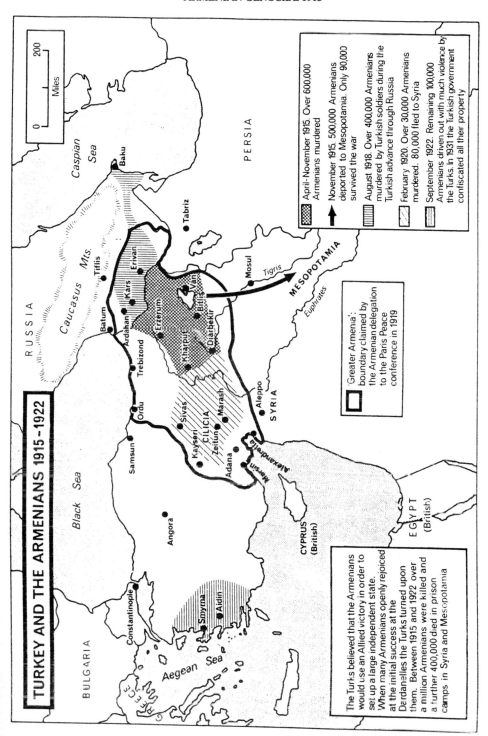

TURKEY AND THE ARMENIANS 1915–1922

April-November 1915. Over 600,000 Armenians murdered

November 1915. 500,000 Armenians deported to Mesopotamia. Only 90,000 survived the war

August 1918. Over 400,000 Armenians murdered by Turkish soldiers during the Turkish advance through Russia

February 1920. Over 30,000 Armenians murdered. 80,000 fled to Syria

September 1922. Remaining 100,000 Armenians driven out with much violence by the Turks. In 1931 the Turkish government confiscated all their property

'Greater Armenia': boundary claimed by the Armenian delegation to the Paris Peace conference in 1919

The Turks believed that the Armenians would use an Allied victory in order to set up a large independent state. When many Armenians openly rejoiced at the initial success at the Dardanelles the Turks turned upon them. Between 1915 and 1922 over a million Armenians were killed and a further 400,000 died in prison camps in Syria and Mesopotamia

In 1920, after the First World War, an Armenian state was created, but it only survived two years.

Today there is still a very strong Armenian nationalist movement. In 1988 there were huge demonstrations in Soviet Armenia, demanding self-determination. 1990 witnessed outbreaks of violence between Armenians and Azerbijanis over land in the former USSR and the declaration of independence by the state of Armenia. And the atrocities continue in 1992 in Nagorno-Karabakh.

At the same time Armenians are still campaigning for the events of 1915 to be recognised as genocide:

> A crime was committed. One and a half million people were massacred. Their land was confiscated, they were scattered throughout the world and there was no justice...nobody did anything about it (*Tatul Somentz-Papazian*, Armenian Revolutionary Committee).

Today, the Turkish government still deny that the genocide ever took place.

> Genocide is a word that sounds bad. It is an international crime and the Turks don't want to be associated with this crime. But the intention of the Turks was in fact genocide' (an 80 year old priest, survivor of the 1915 genocide. Speaking on *Secret History — The Forgotten Holocaust*, Channel 4, 1992).

The US government do not recognise it as a genocide now, for fear of harming USA-Turkish relations (Turkey is an important member of NATO).

---

1. Frank Stone (Source 3) claims that the Western powers did nothing 'substantial to halt the carnage'. What does he mean? What sort of things did they do?

2. Despite the oral and written evidence of witnesses to the Armenian Genocide, the Turkish government still deny it ever happened. Can you explain this? What type of evidence is not available?

3. Had you heard about the Armenian Genocide before reading this chapter? If yes, how? Why do you think it is generally not known about?

Chapter Four

The emergence of Nazism

In the 1920s and 1930s fascist parties emerged in almost every European country including Britain, and in America. Fascists came to power in Italy, Spain and Germany.

What is Fascism?

How and why did this happen? What was it that made thirty seven per cent of German voters support the Nazis (German fascists) by 1932?

The First World War ended in November 1918. German army generals, including the war hero, von Hindenberg, were in favour of surrender. Ten million soldiers from Europe, America, Africa, Australasia, India and the Caribbean, were dead.

The Weimar Republic

The German Kaiser Wilhelm II had abdicated and fled to Holland. Germany was declared a republic. Its new government was led by *Friedrich Ebert,* of the *Social Democratic Party*. At Weimar, a new Constitution was written, promising freedom and democracy.

Violence and Disorder

It was a time of political extremes.

In Russia the bloodshed ended with a Communist Revolution in 1917. The *Spartacists,* the German Communist Party, was led by Rosa Luxemburg and Karl Liebknecht.

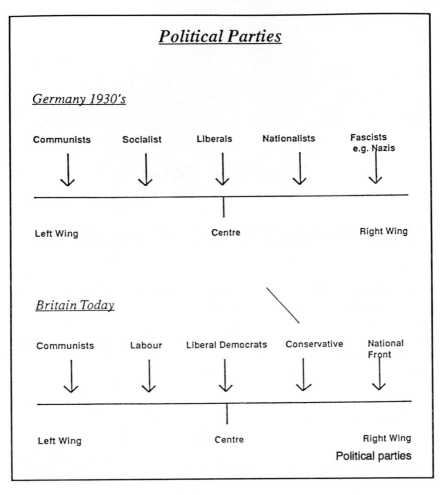

Political Parties

Germany 1930's

| Communists | Socialist | Liberals | Nationalists | Fascists e.g. Nazis |

Left Wing — Centre — Right Wing

Britain Today

| Communists | Labour | Liberal Democrats | Conservative | National Front |

Left Wing — Centre — Right Wing

Political parties

There were a series of uprisings and clashes between the Communists and their opponents, especially the Social Democrats. On 6th January 1919, workers began a revolution in Berlin. Ebert turned for support to the *Freikorps*. Led by former army officers, these were men who had fought in the war, felt appalled by Germany's surrender and were violently anti-communist. On 10th January, 2,000 Freikorps attacked the Spartacist revolutionaries. Street fighting broke out and lasted for three days.

On January 15th they arrested, beat and murdered Rosa Luxemburg and Karl Liebknecht.

The idea of a Communist Revolution terrified German landowners, judges, generals and civil servants. They still had influence but wanted to regain the *power* they had once had.

The Peace Treaties

The victorious Allies (Britain, France, Italy and the USA) wrote the Peace Treaties. They were determined to punish Germany and her allies (Austria, Hungary, Bulgaria and Turkey). Germany was not allowed to participate in the negotiations. Nor was the USSR, because the capitalist countries saw her as a threat. (Russia had made peace with Germany in 1917, giving up twenty per cent of her land and twenty-five per cent of her population).

1. The *Austro-Hungarian Empire* was broken up and Czechoslovakia, Hungary, Poland and Yugoslavia were created as independent countries. Austria became a tiny state, her army to be limited to 30,000, reparations were to be paid and union with Germany was forbidden. Hungary and Bulgaria also lost land. Rumania gained some land (Transylvania) as a reward for joining the allies during the war.

2. *Turkey* was to give up her territory in the Middle East (Syria, Iraq, Palestine) which were to be run by Britain and France.

3. *Italy* had joined the Allies in return for a promise of territory. But they allowed her much less than they had offered. Italy felt cheated.

4. In June 1919, *Germany* signed the *Treaty of Versailles*, facing invasion if she refused.

Source 1

The Treaty required Germany to:

— Admit sole responsibility for starting the war.

— Lose thirteen per cent of her land and population.

— Lose all her colonies.

— Never form a union with Austria.

— Limit her army to 100,000 men.

— Limit her Navy to thirty-six battleships.

— Have no airforce.

— Demilitarise the Rhineland for fifteen years, during which time it would be occupied by Allied troops.

— Pay £6,600,000 compensation, known as Reparations.

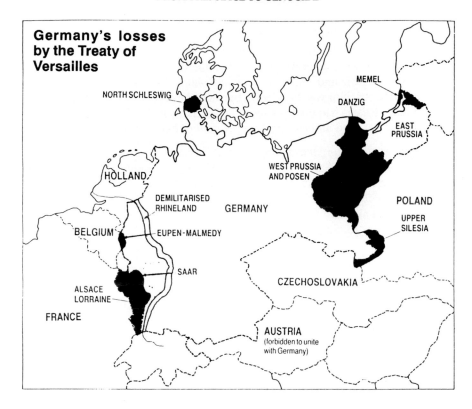

Germany's losses by the Treaty of Versailles

Source 2

The reaction in Germany was fierce. 'Vengeance! German nation! Today...the disgraceful treaty is being signed...Do not forget it! The German people will, with unceasing labour, press forward to reconquer the place among the nations to which it is entitled. Then will come vengeance for the shame of 1919'. (*Deutsche Zeitung* (German News-paper) 28/6/1919)

A number of small nationalist parties formed in Germany, including the *National Socialist German Workers Party* (NSDAP or 'Nazi' Party).

The elections of June 1920 resulted in victory for political parties *opposed* to the Weimar democratic system. The SPD received only twenty per cent of the vote. Some voters wanted Germany to become a monarchy again, others voted for parties promising a strong military government which would ignore the Treaty of Versailles. And a growing minority voted for the Socialist or Communist parties.

There were 20 different governments in 15 years, each serving an average of eight and a half months.

'The problem... was... the absence of any real democratic tradition in Germany'. (J.Tampke)

1. Explain what Tampke means by the above quote.

2. What do you imagine were some of the problems faced by the Weimar governments?

3. Using Sources 1 and 2, write a leaflet or design a poster as if you were a member of the Freikorps in 1920, trying to win support.

Hyperinflation 1923

Between 1914 and 1918, money had been printed to pay for the war effort. After 1918, there was far too much cash in relation to available goods. The currency began to lose its value. Germany failed to pay her war debts. Salaries could not keep up with inflation.

By November, a loaf of bread cost over 200,000,000,000 Marks. People paid for theatre seats with eggs or butter and workers needed wheelbarrows to carry their wages home. Hundreds of thousands of businesses went bankrupt and savings were worthless.

Source 3

Germany had lost the War, but that was not all. The people were famished...men and women who had spent their lives scratching and saving to provide themselves with...security for their old age, were dying in complete destitution. Disabled war pensioners drew no pensions..the War.. had ruined the country's economic life. (Otto Strasser)

Stability restored

Under the leadership of Gustav Stresemann from November 1923, the German economy revived. With the help of loans from America and foreign investment, the currency was restored to normal and the years between 1925 and 1929 even brought new prosperity for some people.

Art, music, theatre, architecture and literature flourished. It was the era of the actress *Marlene Dietrich* and *Bertolt Brecht*, the Communist playwright.

Source 4

William Shirer, an American journalist, writing about Germany in 1925, said: 'Life seemed more free, more modern, more exciting, than any place I had ever seen...One scarcely heard of Hitler or the Nazis except as the butt of music hall jokes'.

Permissiveness

There was more freedom within the family and more education. Attitudes towards sex were more relaxed.

Ilse Kokula (Historian) :

> 'There was open sexual experimentation...it was fashionable for men and women to have homosexual experiences and also for couples to experiment with other couples'.

Groups were set up to worship the naked body and nature. There was more Pornography — 'leatherbars', red light districts, open prostitution, and open discussion of birth control and abortion.

The twentieth century Gay movement originated in Germany, led by Magnus Hirschfeld. In Berlin alone there were 50 bars for women.

'The New Woman'

There were fierce debates between feminists, fighting for equality of rights and freedom from the trap of being housekeepers and 'breeding machines', and for more power in education and in the home. By 1925, one third of all employees were women.

'Except for the Treaty of Versailles, the Woman Question was the most controversial topic in Weimar Germany ' (Claudia Koonz, 1987).

The reaction

For conservative Germans, this was all too much. They described it as 'moral anarchy' and 'undermining Christian values'.

Erich Maria Remarque wrote his famous anti-war novel *All Quiet on the Western Front* and when the film of the book was shown, violent Nazi disturbances led to it being banned.

The usual scapegoats were wheeled out:'the Communists' 'the Feminists' and 'the Jews'. Jewish people were blamed this time for: founding the Weimar Republic, controlling the economy and the liberal Press, being Communists, homosexuals and criminals. Above all, they and the communists were said to have 'stabbed Germany in the back' by signing the Treaty of Versailles. Names of Jewish War Heroes were scratched off some First World War memorials. Nor was this a good time for Gypsies in Germany (see Chapter Two).

---

1. Imagine you were a journalist for the Conservative newspaper *Deutsche Zeitung*. Write an article expressing your alarm at the changes happening in German society. You should include reference to art, theatre, literature, sex and women.

2. Reread the information on the Jews of Germany (pp.4,25-27,34-35). Make a list of the arguments you might use against someone blaming the Jews for changes in German society.

3. In what way were feminists and communists scapegoats too?

THE NAZIS — THEIR RISE TO POWER AND THEIR APPEAL.

In 1929, Stresemann died. October brought the Wall Street Crash, Germany's crippling Depression and the opportunity the Nazis had been longing for.

In 1925, there were 27,000 members of the Nazi Party. By 1928, they had 100,000 members (0.5 per cent of the population) 810,000 votes and a mere twelve seats in Parliament. Only four years later, in July 1932, 13,745,000 people voted for them (thirty seven per cent of the vote) and by January 1933, they were in power.

Why this staggering increase in support? Who were the Nazis, who did they appeal to and how?

Their leader was *Adolf Hitler*, born in 1889, in Austria. His mother was a devout Catholic and Hitler became a choir boy and would practise 'long and fervent sermons' standing on a kitchen chair. Hitler's father was violent and brutal. His sister Paula later described how Adolf would receive daily beatings.

At school, his strengths were in gymnastics and art. In 1907, he failed to get into the Vienna Academy of Arts and was homeless — sleeping on park benches, depending on soup kitchens and charity.

He worked for a while with a man called Hanisch who sold picture postcards drawn by Hitler. (When he became leader of Germany, Hitler ordered the Gestapo to find Hanisch and kill him — to prevent embarrassing stories about his past being told.)

Vienna was then a centre of experimentation — new art, music, drama and ideas. Many of the innovators were Jews eg Sigmund Freud, the psychoanalyst. Hitler read the antisemitic literature on sale and in newspapers.

Source 5

For example, the writings of ex-monk Lanz von Libenfels, who demanded the castration of 'inferior breeds' of people and the mass extermination of 'sub-humans' to ensure 'racial purity' for the 'Aryan culture'. In fact there is no such thing as an Aryan person. The word refers to a family of *languages,* including Iranian, Greek and Latin.

Hitler began to absorb these ideas and to build up a certain view of the world. Later he wrote of his days in Vienna :

Source 6

'Czechs, Poles, Hungarians, Ruthenians, Serbs and Croats...and always the Jew, here and there and everywhere — the whole spectacle was repugnant to me' (*Mein Kampf*, p.114-5)

When the First World War broke out, Hitler was living in Munich in Germany, a country he admired more than Austria. He joined the German army enthusiastically and was awarded the Iron Cross First Class — by a Jewish officer — for bravery shown during the war. This, he said, was 'The greatest day of my life.' He was, however, described by his superior officers as lacking leadership qualities.

Source 7

When he heard about Germany's surrender, Hitler was devastated: 'Everything went black before my eyes. I...dug my burning head into my blanket and pillow...And so it had all been in vain...all the sacrifices...the death of two million...Did all this happen only so that a gang of wretched criminals could lay hands on the fatherland?' (*Mein Kampf*, p.185-7)

---

1. List all the factors which influence a person's behaviour and attitudes from birth e.g. parents, school etc. Using the above Sources and information, next to each factor write a sentence to describe Hitler's experience.
2. Compare Sources 5 and 6. In what way are the thoughts of the two men similar?

Hitler stayed on in the Army after the war and was employed to spy and report on new political groups. He despised the democratic government of Germany and swore revenge on Germany's enemies. In 1919, he joined the German Workers Party, which had a membership of approximately twenty-six people. In 1920, he became their leader and renamed the Party the Nationalsozialistische Deutsche Arbeiterpartei (NSDAP) or NAZI Party.

Hitler organised meetings. He was an effective speaker and the party membership began to grow. To attract a cross-section of Germans, the Nazis drew up a twenty-five point programme, including the following demands:

Source 8

- The union of all German-speaking peoples into a Greater Germany.

- The abolition of the Treaty of Versailles.

- Additional land and territory for the German peoples.

- The denial of German citizenship to Jews.

- A ban on unearned income.

- Nationalisation of major industries.

- Generous old-age pensions.

- The creation of a strong central government.

Which groups of people, or individuals, might have found this programme (Source 8) appealing? Explain your answer.

In 1921, he set up the SA (*Sturm Abteilung*) from ex-soldiers, under *Captain Röhm*. They acted like a private army, keeping order at party meetings.

In November 1923, Hitler led an attempt to overthrow the government in Bavaria. It had some support from politicians and the army, including General Ludendorff (hero of the First World War). It failed and Hitler was sent to prison. He served only nine months of a five year sentence. While there, he wrote *Mein Kampf* (My Struggle), published in July 1925. Some of what he wrote can be summed up as follows:

Race

He said there was no such thing as equality betwen the races. The 'Aryan' race was superior and needed to *act* to protect itself from races he said were 'inferior' — Jews, Gypsies, Slavs and blacks.

Aryans were defined as blond-haired, blue-eyed and: 'tall, long-legged, slim, with an average height...The limbs, the neck, the shape of the hands and feet are slender in appearance...The face is narrow...with a prominent chin'. (from George Mosse (ed), 1990)

Lebensraum
(Living space)

Aryans must have room to live, with their families, and must rule themselves. The East (Poland and Russia) was to provide this living space for Germans. The Slavs there were inferior, he said, and their wishes were of no concern. He promised to restore Germany to greatness.

Party Organisation

Half of *Mein Kampf* was about the need for the Nazi Party to organise itself.

Jewish People

Jews were Hitler's main enemy. He described them as: 'A germ, infecting society' and deliberately trying to bring down governments. This attack on Jews was repeated in his speeches, in Nazi news-

A Danish anti-Nazi cartoon showing Josef Goebbels, who became Hitler's propoganda minister. He is saying: 'High stature, blonde hair, blue eyes, oval-shaped face and a small nose is what characterises the true, the pure Aryan...'

papers and writings. They said that Jews were everywhere and controlled everything. In fact under one per cent of the German people were Jewish. 'In no way could it be argued that the Jews 'dominated' the cultural or economic life of Germany, as the Nazis claimed.' — William Carr, Historian.

'No personal experience has come to light which would explain the intensity of Hitler's obsessive hatred of the Jews. 'The Jew' as he appeared in *Mein Kampf* or Hitler's talk bore no resemblance to flesh-and-blood human beings; he was an invention of Hitler's fantasy, expressing the need to create an object on which he could concentrate his feelings of hatred and agression' (Alan Bullock, 1991).

2% of professional people were Jewish, 16% of lawyers, 11% of doctors, 2.5% of University professors and 0.5% of school teachers.

In 1920, on April 29th, Hitler had declared: 'We will carry on the struggle until the last Jew is removed from the German Reich'.

However, for many supporters of the Nazis, antisemitism was not its main appeal. They were more concerned about unemployment or communism.

Communism

Hitler loathed communism and communists. He was totally opposed to their ideas of equality. He said Jews were communist leaders and referred to 'Jewish Bolshevism' as being the root of all evil.

The 1917 Revolution in Russia and the Communist revolutions and uprisings in Germany after the war had frightened many business people and landowners. For them, the main appeal of the Nazis was their promise to crush Communism.

---

1. Why do most scientists today claim there is no such thing as 'race'?
2. What might Hitler mean by needing to act to protect the 'Aryan Race'? How would he obtain Poland and Russia for the German people?
3. Look at the statistics on percentages of Jewish professionals. How do they support the view of William Carr, historian? How does Alan Bullock explain Hitler's antisemitism?
4. Why was Communism so frightening to so many people in the 1920s and 1930s?

Volk

Hitler wrote and spoke about an 'ideal time' in Germany before the First World war and industrialisation. He promised his listeners that the Germany of farms, rural beauty and happy families could be reborn. If they could only get rid of 'inferior races' and communists, then the 'true Germans' — the Volk — people of the same 'Blood, Race and Soil' could live in harmony. (See p.25 for the effect of industrialisation on Germany). He vowed to rid Germany of the 'permissiveness' of Weimar society with its sexual freedom and its school students demanding their rights.

Women

He said that men were the masters of society and that a woman's place was in the home — as mothers and obedient wives. Women should not wear lipstick or powder, nor should they smoke. Their duty was to have babies, to provide soldiers for the Fatherland.

Führer

Hitler claimed that only a strong leader could ensure the rebirth of this perfect German society. He offered himself as a prophet who would save the German nation.

Source 9

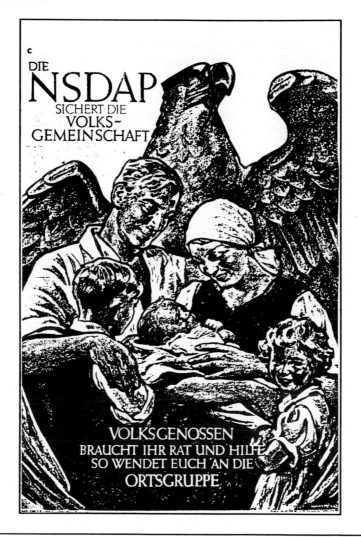

1. Who did Conservatives and Nationalists blame for causing the Industrial Revolution in Germany? (See Chapter 1)

2. How does the Nazi election poster (Source 9) represent Hitler's view of Volk?

3. Read Hitler's views on women. What was he reacting against?

The Appeal of the Nazis

In Werner's opinion:

> Hitler wrote a piece of economic and political garbage called *Mein Kampf*. It was garbage and everyone knew it to be so....But having said that, he kept his word...

However, to their supporters, the Nazis represented Action, Adventure, Movement and Hope.

Hitler with a group of young National Socialists, 1933.

Hitler as a speaker

Hitler was a brilliant orator, addressing massive crowds and whipping them into a frenzy with his words. Often, he would deliberately keep his audience waiting for over an hour, until twilight.

Source 10

At one of the early meetings I was sitting surrounded by thousands of S.A. men and as Hitler spoke I was most interested at the shouts ..of the men around me, who were mainly working men or lower middle class types. 'He speaks for me, he speaks for me.' 'He knows how I feel'. Many seemed lost to the world around them..One man.. with a sort of sob, said, 'He understands'...As I hurried away to go back to my hotel, I heard uncontrolled sobbing beside me and I saw it was a middle-aged woman in a wheel-chair, 'Now you can take me away, I will die happily — I have seen the face of the Führer — Germany will live!' (E.Amy Buller, 1943).

'He had the ability to stop people thinking critically' (Egon Hanfstaengel).

Source 11

see photograph opposite.

Not everyone found his style appealing. *Emmi Bonhoeffer* refers to how he was seen as a 'drunken postman' by some.

Using Sources 10 and 11, explain how the effect of Hitler can be compared to that of a religious leader? Make a note from now on of every reference in the book to the *religious* appeal of the Nazis.

Propaganda

The Nazis realised they needed to do more than hold huge meetings and shout about Jews and communists. Their ideas and image had to be seen everywhere, in literature, art, theatre, films and posters. They used the swastika as a symbol of power. The swastika is an ancient symbol, found in Mayan and early Christian art, but most commonly associated with Hin-

"When you see a cross, think of the

duism. In India, it is a sacred symbol and a sign of welcome. In 1910, the German poet and nationalist Guido von List suggested using the swastika as a sign for all antisemistic organisations.

Masterminded by Dr Joseph Goebbels, the Nazis developed crude but effective propaganda, aimed at certain groups, from industrial workers to the *Mittelstand* rural community. (There is no exact English translation of 'Mittelstand'. Its meaning combines 'middle class' with 'respectability' and has feudal connotations.) Voters were told that the choice was either Communist or Nazi. Goebbels' motto was :

Source 12
IF YOU TELL A LIE, TELL A BIG LIE.
IF YOU TELL IT OFTEN ENOUGH,
PEOPLE WILL EVENTUALLY BELIEVE IT

And some did.

Source 13
I wish I could give you a nice story, that I was against the Nazis,
that I was a hero..
But I believed the movies.
Jews were freaks,
dogs who'd hurt you, cheat you,

though I never saw one...
I believed the principal, my teachers.
We were the Master Race.
We were the deprived ones, crowded, hungry.
We needed room in the East.
The Russians prevented us.
The Poles, the Gypsies, the Jews
They had cruelties. We were not.
The Russians were cruel.
The Poles were cruel, the Gypsies.
The Jews.

(by Eva Klin, born a German Catholic, now a convert to Judaism and living in America, in Julie Heifetz, 1985).

Source 14
see illustration opposite

---

1. Explain how the Nazis used a. fear b. lies c. hope, to win support.

2. What evidence is there in Source 13 that Eva Klin has unlearned the Nazi ideas she heard as a young girl?

3. Hitler did not invent antisemitism, he used it. With reference to Source 14, explain the meaning of this statement (See also p.11-12 Chapter 1).

In fact, the Nazi's policies were very similar to other parties. But their STYLE was different. They appeared more like a religious crusade than a political party.

SUPPORTERS

The Nazis won the support of a wider range of social and economic groups than any other party. Their voters ranged from unemployed labourers to members of the former royal family.

The lower middle classes formed the bulk of support. Civil servants, teachers, small shopkeepers, self-employed artisans, small farmers, pensioners, small investors, they deserted Conservative and Liberal Parties to vote for the Nazis.

These voters were disillusioned with the Weimar governments and liked the Nazi attack on trade unions, high taxes, big business, the banks, money-lenders and large department stores, which the Nazis claimed were dominated by Jewish people. Some Jews did own department stores, but many Jews were the owners of small shops threatened by the larger ones. At the same time, some **industrialists** supported Hitler — because of his fierce anti-communism and nationalism. Industrialists disliked the SDP government, because it believed in welfare payments which meant higher taxes.

Research suggests that the Nazis did extremely well in rural and semi-rural Protestant areas, especially in North and North-East Germany. They did less well in cities, large urban centres or Catholic rural areas in the West or South. The Nazis' highest votes came from wealthy districts.

Women never made up more than five per cent of Nazi Party membership and in the 1920s, only a minimum of women voted for them. But by July 1932, women gave six and a half million of the thirteen and a half million votes for Hitler.

Why did so many vote for a Party which talked about women as inferior to men and promised to restore them to their 'holy position as servant and maid'? Hitler often said: 'The Nazi Revolution will be an entirely male event'. Some were reacting against the Women's Liberation Movement and were attracted by his praise of motherhood. Many referred to Hitler as if he was a religious leader, a Messiah :

Source 15

'Whoever...has a pure heart and hears our Führer speak and looks into his eyes has no choice but to convert to him... *Mein Kampf* became our Bible'. (Maria Engelhardt, quoted in C.Koonz, 1987)

Some have interpreted his appeal as sexual: 'Members of the audience, particularly women, were brought to a state of frenzy which in some ways resembled an orgasm' (Egon Hanfstaengel).

There was an increase in the number of young voters, due to the pre-war 'baby bulge'. Three million **young** voters were added to the electorate after 1928. Many felt alienated from the existing system and were not part of the trade union or Communist movements.

Ex-Soldiers were attracted by the idea of regaining Germany's international pride, after the humiliation of November 1918 and the Versailles Treaty.

The majority of workers did not support the Nazis (10 — 15% of the Nazi voters were workers), though a significant number of SA members were working class. The unemployed workers tended to be more attached to the Communists, Socialists, SPD or Catholic Centre Party. But the German Labour Movement was very divided and therefore weak.

1. Make up a quote for each of the four groups above (women, the young, ex-soldiers and workers), explaining why many of them supported the Nazis.

2. Why did the Nazis particularly try to appeal to young people?

3. Are the two quotes in Source 15 supported by other evidence you have seen in this chapter?

4. How do you imagine Communist women might have reacted to hearing Hitler speak and looking into his eyes?

Nazi supporters who were unhappy about Hitler's rabid racism, said that he would drop it once in power and that his threats towards the Jews were not serious. A typical attitude towards the idea of voting Nazi was: 'Let them have a chance'.

Source 16

Else Wendel, a social worker during the 1930s, supported Hitler. She remembers the hopelessness she felt about the future : 'The despair was so terrible...I felt he was the only one who could do justice to the poor'.

The End of Democracy

In October 1929, the value of shares sold on the Wall Street Stock Exchange in New York collapsed in the *Wall Street Crash*. Thousands of American businesses were ruined and money that had been invested in or lent to German companies was withdrawn overnight. The result was mass unemployment, poverty and misery. Productivity halved and savings were wiped out. Many Germans blamed their government and support for the Nazis soared.

There was a mood of desperation: a feeling that Germany could either descend into total chaos or utterly change.

The Nazis welcomed the crisis. This was what they had been waiting for. *Alfred Hugenburg*, a nationalist newspaper owner, gave them access to his press, cinema and funds.

Homeless workers paid a few pennies for several hours sleep in a Hamburg flophouse.

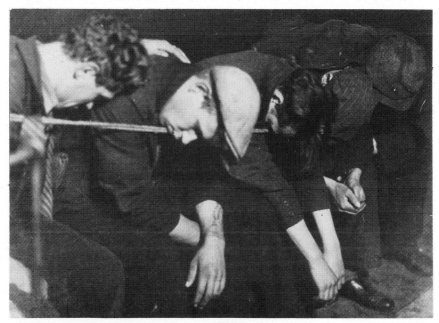

Nazi election poster, 1932. 'We've had enough! Vote Nazi!'

Unemployment

Opposite: Nuremberg Rally.

September 1928	650,000
September 1929	1,300,000
September 1930	3,000,000
September 1931	4,300,000
January 1933	6,100,000

Nazi Support

1928	800,000 votes
1930 (Sept)	6,409,000 votes
1932 (July)	13,745,000 votes

The Communist and Catholic vote also increased.

The Nazis never managed to win a majority of the votes, but the opposition failed to unite. Indeed the Communists warned their supporters that the Social Democrats were more of a threat than the Nazis.

The Nazis promised salvation, hope, strength and answers to Germany's problems. The Nazi Party was everywhere — marching, singing, fighting, in trucks, with flags and rallies every day in a different region.

Chancellor Brüning (Centre Catholic Party) could offer no solutions to the economic crisis and by 1932, Hitler was a national figure.

In 1932, Hitler stood for President of Germany against Hindenburg, the World War One Commander and national hero.

Hindenburg won by 19 million votes to Hitler's 13 million.

1a. Read the quote by the social worker, Else Wendel (Source 16).

1b. Because she voted for Hitler, would you say she was antisemitic? How do the unemployment figures add to your understanding of the period?

2. Hamburg was never a very 'Nazified' city. What sort of solutions to unemployment would the Communists have offered?

3. Can you explain why the Communists regarded the Social Democrats as more of a threat than the Nazis? (Remember the political events of 1919 and the early Weimar years, see p.55-59).

In the elections of July 1932, the Nazis were the strongest party, but received only 37% of the vote, not enough to form a government.

In August 1932 there were pitched street battles between Nazis and Communists. Five hundred people were killed or injured.

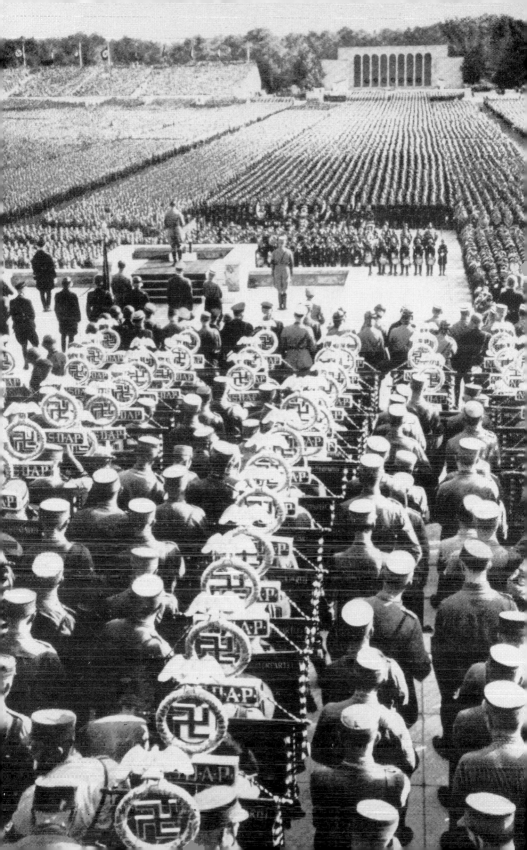

President Hindenburg disliked the way the Nazis ignored the law and how the SA used violence. He refused to make Hitler Chancellor and the Nazis would not make a coalition with any other party. But by the end of 1932, Hindenburg, desperate for a solution and imagining he could control Hitler, invited him to become Chancellor.

The new Cabinet of twelve men included only four Nazis. The rest were Conservatives, who believed that Hitler would calm down in power. Communists hoped that he would bring total ruin to the country, making way for a Communist revolution. They were to be proved drastically wrong.

Werner Mayer (see Chapter One) remembers :

> In the year 1933 I found suddenly that my people and I were turned into vermin. After the Nazis came to power, our lives went sharply downhill. I was twelve years of age, I was scared and worried because I could not understand what crime I had committed. I felt outraged and frightened because there was nothing I could do. My father thought it was a very good job, because Hitler was, after all, an empty-brained loud-mouthed demagogue and he would be shown up to be what he was. My, he was proved wrong...

---

1. Draw a diagram to show all the factors mentioned in this chapter which help explain why the Nazis came to power in Germany in 1933.

2. Can you decide which of the factors were the most (and least) important?

3. In your own words, explain how Conservatives, Communists and people like Werner's father all imagined Hitler's rise to power was not such a bad thing.

Chapter Five

The Nazis in power

On coming to power, the Nazis aimed to set up a TOTALITARIAN society in order to control every person, organisation and institution in Germany. Only healthy 'Aryans' who were active Nazis were acceptable.

In order to achieve this, what aspects of society (e.g. the Press) and which groups of people would you expect the Nazis to control and attack?

Dictatorship

Hitler called a General Election for March 1933. Just before it, there was a fire at the *Reichstag* (Parliament). A Dutch communist was caught and accused of arson, although many historians believe that the fire was deliberately started by the Nazis, so that they could blame and then punish the Communists.

1. Claiming the Communists were plotting to take over Germany, Hitler got President Hindenburg to agree to pass the *Law for the Protection of the People and State.* This banned Communists and Socialists from taking part in the election. In January 1933, 300,000 Germans had belonged to the Communist Party; one year later, half of them were in jails and camps or dead. Most who were free went into exile.

2. The Nazis still failed to secure a majority of the votes, but Hitler managed to get the new *Reichstag* to pass an *Enabling Act* on 23rd March 1933. This gave him the power to make laws without asking for Parliament's consent.

3. Next came a ban on trade unions and a *Law against the Formation of New Parties*.

THE NAZIS WERE NOW THE ONLY LEGAL PARTY AND HITLER HAD BEEN GIVEN THE POWER TO PASS ANY LAWS HE CHOSE

Terror

In 1933, there were 400,000 Stormtroopers, the brownshirted SA. Hitler feared they had too much power and independence. On 30th June 1934, at 3 a.m., he ordered the *Night of the Long Knives*. Ernst Röhm and the other SA leaders were arrested and shot by Hitler's SS (*Schutzstaffel*, Secret State Police Office or Protection Squads), who went on to kill 400 SA members.

Hitler now had control of the SS (headed by Himmler), the *Gestapo* (Heydrich), the SD (Heydrich and Eichmann, Intelligence Service), the police and the Army. With Party officials at every level of government, the machinery of total control was in place.

Why could Communists, Socialists, Liberals and Trade Unionists now be legally arrested?

Concentration Camps

By April 1933, the first concentration camp was set up at Dachau.

> To terrorize political opponents, Churchmen, Communists, homosexuals and Jews, the new government set up concentration camps ...In each of these camps, daily beatings and harsh treatment quickly became the rule. (M. Gilbert, *The Holocaust*, 1986)

Every prisoner was identified by a different colour badge: red for political prisoners; pink for gays; green for 'habitual criminals; yellow for Jews; brown for gypsies and purple for Jehovah's Witnesses.

Why were camp prisoners labelled in this way?

Source 1

The camps had the desired effect on most people. Egon Hanfstaengel remembers a schoolchildren's saying from the time: 'Dear God, strike me dumb, so that I shan't be sent to Dachau'.

1. What is the meaning of the saying in Source 1?

2. Why did many Germans not object to the mass arrest of Communists, trade unionists etc?

3. There were thousands of people in the concentration camps before 1939 — does this mean that the Nazis failed to impose total terror?

Education

In 1938, Bernhard Rust, Minister of Education, announced that: 'The whole function of all education is to create a Nazi'. Children in Kindergarten, aged 3, began the day with 'Hands together, bow your heads and think of Adolf Hitler'. Schools and Universities were told what to teach.

Pictures of Hitler were displayed in every classroom and each day began with the Nazi salute and 'Heil Hitler !'

Mein Kampf became the text-book for schools. The pupils read and discussed it, chapter by chapter and when they had finished, they started it again. By 1937, 97% of teachers belonged to the Nazi Teachers Association.

Source 2

The following is an example of a Math's problem set for German children in 1936: A mentally-handicapped person costs the public four Reichsmarks per day, a cripple costs 5.50 Reichsmarks...300,000 persons are being cared for in public mental institutions. How many marriage loans at 1,000 Reichsmarks per couple could be annually financed from the funds allocated to these institutions?

---

1. Why did the Nazis want 3 year-olds to start the day by thinking of Hitler?

2. What did they hope would be the effects of using materials such as Source 2?

3. Is school the most important influence on your life and attitudes?

4. Why did many children remain anti-Nazis?

A new subject, *Race Science,* was introduced to the curriculum.

Source 3

Frank S. was a twelve year old boy in 1933, living in Breslau, Germany. He was one of two Jewish students in a class of fifty-three boys. Frank remembers one class in which the teacher ordered him to the front of the room as the example of a Jew. The teacher pointed to Frank's features, explaining that they marked him as an inferior human being, while the features of a blond-haired, blue-eyed student represented the perfect Aryan...Frank encountered repeated insults from non-Jewish students who wanted to pick a fight with him. (M. Johnson and M Stern Strom, 1989).

Source 4

I was chased out of school when I was fourteen years of age and I went to a Jewish College. Just before my sixteenth birthday, our school was ransacked, destroyed in the so-called Kristallnacht (see p.83-84) and I found myself in a concentration camp called Dachau...that was hell, but I survived. (Werner Mayer)

Think of some of the reactions Frank (Source 3) and Werner (Source 4) and their non-Jewish classmates might have had to the incidents they describe.

THE TREATMENT OF THE JEWS

Hitler said: 'Antisemitism is the most important weapon in our propaganda arsenal'. A popular Nazi song included the lines:

> 'When Jewish blood spurts from under the knife, things will be twice as good as before.'

A total of 400 anti-Jewish laws was passed.

---

1.   What did Hitler mean in the above quote?

2.   Draw a chart. On the left hand side make a list of the following laws (Except for the two in capital letters). On the right, put the effect you imagine the Nazis wanted to have by passing each law.

Source 5

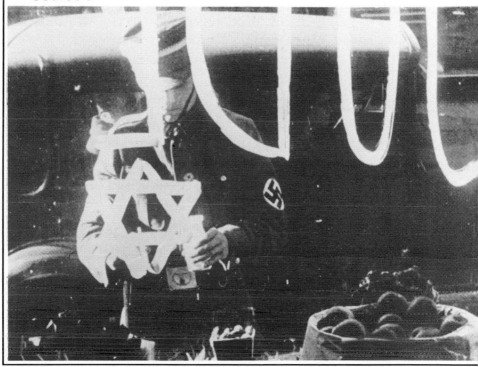

Nazi painting 'Jude' (Jew) and star of David on Jewish-owned shop.

1933	Public burning of books by Jewish authors.
1-4-1933	A one day boycott of all Jewish-owned shops.
15-9-1935	*Nuremberg Laws.* Jews are deprived of German citizenship. It is illegal for Jews and Gypsies to marry or have any sexual relations with Aryans.

Jews were encouraged to emigrate. They had to pay a tax on leaving. (By 1938, 250,000 or half the total German Jewish population had left).

7-3-1936	Jews may no longer vote.
2-7-1937	Most Jewish students removed from German schools and Universities.
16-11-1937	Restrictions are placed on Jews travelling abroad.
27-7-1938	All 'Jewish' street names are to be replaced.

17-7-1938	All Jews must add either 'Israel' or 'Sarah' to their name.
9-11-1938	KRISTALLNACHT — DESTRUCTION OF SYNA-GOGUES, MASS ARRESTS AND THE MURDER OF A THOUSAND JEWS
23-11-1938	All Jewish business are closed down and taken over by Nazis.
23-9-1939	All Jews must hand their radios in to the police.
29-7-1940	Jews may no longer have telephones.
31-7-1941	THE BEGINNING OF THE ATTEMPT TO MURDER ALL THE JEWS OF EUROPE.
1-9-1941	Every Jewish person in Germany must wear a yellow star of David.
15-10-1941	Jews are forbidden to keep dogs, cats and birds.
17-7-1942	Blind or deaf Jews may no longer wear armbands identifying their condition in traffic.

In order to be employed in certain jobs within the Nazi regime, Germans had to prove there was no 'Jewish blood' in their family since 1850. So population records were very well kept.

1. Imagine you are a Jewish child in Berlin, October 1941. Write a letter to a pen pal in England describing how your life has changed over the past 8 years and how your family and friends (Jewish and non-Jewish) have reacted.

2. Look again at p.15-16 Chapter 1. Find all the similarities and differences between the medieval and the Nazi anti-Jewish laws.

3. The Nazis claimed that Jews had certain obvious physical characteristics. How does the order making all Jewish people wear yellow stars contradict this claim?

4. Look at the photo of Jewish Austrian athletes on p.3. It was taken before the Nazis came to power there. Think about how some Jews actually *chose* to wear the Star of David. What does it represent for Jews in pre- and post-Nazi times? What did it represent under the Nazis?

5. Why did the Nazis introduce their antisemitic laws over a period of six years, rather than all at once?

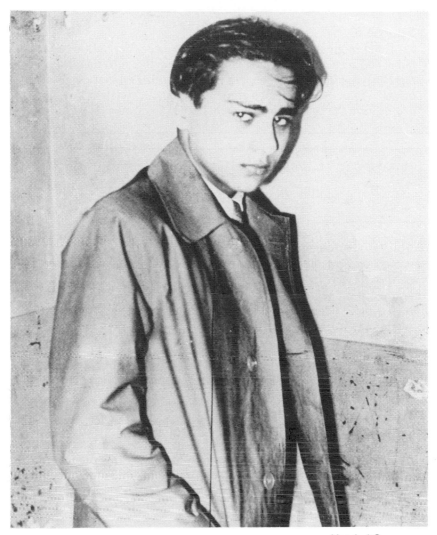

Herchel Grynszpan

Kristallnacht, November 1938

On October 28th 1938, all Polish Jews living in Germany were sent back to Poland. Most of them were literally dumped on the German/Polish border.

Herchel Grynszpan was a student in Paris at the time, his parents were among those deported. When he heard the news, he went to the German Embassy in Paris on November 7th and shot dead Ernst vom Rath, an Embassy employee.

Source 6

I was not motivated by hatred or by vengeance... but by love of my father and my people, who have endured unbearable suffering. I deeply regret having injured anyone, but I have no other way of expressing myself...To be Jewish is not a crime! We are not animals! The Jewish people have the right to live! (Herchel Grynszpan, aged 17)

---

1. In your opinion, was Herchel Grynszpan's action justified?

2. What did he mean by saying : 'I have no other way of expressing myself'?

Two days later, on the orders of the *Gestapo*, synagogues throughout Germany were set alight, 92 Jews were murdered, 7,000 shops owned by Jewish people were looted and destroyed, as well as 800 houses. 31,000 Jews were arrested and sent to concentration camps — one thousand of them were murdered there. Children were dragged from orphanages, patients from hospitals and old people from their homes.

The amount of broken glass on the streets next morning, led the Nazis to call that night 'the Night of the broken glass' or *Kristallnacht*. The Jews were fined one billion Marks to pay for the damage done. For many Jews, it was too much to bear.

'After *Kristallnacht*, no German could any longer be under any illusion' (ex-Hitler Youth member).

The Nazis were surprised at how strongly many Germans opposed this violent attack on their Jewish neighbours. For example, the mayor of Fishbach stopped the burning of the town's synagogue. People were arrested for making pro-Jewish comments and criticising the Nazis' action.

---

1. Why might some non-Jewish Germans have opposed *Kristall-nacht*, when they had not objected to antisemitic laws passed before 1938?

2. What did the ex-Hitler youth mean?

Work and Leisure

For some Germans, life became more bearable under the Nazis.
Between January 1933 and January 1939, the number of (officially) unemployed people fell from 6 million to 302,000.
How was this achieved?

1. Jobs were created for unemployed men by the removal of women and Jewish people from their work.
2. All men aged between 18 and 25 were forced to build schools, hospitals, roads and forests.
3. Two million jobs were created in the army, airforce and weapons' factories.

Trade unions were banned, strikes made illegal and there were no limits on working hours per week. However, holidays, trips, theatre and concerts provided by the Nazi *Kraft Durch Freude* (Strength Through Joy) kept some workers content.

---

1. For many German individuals and families, these were happy days. Why?
2. However, some people were not satisfied with their working conditions. Why did most of them not complain?

Women

From 1933, Feminist organisations were made illegal and Nazi Women's Organisations set up. By 1940, the League of German Women had 8 million members. Many women judges, teachers, civil servants or MPs were dismissed. They were discouraged from having any form of employment.

Gertrude Scholtz-Klink, was the chief of the Women's Bureau under Hitler. In 1937, her portrait appeared on the cover of the magazine for Nazi women. During an interview with Claudia Koonz in 1981, she said:

'Our job (and we did it well) was to infuse the daily life of all German women — even in the tiniest villages- with Nazi ideals...How often they told us with shining eyes, 'No one has ever talked to us like this, except possibly in religious services'.

In Hitler's opinion, women were only suited to: *Children, Church and Cooking* (KINDER, KIRCHE UND KUCHE). The image of Woman as Eve and Mother was promoted everywhere.

Source 7

Gertrude Scholtz — Klinks' portrait on the cover of the magazine for Nazi women (*Mutter und Volk*)

Source 8

The mission of the woman is to be beautiful and to bring children into the world...the female bird pretties herself for her mate and hatches the eggs for him (Joseph Goebbels, Minister for Propaganda, 1934)

Hitler compared a woman's duty to produce children for the Fatherland with a man's duty to fight and die. Medals were awarded to women bearing more than four children and abortionists were hunted down.

1. How did the name of the women's magazine in Source 7 fit in with Nazi ideology? You should refer to Source 8.

2. The Nazis claimed to be in favour of The Family. How did their policies on Work, Party activities and Youth (see below) actually break up the family?

The Hitler Youth

From 1933, there was pressure on young people to join the Hitler Youth movement. There were separate organisations for girls and boys. Admission was to be on April 20th each year, Hitler's birthday. But millions did not join and in 1939, membership became compulsory for all young people aged ten to nineteen. Any parent preventing their child from joining could be fined or imprisoned. To parents unwilling for their children to join, Hitler said : 'Your child belongs to us'.

There were weekly meetings, trips and camps. Physical fitness was emphasised and they were indoctrinated with the ideas of Nazism. Hitler described the sort of young people he hoped would come out of his camps:

Source 9

'The weak must be chiselled away. Young people will grow up who will frighten the world. I want a violent, arrogant, unafraid, cruel youth who must be able to suffer pain. '

Alfons Heck, a former Hitler Youth leader remembers :

> He spoke to us like a father to a son — 'You all belong to me...one day you are going to rule the world' and from that day on, I was bound to Adolf Hitler. So devoted were some, that they were willing to inform the police if their own parents spoke out against the Nazi regime.

The BDM (Bund Deutscher Madchen — *German Girls League*) also spent their time at camps, keeping fit, memorising information about the Nazi leadership, the Treaty of Versailles and the words of Nazi songs. They were expected to conform to a certain sort of beauty — anyone who permed their hair instead of wearing plaits or braids, had it shaved off.

The Press image of the League did not always fit with the image they had in some people's eyes. Their organisation was known unofficially as Bund Deutscher Matrazen (German Mattresses League).

Source 10

In 1936, when approximately 100,000 members of the Hitler Youth and the Girls' League attended the Nuremberg Rally, 900 girls between fifteen and eighteen returned home pregnant. (Richard Grunberger, 1971)

Some young people not only refused to join the movement, they set up their own anti-Nazi youth groups (see Chap 6).

Judges of the Berlin Criminal Court display the emblem of the Nazi state on their robes, 1936.

The Courts

To the Nazis, the law, the Courts, judges, lawyers and police existed purely to help them achieve their aims.

A *Nazi Lawyers Association* was set up and the judges proved quite easy to control, sending people to their death for 'race defilement' (sexual intercourse between Jews and non-Jews) or, for example, executing a Berlin pastor for telling an anti-Nazi joke.

Most judges were Right-wing and Nationalist. Any judge who displeased the government was sacked. On 1st November 1937, a lawyer who had failed to give the Heil Hitler salute had to appear in Court.

Why in a democracy, is it considered so important to make sure that judges and lawyers are independent of the government?

The Media And Propaganda

Joseph Goebbels was Reich Minister of Propaganda. The image of the Fuhrer was promoted everywhere as strong, caring and magnificent:

1. Why was this a powerful image for some Germans?

2. If you were employed as Hitler's Propaganda Minister, what other images of him would you use?

3. Remember that Jewish Germans formed under one per cent of the population. Many Germans had never met a Jew. Would this have helped or hindered Goebbels? Explain your answer.

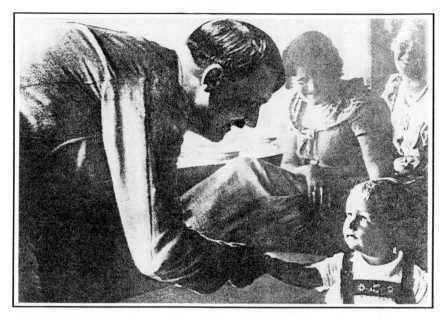

Hitler with a little boy. This picture was distributed all over Germany as a postcard entitled: *A Child's Gaze.*

Hitler believed in the power of the spoken word and the Nazis had total control of: radio, cinema, theatre and effective control of the newspapers. Novelists, playwrights, magazine editors and publishers were suppressed and controlled.

Cheap radios were manufactured and by 1939, 70% of German homes had one, the highest percentage of radio ownership in the world. In order to broadcast rallies, speeches and orders, radio loudspeakers were set up in village squares, Department stores, pubs and blocks of flats. It was compulsory to attend propaganda sessions in the factories.

Der Stürmer (The Stormer) was a weekly Nazi paper owned by *Julius Streicher*. It became phenomenally popular, selling over half a million copies every week by 1935. It was violently antisemitic, with a banner headline reading: ' The Jews are our misfortune'. Names and addresses of Germans who continued to employ Jews, or attend the weddings of Jewish friends were published in it:

Dear Stürmer!
The engincer Dr A.Kleinlogel is a part-time professor at the Technical High School in .....[He] lives at 33 Roquette street in Darmstadt. He employs the Jew Hajnal in a leading position as Chief Engineer. This Jew often conducts negotiations with various government authorities on behalf of Mr Kleinlogel...It is time to put a stop to the activities of the

Jew Hajnal and the Jew-lover Kleinlogel. (Translation of part of a letter from *Der Stürmer* of April 1936)

In 'September 1938, Streicher began writing articles which called for the annihilation of the 'Jewish race'.

Source 11

My way to school took me past the local Nazi Party Headquarters (the former Jewish Community House). In a glass case.....there was displayed a complete issue of 'The Stürmer'....I found the grotesque cartoons and the almost pornographic text deeply offensive. Nobody in my family or among my friends and relations looked, thought or acted as described in the paper, but I realised that it would create much hatred. (Herbert Loebl)

The paper published regular illustrated stories about Jewish men raping blond German girls.

Source 12: (Stürmer)

Der Stürmer, May 1934.

On May 1st 1934, a special fourteen-page issue came out, full of the medieval accusations about Jews (see Chapter 1). 130,000 copies were printed and sold. Some were displayed on public noticeboards.

Source 13 : The poisonous mushroom:
Propaganda for children

One of the pictures in *The poisonous mushroom*, in Nazi propaganda book for children, published by Julius Streicher.

Written by Ernst Heimer, illustrated by Fips, this children's book was also published by Julius Streicher.

---

1. What does the German sentence at the bottom of the front cover (Source 12) mean?

2. Why did Streicher publish the names and addresses of Germans who continued to be friendly to Jewish Germans?

3. Even without the words, the message of the children's book (Source 13) is very clear. What sort of images of Jewish men does it convey?

4. Why did the Nazis have to use cartoons of Jewish people, rather than photographs?

5. Can you think of books you read as a child which have influenced your attitudes in any way?

THE JEHOVAH'S WITNESSES

The Jehovah's Witnesses were another target for the Nazis. Because they refused to join the army and swear allegiance to Hitler, they were persecuted.

Elizabeth Dopazo was four when Hitler came to power. Her father was arrested for the first time in 1934 :

> My father wouldn't join the Nazis because of his religious convictions; it was totally against the principles of the Bible to be militaristic...My father spoke five languages. He also corresponded with people all over the world and that already made you suspicious...We had breakfast one morning and the Gestapo came in and arrested him at gunpoint. I was seven...and that's the last time we saw him.

How did Elizabeth's father's religion make him an anti-Nazi?

THE CHURCHES

It was very important for Hitler to ensure control of the Churches. Why?

In 1933, the Pope signed a Concordat (agreement) with Hitler's regime. In return for a guarantee that it could continue to function and keep control over Catholic education, youth groups etc., the Catholic Church promised not to oppose Hitler. Many Catholic bishops and priests collaborated enthusiastically with the Nazis. 'The aims of the Reich government have long been those of the Catholic Church', claimed the Roman Catholic Bishop Burger.

Hitler ignored the Concordat. To him, it was just another 'piece of paper', and he suppressed the Catholic Press, schools and youth movements. There were individual priests who were anti-Nazi and who suffered as a result.

The Lutheran (Protestant) Churches were in the majority. There were many pro-Nazi 'German Christians' who gave sermons supporting the new regime. A leading Protestant, Didelius, lent his support to the Nazi boycott of Jewish shops in April 1933. Most Church leaders were Conservatives, not Nazis.

Source 14

The Nazis set up the *National Reich Church* in 1936. Among its rules was the following order : 'The National Reich Church will remove from the altars of all the churches, the Bible, the cross and religious objects.

On the altars there must be nothing but *Mein Kampf*, and to the left of this a sword'.

Crosses and crucifixes were removed from classrooms.

Some of those in the Protestant Church who opposed Hitler, set up the *Confessional Church* in 1934. 5,000 clergy eventually joined. It was led by a Swiss theologian called Karl Barth, who was expelled from Germany in 1935. Individuals within the Confessional Church were prominent in the resistance to Nazism (see Chapter 6).

1. Why might you expect Church ministers and priests to be anti-Nazi?

2. How does Source 14 fit in with other evidence you have read referring to Nazism as a sort of religion?

Sterilisation and Organised Murder

70,273 ordinary Germans, including old people and babies were gassed in Germany between 1940 and August 1941. WHY?

They were seen as 'undesirable' or 'racially unhealthy' by the Nazi regime because they were mentally ill, incurably sick or disabled. They did not fit the perfect Aryan ideal and so were considered 'unworthy of life'. They were considered too expensive. Sterilisation of people who were deaf, blind and epileptic, also of unwed mothers, had been urged by serious German writers in the 1920s. The American historian Stephen L. Chorover, in his book *From Genesis to Genocide*, describes how, in 1923, the German Foreign office requested information from the USA about the practices of certain American mental institutions and prisons.

'It should be clear that much of the ideological groundwork for genocide was laid in Germany well before the Nazis came to power and that Nazi sociobiology did not arise out of thin air'.

The British Sunday *Observer* of 19th November 1989 featured an article about the Nazis' sterilisation and euthanasia policy:

> It was from America's...sterilisation programme that the Nazis drew inspiration for their own laws. Indiana passed a sterilisation bill in 1907 which provided for the sterilisation of the mentally ill and the criminally insane, and by 1930, twenty-eight states had followed.

In January 1933, Hitler's Cabinet began a sterilisation programme with the Act for the Prevention of Hereditarily Diseased Offspring. Gypsies and black people were also targets. Hitler's Euthanasia Order came in October 1939, backdated to 1st September 1939. Its aim was the mass killing of German mental patients, described as 'useless eaters'. He called his doctors 'biological soldiers'.

Special hospital departments were established, where disabled children were murdered, usually by poison or starvation, and their parents were not only lied to, but also *charged* for the 'operation'. The criteria for killing eventually included children with malformed ears and bedwetters.

Then came the murder of adults. Five euthanasia institutions were set up for the purpose. The gassings were organised by Dr.Kalinger — a trained chemist. People living nearby saw the darkened buses arrive full and leave empty. Children living nearby began calling out: 'They are taking some more people to be gassed'. Staff were specially trained and 'hardened' for the job.

> Students who didn't complete the course because they cracked...were sent to the war front where the Commander in charge of the unit would assign them to a 'suicide' squad....[The] schooling produced perfect murderers who were used to the smell of burnt flesh...Pupils were naturally rewarded with alcohol, women....and medals. (B.Schrieber)

Members of the public, especially in the Catholic and Confessing Churches, protested very strongly about this Euthanasia programme. Cardinal Galen told his congregation: 'These are our brothers and sisters'.

In 1941, as a result of public protest, the Nazis put an official stop to the gassings. But they continued unofficially until 1944. The Euthanasia Programme exterminated an estimated 100,000 inmates of institutions.

---

1. Why did the murder of disabled people provoke such a loud protest by those who did not speak up against other Nazi policies?

2. What does B.Schrieber mean by 'suicide' squads?

Gays

The Nazis believed that there was such a thing as a 'normal man' — a masculine/father/soldier type. They saw gay men as unacceptable and 'degenerate' and singled them out for persecution, beginning in February 1933 when homosexual rights groups were banned.

Michael Ritterman, an actor, was arrested and beaten by ten men in a police cell. The authorities had his address book and wanted information about the names in there. He refused to tell them and eventually escaped from Germany.

Lesbianism was not forbidden by law. But there were many lesbians in concentration camps, put there as 'prostitutes' or 'communists' or 'bad for the German community'.

In October and November 1934, there were large-scale arrests of gay men in Germany. The Nazis had waited until after the *Night of the Long Knives* (see p.78) because Ernst Röhm, the leader of the SA was well-known as a homosexual. A decree passed in 1935 provided for the compulsory sterilisation of homosexuals.

In October 1936, the *Gestapo* leader, Himmler, said homosexuals must be eliminated as a danger to the German race. Estimates of the number of prosecutions (for homosexuality) vary, from 33,000 to 63,000 between 1933 and 1939. Heinz Heger has written about the experiences of an anonymous gay victim of the Nazis, an Austrian, in *The Men with the Pink Triangle*. He was arrested and sent to prison and then to Sachsenhausen concentration camp:

> 'And what had I done to be sent off this way? What infamous crime or damage to the community? I had loved a friend of mine, a grown man of 24... I could find nothing dreadful or wrong in that.'

From Sachsenhausen, he was sent to work in the Klinker brick-works:

> 'This clay-pit, known among us prisoners as the death-pit, was both famed and feared by all prisoners in all other concentration camps, as a factory of human destruction...'

By February 1942, the death penalty had been introduced for any German male having sex with another male.

Why did gays not fit in with the Nazi ideal? What does the man above mean when he says: 'What crime to the community'?

Black People

Chapter Four outlined the Nazi theory of 'race' and noted how black people were described as inferior to 'Aryans'. A small number of black children were living in Germany when the Nazis came to power, the children of German women and Senegalese (African) troops used by the French during the First World War to patrol the Ruhr Valley. There were also black residents in Europe from German ex-colonies in Africa. In 1937, on Nazi orders, 385 of these children were taken to hospitals and sterilised, without them or their parents knowing what was being done.

The Nazis disapproved of jazz and swing music, labelling it 'Jewish Negro' music. Jewish and black art and music were banned. The Nazis tried to ban the saxophone and control which tunes were played by German orchestras. Yet, Joseph Goebbels gave huge jazz parties at his mansion on Peacock Island near Berlin, to impress visiting foreign officials during the 1936 Berlin Olympics

The Olympics and Football

The 1936 Olympics were held in Berlin. German Jewish sportspeople, like *Greta Bergmann*, the high-jump champion of Wurtemberg, were not allowed to take part. There was talk of boycotting the Games, as a protest against how the Nazis were treating so many of their people. But the Games went ahead. Governments were anxious to avoid an 'international incident'. While the games were on, Hitler ordered anti-Jewish slogans and posters to be removed. The attacks on gays were relaxed and visiting journalists were showered with German culture and evidence of great Nazi achievements. During the opening ceremony, the French team gave the Nazi salute, while the British and American teams refused, greatly displeasing Hitler.

When *Jesse Owens*, the black American long-jump and sprinting champion won four gold medals, Hitler re-

Jesse Owens

fused to present him with his medals. Owens had proved that the Nazi theory of Aryan superiority was nonsense.

1. What are the arguments for and against refusing to have sporting links with certain countries? e.g. 1990 South Africa and the English Cricket team; 1992 Yugoslavia and the European Football Championships.
2. In your opinion, was the victory of Jesse Owens at the Berlin Olympics as effective as a boycott of the games would have been? How did his success challenge the Nazis' racism?

In 1935, the German Football team played an international against England at White Hart Lane. Local trade union and community groups protested, saying that the Nazis were trying to win international credibility. Only three years later, when the English Football team played Germany in Berlin, they gave the Nazi salute before the game.

The English football team give the Nazi salute at the Olympic stadium, Berlin, May 4th 1938 before a crowd of over 100,000. England beat Germany 6–3. (Stanley Matthews is fifth from the left).

Source 15

An FA official visited the dressing room and instructed the players to give the Nazi salute — an order which caused every one of us to stop what we were doing and look up with some alarm...It was pointed out that when the British athletics team had given the eyes right salute at the Olympic Games in 1936 many Germans took it as a deliberate snub. So much as the boys hated this gesture towards Hitler we agreed to abide by the decision of the FA...Whenever I glance through my scrapbook and gaze on that infamous picture of the England team lining up like a bunch of robots I feel a little ashamed. (Stanley Matthews)

1. Did the British football team have a choice about whether or not to give the Nazi salute in 1938?

2. Why did Stanley Matthews describe the team as 'a bunch of robots'?

ANSCHLUSS

In March 1938, the Nazis began their occupation of the countries they said were rightfully theirs. The German Army marched over the border into Austria and entered Vienna, to create 'Greater Germany'. They were welcomed by cheering crowds of Austrians and their own Nazi leader Seyss-Inquart. 99.75% of Austrian people voted their approval of the Nazi takeover (excluding all those who had fled, been arrested or were otherwise unable to vote against).

183,000 Austrian Jews were immediately subject to laws which had been passed over a number of years in Germany. Overnight, Jewish shops were branded with the word 'Jew' and Jewish people deprived of the right to own property, be employed, work, visit cafes, public pools or parks. They were physically attacked and publicly humiliated.

Opposite: Austrian Jews forced to scrub the streets of Vienna, 1938.

1. Summarise how the Nazis tried to achieve total control in Germany.

2. Identify the groups who were treated as 'unworthy of life' by 1939.

3. What choices did they have about how to respond to this treatment?

4. What choices did 'ordinary Germans' have about how to respond to the Nazi regime?

Chapter 6

Responses to Nazi rule from 1933 to 1939

Inside Germany: Nazi sympathisers and opponents

In the face of Nazism, people reacted in different ways. Many actively supported the regime (see Chapter 5). Some people agreed with the Nazi ideas; they believed Hitler would make Germany strong again. Some liked the uniforms, slogans and mass rallies, but disliked the violent methods the Nazis used. Other people were attracted to the Nazis because of their violent methods.

There were certainly many who did not know about the most brutal acts of the Nazi Party, since they lived in rural areas, and did not travel. For many Germans, 1933–1939 were years of stability and fond memories. Henry Metelman ex-Hitler Youth:

> You felt you belonged to a great nation which had found its feet and you were in good, safe hands....it was a lovely feeling.

Protesters

Opposition was demonstrated in numerous ways, for instance: strikes, factory lavatory walls daubed in human excrement with anti-Nazi slogans and swastikas; refusal to contribute money for a new Nazi employer's wedding present after he had taken over from a popular Jewish employer; a village in Bavaria which defied the anti-Jewish boycott by hoisting a banner saying: 'Jews very much wanted here'. All these acts risked harsh penalties. Newspaper reports in 1935 tell us of people imprisoned for not giving the Nazi salute when a band played the Nazi anthem.

John Heartfield used his artistic skills as a form of political protest and designed posters to demonstrate his opposition to the Nazis:

Source 1   Göring der Henker ('Göring, the Butcher')

IN DEUTSCHEN VOLKE

GÖRING, DER HENKER

There are very few records of protest marches against the Nazis and there was never a unified resistance movement. Members of the Communist and Social Democrat parties planned attacks on the government and some individuals showed their opposition by murdering Nazis:

Source 2

Prisoners Kill Nazi Guard at Concentration Camp

Special Cable to The New York Times

BERLIN, May 17 — A notice in the obituary column of the newspaper, Veelklscher Beobachter of the death of Albert Kallweit, a Storm Trooper who on May 13 was the victim of cowardly attack during the performance of his duty at a lonely post in the Thuringian Forest, is taken here as confirming a report of the first known outbreak of violence in a German concentration camp.

The report said two prisoners had killed the guard with a spade and that their escape probably had been facilitated by villagers.

The New York Times, 5/18,38.

Others, like the former heavyweight boxer Max Schmeling, demonstrated their opposition by individual acts. Schmeling became world heavyweight champion in 1930 and was once Nazi Germany's most famous sportsman:

Source 3

At a special tribute recently... for the now 84-year-old Schmeling, Mr (Henri) Lewin, with tears in his eyes, recounted what happenend. Pointing to Schmeling, ...Mr Lewin said: 'I am going to tell you what kind of a champion Max Schmeling is. Beginning on November 9th [1938], for four days, Max hid my older brother Werner and me in his Berlin flat. He risked everything for us. If we had been found in his apartment, I would not be here this evening and neither would Max. (*Jewish Chronicle,* 5th January 1990)

1. How effective do you think the poster in Source 1 is as anti-Nazi propaganda?

2. What does the obituary writer in Source 2 think about the murder of the guard (quote from it to support your answer)?

3. To what event (9th November 1938) is Henri Lewin referring in Source 3 (see p.83-84)?

Some people, (German and non-German) chose to show their opposition by helping to rescue victims of the Nazis.

Indifference

According to Professor Ian Kershaw (a British historian): The majority of Germans were probably 'neither full-hearted Nazis nor outright opponents'. They did not care either way when they heard about Nazi attacks on Jews or anyone else. They did not necessarily approve, but they let things happen and were bystanders. They were indifferent. Guenther Triedwindt, then a schoolboy, remembers:

> The teachers told us: 'Don't worry about what you see, even if you see some nasty things, always think....Hitler wants to create a better, cleaner Germany....everything will work out fine in the end'.

Outside Germany

There was wide reporting of the sufferings of the victims of Nazi rule in newspapers, personal accounts, films and photographs. This resulted in various forms of written and verbal protests to Germany by individuals, organisations and governments in, for example, Britain and the United States, Canada, Poland, Australia, Czechoslovakia and Turkey. There were world-wide campaigns to boycott German goods.

Source 4 : Protest in the U.K. and U.S.A.

TREATMENT OF JEWS IN GERMANY AMERICAN PROTESTS

Protests against persecution of Jews in Germany are growing throughout the US... The American Jewish Congress yesterday issued an appeal to Jews in all lands to... hold protest meetings on Monday night... The protest meeting in New York will be held in Madison Square Garden. Many Christians are to be among the speakers... and Mr Alfred F. Smith, former Governor of New York State.

The Union of Jewish Congregations is urging the Secretary of State,... to afford victims of persecution easy admittance to the USA... (*The Times* 24th March, 1933)

PROTESTS TO EMBASSY

A letter denouncing 'organised ferocity' against Jews in Germany was sent to the German Ambassador in London by the Independent Labour Party on Saturday... At a Communist demonstration in Hyde Park yesterday, a resolution was passed denouncing 'the campaign of terror now being waged against Jews in Germany'. (*The Times*, 14th November, 1938).

Protest meeting against Hitler's persecution of the Jews, USA 1933.

The Battle of Cable Street

Elsewhere in Europe, there were smaller fascist parties, for example the British Union of Fascists. Its main target was British Jews, but the fascists were widely opposed and on October 4, 1936 a huge anti-fascist demonstration prevented a BUF march through London's East End (where there was a big Jewish community). The demonstration was led by Jews, many of them communists, joined by dockers and other local people. This victory became known as the Battle of Cable Street. The British government then passed the Public Order Act, which banned poltical uniforms and restricted processions. This was to apply to all groups, fascist and anti-fascist.

British visitors to Nazi Germany reacted in various ways. David Lloyd George (former British Prime Minister) was reported in the *Daily Mail* of November 1936 as saying:

Source 5a

'I have just returned from a visit to Germany....I have now seen the famous German leader and also something of the great change he has effected. Whatever one may think of his methods...there can be no doubt that he has achieved a marvellous transformation in the spirit of the people...He is a born leader of men.'

Others saw much to condemn:

Source 5b

I believe that if Germany continues the policy which she is now pursuing with regard to the Jews and other refugees, she will bring about an impediment to that peace which we all desire to see established...the persecution which is carried on in Germany is not that of persecuting opinion, but of persecuting blood (Lord Allen of Hurtwood, speaking to the House of Lords on 27th July 1938, quoted in Martin Gilbert (ed) *Plough My Own Furrow. The Life of Lord Allen Of Hurtwood*, 1965)

---

1. Why did some people organise a boycott of German goods in the 1930s?

2. How could you find out whether the boycott was successful or not?

3. Identify and name the groups mentioned in the UK and USA who protested about the persecution of Jews in Germany (Source 4). Can you think of any reasons why these groups were amongst those who spoke out?

4. What reasons can you think of to explain why the local community was able to stop the British Union of Fascists in October 1936?

5. Do you think political uniforms should be banned? Should marches (organised e.g. by the National Front or Ku Klux Klan) be restricted? Explain your answer.

6a. What sort of things do you think Lloyd George saw in Germany to make him describe it as a 'marvellous transformation' (Source 5a)? Information in Chapter 5 might help you answer this question.

6b. What sort of things would he probably not have seen?

7. What did Lord Allen (Source 5b) mean when he accused the German government of 'persecuting blood'?

The difficulty of resistance in Germany

Why was there not more resistance in Germany? In order to appreciate the courage of those who did make a stand against the Nazis, imagine the circumstances they were in:

The atmosphere of fear and distrust

In most places there were spies. Not just police spies, but people's neighbours and workmates. There are reports of children telling the authorities about anti-Nazi comments made by their parents.

Source 6

Bernt Engelmann (a journalist, born in Berlin in 1921), remembers a New Year's Eve party in 1934 held at a hotel in Westphalia. A drunken Nazi made a speech ending with 'God save our Führer!' and an elderly guest said: 'And us from him!' quietly, but loud enough so that a few people stared at him in horror. A few days later, the man was arrested by the *Gestapo*, taken to a concentration camp and his ashes were returned to his family.

Families of individuals who spoke out were often punished. Those found helping Jews people, doing business with them, or going out with them, were humiliated in public.

The concentration camps and prisons

Fear of these camps and prisons prevented most people from showing any opposition. The *Manchester Guardian* described the growing terror in Germany in a series of reports. The following is an excerpt from an article published on 1st July 1935. It recounts the ordeal of a political prisoner detained by the Hamburg *Gestapo*:

> As the prisoner refused to give information he was wrapped in a wet cloth that was knotted so tightly across his mouth that his teeth cut into his lips and his mouth bled profusely. He was held by three assistants while the official and another assistant took turns in beating him with a flexible leather-covered steel rod. When he fainted from pain and loss of blood he was brought to by means of various other tortures... He was released some time afterwards. (Quoted in Martin Gilbert (ed), *Britain and Germany between the Wars*, 1964)

The Nazis were very good at breaking up organised resistance. The State was geared to preventing resistance.

Insecurity

Thousands of Jews, communists, socialists, gay people and others had lost jobs, income, friends, access to education and public places. Jews especially, felt cut off from the society they were born into. Many of the working class were also unemployed or on very low wages, which made them afraid to speak out for fear of losing their jobs.

Having read about the difficulty of resistance, discuss to what extent people living in Nazi Germany had choices as to whether or not they should oppose the government.

Yet, despite these circumstances, hundreds of men and women risked and often sacrificed their lives, in the struggle against Nazism. In 1939, 300,000 Germans were in prison for political reasons.

Some young anti-Nazis formed the Edelweiss Pirates. Boys and girls aged between 14 and 18 attacked Hitler Youth groups and daubed 'Down with Nazi brutality' on walls. The Gestapo established a youth concentration camp at Neuwied on the Rhine and publicly hanged twelve Edelweiss Pirates.

Source 7

Women (many of whose husbands were in jail or underground) could meet for Kaffee und Kuchen (coffee and cake) in the afternoons without causing suspicion. While appearing to gossip, they exchanged vital and secret information, concealed in shopping bags, books or napkins (Claudia Koonz, 1987).

---

1. In your opinion, were the Edelweiss Pirates justified in (physically) attacking Hitler Youth groups?

2. Do you think there are any occasions when it is acceptable for people to break the law?

3. What sort of 'vital and secret information' would the women in Source 7 be exchanging?

The Churches

When the Nazis tried to reduce the power or independence of either the Protestant or Catholic Church, Christians protested very strongly. They met with Nazi officials, wrote letters or spoke out from the pulpit, for example in 1936-37 when the Nazis tried to close down Catholic schools. Also, some Catholic bishops opposed the Nazi policy of killing mentally ill and disabled people (see Chapter 5). But there was relatively little protest about the persecution and killing of Jews.

Of course, there were exceptions, for example the *White Rose* group of Christians, led by Hans and Sophie Scholl, brother and sister, in Munich University. They circulated anti-Nazi leaflets, calling on their fellow students to rise up in protest. Both were executed in 1943.

Bishop Würm of Würtemberg wrote to the German government in July and December 1943 condemning the persecution and execution of Jews. Hundreds of individual pastors and priests were arrested and thrown into concentration camps, either for speaking out or as part of the Nazi attempt to control the Church. Two of the most famous of these churchmen are *Pastor Martin Niemoeller* and *Dietrich Bonhoeffer.*

Bonhoeffer was imprisoned and hanged by the Nazis on 9th April 1945 as a punishment for his continuous and very public protests against Hitler and his policies. He chose to return to Germany from the USA and wore a yellow star in order to identify with the Jews.

Right: Sophie Scholl

Niemoeller was arrested in 1937 and spent seven years in a concentration camp for his anti-Nazi activities. His arrest led to the first public mass demonstration against the Nazis in Germany. Niemoeller was liberated from Dachau concentration camp at the end of the war. He later regretted that he was silent on the persecution of the Jews and only spoke out about Jews who had become Christians. This poem is attributed to him:

Source 8

First they came for the Jews
and I did not speak out —
because I was not a Jew.

Then they came for the communists
and I did not speak out —
because I was not a communist.

Then they came for the Trade Unionists
and I did not speak out —
because I was not a Trade Unionist

Then they came for me
and there was no-one left
to speak out for me.

---

1. Can you summarise what Niemoeller is saying in Source 8?

2. This poem is often quoted today — it appears on wall posters and is used in school assemblies. Why do you think this is? What relevance has it for people today?

3. Why might the Nazis see literature and poetry as a threat?

Jewish responses to antisemitism

Jewish communities in Germany also reacted in different ways. Suddenly they were struck by these laws of discrimination and violently attacked. Many could not believe what was happening — in the country they loved and by people they felt were their fellow citizens.

Religious and cultural responses

Some Jews believed that if they kept calm and quiet, the government would ignore them. They were sure the Nazis were just another unfortunate episode in the history of European antisemitism (see Chapter 1). Even those Jews who did not actively oppose the Nazis, made responses. A committee was set up, called the *Reichsvertretung der Juden in Deutschland* (Federal Representation of the Jews in Germany). It was led by *Rabbi Leo Baeck*, one of Germany's most famous rabbis, a teacher and a scholar. He helped evacuate children from Germany after *Kristallnacht* and was eventually arrested and sent to Theresienstadt concentration camp in Czechoslovakia. He survived the Holocaust.

The *Reichsvertretung der Juden in Deutschland* organised social and cultural activities, encouraging people to be proud of being Jewish. Synagogue attendance increased. They later organised emigration, education and social welfare but did not agree with Jewish people who set up underground resistance groups. A small number of Orthodox Jews felt that the persecution was all God's punishment for those who had neglected their religion.

Many Jewish people found new support through contacts with the Jewish communities with which they had perhaps lost touch.

> We were driven in upon ourselves. We lost our non-Jewish contacts. The family united, because we knew we were on the edge of being broken up, which happened in due course. (Werner)

Although of course some non-Jewish Germans remained friends and allies of Jews, it was not easy.

Source 9

Werner was released from Dachau concentration camp in 1936. Here he describes a chance meeting with his old (non-Jewish) best-friend Willi:

As the Nazi hold on people increased, our contacts began to diminish. It became more and more unwise to lay yourself open to the accusation of being a Jew-lover. In 1936 Willi's parents transferred him to a Catholic boarding School, to protect him from too much exposure to Nazi brainwash, and we seldom saw one another [but] here we were on the same pavement, coming towards one another. I pretended to look at the display in a shop window, and for the briefest of moments Willi's body brushed against me. A little later I was lining up in front of a bank counter, when I felt a hand on my shoulder, and heard a whisper: '*Viel gluck*, Werner — good luck'.

Emigration

A growing number of Jews felt that the Nazis could not be ignored and that the Jewish communities and all those opposed to fascism should do something and prepare themselves for much worse to come. In 1933, Leo Baeck said: 'The thousand year history of the German Jews has come to an end'. Some felt the answer was emigration. 37,000 Jewish people (out of 500,000) left in 1933, most of them hoping to return. From 1933 to 1938, the German government encouraged Jewish emigration. It has been estimated that 226,000 Jews left Germany and a further 134-144,000 left Austria and Czechoslovakia between March 1938 and May 1939. But they had to pay a tax on leaving and many could not afford to go. Numerous German and Austrian scholars, scientists and artists left during this time, among them Albert Einstein in 1933 and Sigmund Freud in 1938.

> Above all, we were worried about one thing...
> *Where shall we go? (Werner)*

---

1. Why did synagogue attendance increase after 1933?

2. Read Source 9. How did Willi's parents show their opposition to the Nazis?

3. What does the Source tell you about the power the Nazis had over everyday life?

4. What did Willi mean by 'Good luck, Werner'?

People in countries all over the world put pressure on their governments to admit Jewish people leaving Nazi Germany. Thousands were allowed in, but most countries put strict limits on the numbers and on who they allowed to enter. This was partly due to the world-wide economic depression of the 1930s and partly due to anti-immigration policies and antisemitism. On one occasion a boatload of refugees was sent back to Germany:

On board the *Etrato*, on the way to Palestine, 1938. Members of the Jewish Youth movements sailed from Italian and Rumanian ports.

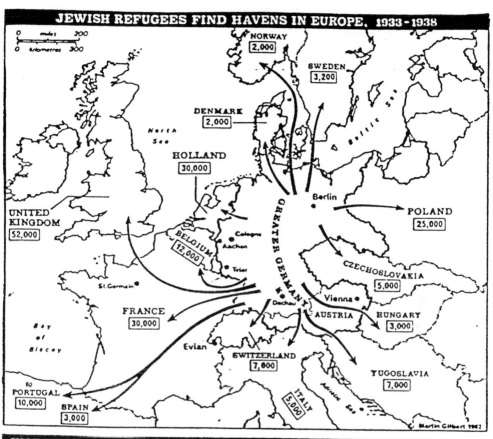

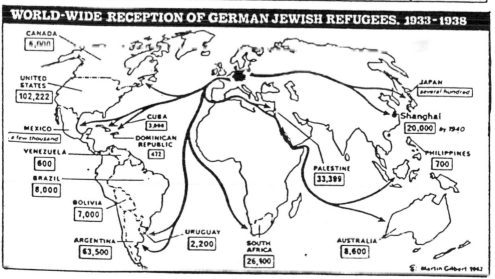

113

Source 10 : The St.Louis, 1939

On 13th May, 1939, the ship *St.Louis* sailed from Hamburg, with 936 Jews. It was enroute to Havana, Cuba. Upon arrival, they were refused landing and the ship was shunted between Florida and Cuba as US officials argued over its admittance. Entrance to the USA was finally denied and the *St Louis* forced to return to Europe. France, Belgium and Britain took in refugees from the *St Louis*, but others found no refuge and many of the passengers did not survive the Holocaust.

Shanghai, China was one of the few places to allow unrestricted Jewish immigration. This was because it was a Free Port and there was no need for immigrants to have visas.

The *Evian Conference* was called by President Roosevelt of the U.S.A. in July 1938. The main discussion was: what to do about future Jewish refugees. Hitler suggested Madagascar, Roosevelt suggested Ethiopia, Mussolini favoured 'the open areas of Russia' and the Soviet Union thought Alaska a suitable place of refuge. At the Conference, the representatives made their countries' feelings clear:

Source 11

see world map opposite.

---

1. List some of the reasons given by countries for not allowing unrestricted Jewish immigration (Source 11).
2. What other reasons might there have been?
3. After Evian and the *St.Louis* episode, a Nazi journal commented: 'We are saying openly that we do not want the Jews while the democracies keep on claiming that they are willing to receive them and then leave the guests out in the cold. Aren't we savages better men, after all?'
   What does this quote mean? How could it be argued that the outcome of Evian only encouraged the Nazis towards a policy of mass murder of the Jews?
4. Find out about the reaction to the immigration of refugees to your country e.g. Kenyan and Ugandan Asians to Britain in the 1970s; the treatment of Haitians in the United States after the 1991 coup; Bosnian refugees 1992.
5. Do you think your country should allow unrestricted immigration?

MAP EVIAN CONFERENCE, 1938

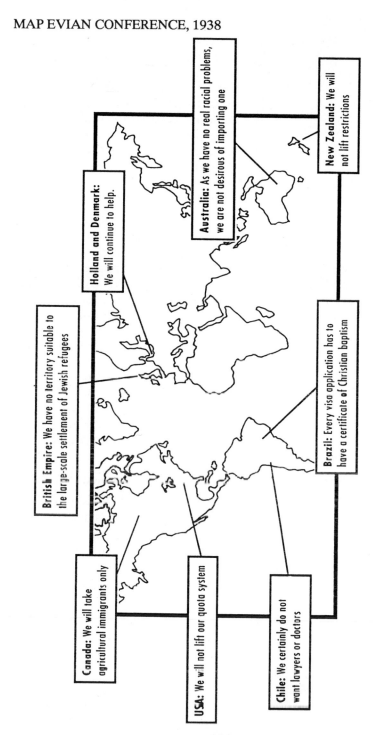

Australia: As we have no real racial problems, we are not desirous of importing one

New Zealand: We will not lift restrictions

Holland and Denmark: We will continue to help.

British Empire: We have no territory suitable to the large-scale settlement of Jewish refugees

Brazil: Every visa application has to have a certificate of Christian baptism

Canada: We will take agricultural immigrants only

USA: We will not lift our quota system

Chile: We certainly do not want lawyers or doctors

German Jewish children leaving Germany, on their way to Holland.

The Kindertransport

Between 1938 and 1939, 9,354 European children were sent from Germany to Britain (7,482 were Jewish). The rescue was organised by the World Movement for the care of children from Germany. Once in England, they were either taken in by families or looked after in camps or hostels. In Newcastle-upon-Tyne, the Quakers were particularly active in raising funds and providing homes for the refugees.

Werner Mayer escaped thanks to the Feilelmann family who had emigrated from his home town, Landau, (see Chapter 1) in 1933. They had set up in business in Manchester. His visa was issued 'pending his emigration to the USA... may not accept employment paid or unpaid'. He was seventeen years old and, instead of going to America, became a trainee in an electric components factory in Manchester.

Helga Samuel arrived with her sister in December 1938:

> The love and affection I received were boundless and I will still be indebted to my wonderful foster-family for the rest of my life. I found peace and happiness and contentment in this wonderful free country — England. But I was one of the lucky ones.

Some children found themselves in far less welcoming homes.

Adults were only allowed to fill jobs which English workers would not take. Many became servants. Others were allowed in if they set up businesses in 'deprived' areas of the country. By 1947, there were 1,000 factories owned by Jewish refugees in the North-East, South Wales and Clydeside. Between them they employed 250,000 people.

During the war, thousands of these Jewish refugees were interned on the Isle of Man, along with non-Jewish Germans, suspected of being 'enemy aliens'.

---

1. How do the photographs above and below add to your understanding of the children's experience?
2. There were loud objections to Jewish people being interned for part of the war. Why?

Suicide

As thousands of Jewish people in Germany and Austria lost their jobs and hundreds were attacked, murdered, sent to prison or camps, some were so terrified and depressed about what was happening, that they took their own lives. It is thought that 350 killed themselves in the three years 1932 to 1934.

Active resistance

There were protests against the Nazis. Jews let friends in other countries know details of what was happening. Still others, most of them already politically active as communists or socialists, turned to organised resistance. They tried to wreck Nazi plans by attacking their buildings, or individual and groups of Nazis, distributing secret newspapers and organising escape lines. One such group was the *Herbert Baum Group*, who were active over the six years 1937 to 1942.

Source 12

The group was based in Berlin. There were thirty-three members and nearly all were Jewish communists. Some were as young as eleven in 1933. The leaders, Herbert and Marriane Baum, and Sara and Martin Kochmann, were nineteen. Most worked together in the Siemens electrical motor plant and met in the Baum's home. The Baum Group began as a social and cultural group, trying to keep up the morale of Jews in despair. They worked with other resistance groups, distributing anti-Nazi literature and posters.

In 1942, members planted bombs at a Nazi exhibition but were betrayed, probably by a Gestapo spy. Herbert Baum was arrested and nearly beaten to death. He was taken to the Siemens factory and told to identify others. He betrayed no-one. On 11th June, the Gestapo announced his suicide. Witnesses say he was tortured to death. Sara Kochman could not withstand torture and fearing she might break under the strain, threw herself from the window. She did not die but was later executed. Twenty two members of the group were executed, nine died in concentration camps. Two survived: Charlotte and Richard Holzer.

---

1. Look at the ages of the members of the Baum group on the monument. What was their average age in 1942? What was their average age when Hitler came to power? Do you think it is significant that their average age was so young?

2. It is May 1936. You are with friends — Rosa, Karl, Herman and Lisa (Jewish and non-Jewish) in a cafe in Munich. You are all aged between 15 and 18. None of you supports Hitler, though some of your friends and relatives do. The conversation turns to what can be done to oppose the government. Later that night, you record what you remember of the conversation. Sum up what was said. What suggestions were made? Make it clear that some of you were more afraid than others. Some had contacts with people already involved with anti-Nazi activities. Some were willing to use violence, some not.

Even within the concentration camps, small Jewish resistance groups were set up before the war. For example: the group led by Olga Benario and Charlotte Eisenbletter in Ravensbruck (the women's concentration camp); the Buchenwald group led by Rudi Arndt and a group in Dachau led by Heinz Heshen and Hanz Litten.

Monument to the Baum Group in the Weissensee Cemetery, Berlin.

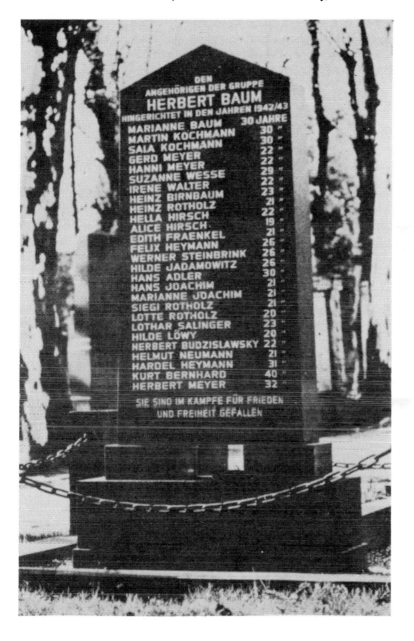

At first, some of the opposition groups included Jews and non-Jews, e.g. the Red Union Opposition, but this became more difficult. German resistance groups were isolated, and had to work in secret, trusting few people. Jewish resistance groups were even more isolated. There were special barracks for Jews in concentration camps; in the cities, separate factory departments were created after November 1938. Later, with Jews having to wear the yellow star and travelling and eating separately from non-Jews, it was incredibly dangerous to meet with non-Jews, for everyone involved.

Jewish people had formed under one per cent of the German people, before some chose to emigrate — there was nothing they could do alone.

1. List the reasons which made opposition to the Nazis difficult.

2. Give six examples contained in this chapter of the many ways in which people responded to Nazi rule before 1939.

3. Why will we never know the exact number of German people who spoke out or did anything to show their opposition to the Nazis?

4. 'There was no use in showing opposition to the Nazis, it made no difference'. Do the Sources in this chapter prove or disprove this statement?

Chapter Seven

The Second World War, Occupation and Ghettos

Mr Speaker, we seem to be moving, drifting steadily, against our will, against the will of every race and every people and every class, towards some hideous catastrophe. Everybody wishes to stop it, but they do not know how. (Winston Churchill, speaking in Parliament, 1938)

Churchill was referring to the tension building up in Europe, as a result of German rearmament and aggression.

Meanwhile, another pending 'hideous catastrophe' was preoccupying Roman Vishniac. He was a Russian Jew who had fled to Germany in the 1920s. Witnessing the Nazi's rise to power, he became obsessed with Hitler's *Mein Kampf*, sure that it meant what it said about destroying the Jews :

Source 1

I took those wicked threats seriously from the very start...I decided to start photographing the Jewish communities; because I knew then that they were doomed...I want to show a life that once existed and then was utterly destroyed...I wanted to save the faces..

(Roman Vishniac, quoted in *Sunday Times* Magazine, Nov. 20, 1983)

He set off in 1936, travelling 5,000 miles in Poland, Latvia, Lithuania, Hungary and Czechoslovakia, (see map, p.2) wherever there were Jews. Speaking Yiddish, he gained acceptance in the *shtetls*. Before the war, antisemitism was particularly strong in Poland and he was regarded as suspicious by the authorities and often arrested. Vishniac took 16,000 photographs. 2,000 of them survived the war, having been hidden by his father in France.

Source 2 Cheder, Jewish School, Slonim, Poland 1938.

What sort of 'wicked threats' was Roman Vishniac referring to? Find sources and information from earlier chapters to support your answer.

Countdown to war

From the moment he came to power in 1933, Hitler had made it clear that he had no intention of sticking to the details of the Treaty of Versailles (see p.57).

In 1933 he began to build up a massive Army, Navy and Airforce and was determined to regain land taken from Germany in 1919 and obtain 'lebensraum' for the 'Master Race' in the East (see map of German losses, p.58 Chapter 4).

By 1936 the German airforce was larger than that of Britain.

1935	Germany withdrew from the League of Nations and Disarmament talks. Conscription was introduced.
1936	Germany re-militarised the Rhineland. Rome — Berlin Axis (German alliance with Fascist Italy).
1937	Germany, Italy and Japan signed the Anti-Comintern Pact.
1938	Anschluss — German occupation of Austria.

Nor, despite the possibility of war in August 1938 had Hitler invaded Czechoslovakia, were Britain and France willing to challenge Hitler when, a month later, he insisted that his demands were limited to the German-speaking areas of the country. So an agreement was reached between the British and German governments — at the expense of the Sudetenland. The Czech government felt betrayed by Britain and France. On 1st October 1938, Hitler's army annexed the Sudetenland. Three million Germans lived there and Hitler claimed it belonged to Germany. He promised that this was: 'The last territorial demand I have to make in Europe' and many believed him. By early 1939, it was clear that he wanted the Czech capital, Prague and the two western provinces, Bohemia and Moravia.

Source 3

In January 1939, Hitler declared publicly that if war broke out:

The result will not be the Bolshevisation of the earth, and thus the victory of Jewry, but the annihilation of the Jewish race in Europe....I would achieve a solution of the Jewish problem.... the extermination of the Jewish race.

15th March 1939 saw 'The rape of Czechoslovakia'. German troops occupied Bohemia and Moravia. The country was carved in two. The Sudetenland, Bohemia and Moravia became part of Greater Germany, leaving Slovakia as a new state, under German control, but run by a Slovak Fascist Party led by a Catholic priest, Father Tito. 300,000 Czechs were to die in the following years and thousands were forced into slave labour.

Why was this 'appeasing' of Hitler referred to frequently in August 1990?

Czechoslovakia, Oct. 1938

When German troops occupied the Sudetenland, they were met with flowers by the German Czechs. But for other Sudetens, it was the beginning of the end.

Liesl Fischmann

Liesl was twelve years old in 1938. Born in 1927 in the Sudetenland, her parents were Willy and Friedl and she had one brother, Heini, who was six years older. They lived in the town of Teplice-Sanov (see map p.2)

Liesl with her parents and brother.

Liesl

Source 4

It was a very secure life. Life was good, we were well-to-do as the family owned the largest glassworks for window panes and bottles, yet I was not spoiled. I did well at school. At weekends we would go into the mountains to ski or ramble. I was a Daddy's girl, he loved me very much...[but] we couldn't see what was coming. When the Germans occupied the Sudetenland, we fled to Prague. And at that time all the Jewish people were just trying to get out. But my parents weren't able to do that. There was a scheme to allow children under 16 to get out. So I was able to get out on the last train to leave Prague before the war [August, 1939]. Not my brother, he was too old... So, I came to England and at the railway station my parents said: 'See you soon'. I didn't really want to go.

22nd March 1939	Germany occupied Memel in Lithuania.
23rd March 1939	Germany demanded Danzig and the 'Polish Corridor', threatening Poland.
31st March 1939	Britain and France promised to help Poland if Germany attacked her.
23rd August 1939	Nazi-Soviet Pact. Agreed to a 10 year non-aggression Pact and secretly arranged to divide Poland between them.

This Pact stunned the world, since the Nazi and Communist regimes had been such bitter enemies. The Pact made war inevitable because it freed Germany to invade Poland without fear of having to fight the Soviet Union in the East. On the 1st September 1939 Germany invaded Poland.

Before the invasion, Hitler made the following statement:

Source 5

The destruction of Poland is our primary task...Be merciless ! Be brutal!...I have sent to the east only my 'Death Head Units', with the order to kill without mercy all men, women and children of Polish race or language. Only in such a way will we win the vital space that we now need. Who still talks nowadays of the extermination of the Armenians? (see p.49)

Source 6

German soldiers on a train leaving for the east, Sept. 1, 1939. The inscription on the train reads: 'We're off to Poland — to thrash the Jews.'

On September 3, Britain warned the German Government that unless they withdrew their troops by 11.00 a.m. a state of war would exist between Britain and Germany. When this ultimatum was ignored, Britain and France immediately declared war on Germany.

The Second World War had begun.

1. At the age of twelve, what sort of things might have been going through Liesl's mind as she left Prague?

2. What does Hitler mean by: 'Who still talks nowadays of the extermination of the Armenians'? (Source 5).
   Refer back to Chapter Two for details of the Armenian Genocide of 1915.

3. In an interview broadcast in 1989, Henry Metetman, ex-Hitler Youth, said : 'I believed Hitler was ...like a second God...I believed that I was superior to people of other nations...you felt like marching...marching into other people's countries..I know now that it's all foolish'.

   How does this and other information you have learned help you to understand Sources 5 and 6?

Poland under Nazi rule

Twenty-two million Polish Christians and two million Polish Jews came under Nazi control. Among the Jews was Esther Zylberberg (see Chapter 1) and her family.

Source 7

My town was invaded and we were terrorised from the very beginning. I was very scared, but I also had a kind of childish excitement that 'It's going to be over soon and my, won't there be a lot to talk about'. The first painful thing for us as a family, was my father had to flee our town because he was an active member of the Bund. The last time I saw him was at the age of 11 (Esther).

Because of his socialist activities, Philip Zylberberg was warned he would be a prime target for the Nazis. He ran away to another town in Poland and Esther's brother David escaped to Russia. Both were eventually shot by the Germans.

Part of Poland was incorporated into the German Reich. The rest became known as the General Government and included Warsaw, Lublin and Cracow. Hans Frank, a Nazi legal expert, was appointed its General Governor.

Right. Esther's father Philip Zylberberg.

Source 8

Hans Frank's son Niklas remembers: 'My father felt he was the King of Poland... when we visited him there... I saw a young boy wearing a star of David... I stuck out my tongue at him and he went away... I felt I was a victor... For me the war was a wonderful time... I had a personal servant... and I loved driving around in a huge Mercedes.'

Untermenschen

After three weeks of fierce fighting, the Polish government surrendered and German rule began. The Polish troops had been seriously outnumbered and were poorly prepared for war. To the Nazis, Poles were *untermenschen* — sub-human Slavs, useful only as slaves for Germany. 300,000 able-bodied Poles were transported to Greater Germany Reich to work in German industries. Polish factories became geared to Germany's war needs.

Tens of thousands of Poles were taken as forced labour to southern Poland. Their land was then given to people Hitler called 'ethnic Germans'. Tens of thousands of Poland's writers, journalists, artists, aristocrats and clergy were murdered.

The Nazis were also eager to arrest gay men in Poland: 'They must be evicted and transported to an area where their activities present no danger to Germandom' (part of a secret memorandum issued by the Gestapo in March 1942, cited in R.Plant, 1987)

Some schools were closed and in those that remained, the Polish language was forbidden.

Source 9

Typical of the New Order in Poland was a notice posted in the streets of Torun on October 27th 1939:

All Poles must leave the pavement free for Germans. The street belongs to the conquerors, not to the conquered. Germans must be served first in shops and male Poles must raise their hats to Nazis. (Martin Gilbert, *Second World War*, 1989)

While killing the 'inferior race' of Poles, the Nazis continued with their attempt to create a Master Race. Himmler set up *Lebensborn*, breeding farms where young Polish women, chosen for their Aryan looks, were sent to have sex with SS men to produce 'superior Aryan babies'.

Soviet occupation

In 1939, the Soviet Union invaded Finland and Poland.

Poland's history is one of constant invasion and division by surrounding hostile countries. Historically, most Russians saw and treated Polish people as their inferiors.

When Soviet troops occupied Eastern Poland, they were followed by the secret police, the dreaded NKVD. The NKVD were responsible for the death and 'disappearance' of countless millions during Stalin's Purges. Stalin saw the Polish army officers as the 'backbone' of Polish society. The officers corps was made up of professional men from all walks of life. The Russians captured 15,000 officers and put them in prison camps. Months later, they were tied up, then shot and buried in three different locations, one of them the forest of *Katyn*. Among the 15,000 murdered officers were more than five hundred Jewish men including top doctors, surgeons, dentists and veterinarians. In 1943, when the Nazis invaded the area, they discovered the mass grave. For years, the Soviet government denied responsibility for the massacre. It was only in April 1990 that they confessed to this 'evil deed.'

1. Philip and David Zylberberg were socialists. Why did they have to flee?

2. What was the Nazis' reason for killing Poland's intellegensia? (writers, artists etc.)

3. Hitler said he was going to murder all the Poles. Using Source 9 and the text, explain why they were made into slaves instead. Describe what the Nazis did to the Poles to turn them into slaves.

   If he never intended to kill them all, why do you think he threatened to?

The treatment of Polish Jews

Religious Jews were singled out for the harshest treatment. Laws were passed forbidding kosher slaughter, beards and earlocks, prayers, study of the Torah and other religious books. Nazis attacked Jews who had beards and earlocks, cutting them off with blunt instruments, sharp knives and scissors, pulling away flesh and setting fire to their hair. They often took photos as they harassed people:

Source 10

The rabbi of Rawa Mazowiecka, near Lodz (see map p.2) requested to be allowed to continue wearing his beard. The Gestapo chief gave him the choice of buying this right in exchange for one hundred lashes of the whip. The rabbi accepted. He fainted at the tenth stroke and spent two weeks in hospital.

'Of 16,336 Polish civilians executed in 714 localities in the first six weeks of the war, at least 5,000 were Jews'. (M. Gilbert, *Atlas of the Holocaust*)

Ghettos

Joseph Goebbels, visiting Lodz on November 2nd, wrote of the city's 200,000 Jews :

Source 11

They are no longer people, but beasts. There is therefore not a humanitarian, but a surgical task. Here we must make radical incision. Otherwise Europe will be ruined by the Jewish sickness.

Some Polish children pointed out their Jewish classmates to the German authorities. Many Jews were forced to abandon their homes, businesses and possessions. They were crammed into ghettos, which were created in the most run-down streets of the main cities. Jews whose homes were in ghetto-designated areas did not have to abandon them. For example 280,000 or Warsaw's Jews stayed where they were. The journey from home to the ghetto was usually made by road. Handcarts were used to carry the few possessions the Nazis allowed the Jews to keep. They were obliged to wear a white armband with a blue star of David.

Martin Gray remembers: 'Young Poles yelling in the streets, 'Long live a Jewless Poland! We want a Jewless Poland!' (M.Gray, 1972)

Esther, her mother and remaining brother Peretz were among those forced into the Lodz ghetto in 1940. The majority of people forced into the ghetto were working class traders and labourers and could not afford to pay for anywhere decent to rent. Most had to settle for a corner of a landing or a cubby hole under a staircase. Many people died on the pavement.

Jewish people from Germany, Austria and Czechoslovakia were deported to Poland. Many were forced into the Lodz ghetto, where 165,000 Jews had to live. The Warsaw Ghetto was the largest. Just under 400,000 Jews were forced to live in an area of the city where 280,000 previously.

Jewish Councils

Jewish Councils (The Judenrat) were set up by the Nazis to run the ghettos. They were ordered to collect money from the ghetto population, supply men for labour and later, to organise Jews to be 'resettled'. They also organised the Jewish police, hospitals, food and fuel distribution, sanitation and the continuation of religious functions (circumcision, marriage, burial etc). If they did not carry out orders, members of the Council were severely punished, or killed.

Emmanuel Ringelblum was among the thousands of people in the Warsaw ghetto. He was an internationally famous historian and active in the Jewish resistance. He was also one of the many people to keep a detailed diary, until February 1943. It was hidden in ten metal boxes and two milk churns. Ringelblum survived the Warsaw ghetto Uprising (see Chapter 9), and hid in a bunker with thirty others, including his son. He was betrayed to the Nazis on 7th March 1944, tortured and murdered.

Source 12

From his diary we learn a great deal about life in the ghetto and how people responded to their situation: in his notes for April 17th 1941, he recorded how a German guard had taken a sack of potatoes away from a Jewish woman:

Ginsberg, a Jewish Policeman from Lodz, asked the guard to give the potatoes back to the poor woman. As a punishment... the guard knocked him to the ground, stabbed him with the bayonet and shot him as he lay there. The most fearful sight is that of freezing children, dumbly weeping in the street with barefeet, bare knees, and torn clothing stand dumbly in the street weeping... Child in arms, a mother begs — the child appears dead.

Source 13

Warsaw Ghetto, 1941.

This photo was taken by *Joe Heydecker*, an ordinary German soldier. On arriving in Warsaw, he had looked up some old Jewish friends, heard they had been 'relocated' to the ghetto, went to find them and found himself amidst the most appalling conditions. He made several trips back, in order to record what he saw.

In every ghetto, living quarters were dangerously overcrowded and food was rationed at starvation level. The average working adult needs up to 6,000 calories per day. Jews in the ghetto were allocated 200 calories per day. There was mass unemployment and thousands of people died from disease, hunger, cold and terror raids. Some worked in the German factories, making uniforms, ammunition or carpets. Others created work, making clothes out of prayer shawls and continuing their crafts. But wages were pitiful and children turned to smuggling food and medicine, in order to keep their parents alive. Leaving the ghetto without permission was punishable by death.

Source 14

Their thin little bodies could be pushed through a crack in the Ghetto wall, or through a sewer, to the other side to beg for bread or some flour among Poles...as a German sniper aimed a gun at the easy mark climbing down the wall. So went a provider of many a Jewish family...Sometimes the child was successful...only to be attacked by another hungry child or even an adult upon his return to the Ghetto. (David Wdowinsky in I. Tatelbaum, 1985)

The Nazi records reveal how amazed they were at how strong was the will to live among Jews in the ghettos. They were also surprised to discover that there was a thriving Jewish cultural life. The Nazis had been told that the Jews had no culture.

Skilled teachers, talented actresses, singers and workers from all trades and professions were crowded together and the result was Ghetto theatres, schools and libraries. People married, had babies (even in the ghettos where the Nazis specifically forbade women to have children) and when there was nothing else to eat, they dug up the pavements to plant radishes and cabbages.

1. Why do you think the Nazis took the photograph in Source 10?

2. What does Goebbels mean by 'surgical task' and 'humanitarian'? Why does he not say exactly what he means?

3. Using the text, list the ways Polish Jews were treated like 'beasts'.

4. Many Jews despised the men who joined the Jewish ghetto police. What motives do you think those who did join might have had?

5. Joe Heydecker was risking punishment by visiting and photographing in the Warsaw Ghetto. Why do you think he did?

6. A child is going to try smuggling supplies into the ghetto. In pairs, using Source 14 and any other information write a dialogue between the child's parents as they debate the risks involved.

Occupied Europe

Meanwhile, the German Army continued its conquest of Europe. Hungary, Bulgaria, Rumania, Slovakia and Croatia were already allied with Germany. In April 1940, Germany occupied *Denmark* and *Norway* to secure her iron-ore imports from Sweden, which were vital for the war effort. On the 10th of May, the German Army invaded *Holland, Belgium* and *France*. The armies of these nations resisted but could not avert defeat and by the Summer of 1940, Hitler was at the height of his power. *Yugoslavia, Greece* and *North Africa* were occupied in Spring 1941. The German Army was assisted by the Italian Army.

For the vast majority, the presence of an enemy invader was unbearable, but the populations responded to their occupiers in very varied ways (see Chapter 9). Tens of thousands of Czechs, Poles, Belgians, Dutch, Norwegians and Greeks were killed solely because they were Czechs, Poles, Belgians etc. Many were caught up in the terrible punishments inflicted on villages where there were suspected resistance fighters. Nazi ideology was imposed in every occupied country. Jews were dismissed from their jobs required to register their names and addresses with the local authorities. Antisemitic films such as *The Eternal Jew* were shown in cinemas throughout Europe, playing to packed audiences.

Source 15

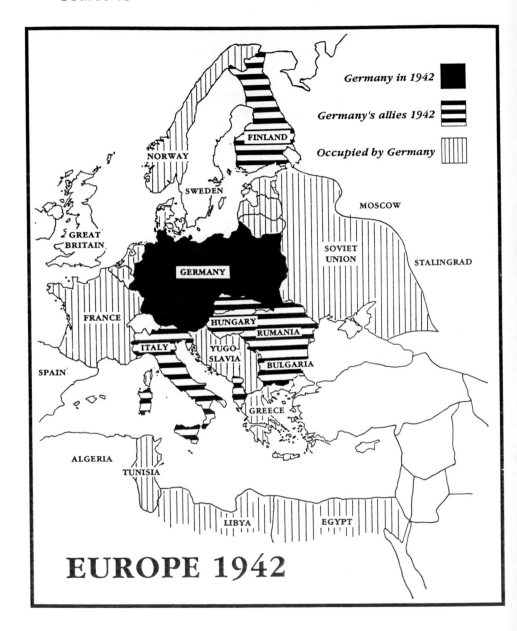

The Gypsies in occupied Europe

Gypsies had to wear yellow arm-bands in parts of occupied Europe.

Source 16

Gypsies were deported [from the Reich] to Poland in 1939 and 1940. After 1941 their situation became still more serious and in the areas occupied by the German army murder of Gypsies was common. ...In Austria, a Gypsy census was carried out on March 13th 1938. In April, Gypsies were deprived of the right to vote. In May, children were no longer allowed to attend school, and all men not working on farms were sent to Dachau or Buchenwald. In July, marriage with a non-Gypsy was prohibited...In 1941, 2,000 Gypsies were deported to Lodz. (Jean-Pierre Liégeois, 1987)

In May 1941, the German army commander in Yugoslavia, General Bohme sent out the following order :

Source 17a

'Gypsies are to be treated as Jews.' Dushano, a Yugoslavian Gypsy was told by the police: 'Now the partisans and the communists and the Jews are being killed, then it will be your turn...It isn't time yet...Hitler hasn't yet fixed the day'. (Quoted in D.Kenrick and G.Puxon, 1972)

Source 17b

It all began to happen in 1937-38. First with the Jews. Then we noticed on our travels that we were more and more discriminated against. Despite this we went on hoping that we travellers would be safe. After all we were still Germans....They decided that all travellers should be sent to Poland...Then I joined the army....Meantime my family and relatives were all interned in Frankfurt...My Dad wrote and said there was no point in my being in the army — it was no protection. Either they'd find out I was a gypsy and throw me into a camp or they'd send me to the front and I'd be shot. (B. Stembach, 1986)

Source 18
In Holland :

After May 1940 good times rapidly fled... Anti-Jewish decrees followed each other in quick succession... Jews must wear a Jewish star, Jews must hand in their bicycles, Jews are banned from trains... Jews may not visit Christians... (Anne Frank).

When Jews resisted the persecution of the Dutch Nazi Party, 425 Jewish men were arrested at random on 22nd February 1941. The men were beaten up and taken away in trucks. On 25th February, groups of Amsterdam citizens called a general strike as a protest against the arrest of the Jews. The strike was brutally suppressed.

Source 19
Rumania
The Rumanian government imposed Anti-Jewish laws before the war. On August 10th 1940, Nazi racial laws were introduced. The introduction of these laws coincided with an outburst of anti-Jewish violence: 'Every day Jews are being thrown out of railway carriages.' (Quoted in Martin Gilbert, *The Holocaust,* 1986).

Source 20

French Jews wearing the Yellow Star.

1. Using Sources 16 and 17a and 17b, list the similarities between the way Gypsies and Jews were treated by the Nazis.

2. How informative is Source 17b?

3. Using Sources 18, 19 and 20, what evidence is there that antisemitism existed outside Germany?

By 1940, Liesl and Werner were in England, both separated from their parents. Liesl was thirteen and Werner eighteen. Esther, her mother and brother Peretz were in the Lodz Ghetto. Esther was twelve.

Organising Genocide

Chapter Eight

The Holocaust

This chapter describes the Holocaust and records the experiences of some who were eye-witnesses, as victims and perpetrators. *Part One* covers the period June–August 1941 when approximately two million Jews and thousands of Gypsies were shot dead by the *Einsatzgruppen* (killing squads) in the Soviet Union and Baltic States. *Part Two* is about the *'Final Solution'*, when the Nazis attempted systematically to annihilate all the remaining Jews of Europe in specially built death camps. Gypsies, gays, Poles and thousands of others were also murdered in concentration camps.

PART ONE: THE *EINSATZGRUPPEN*

In his first speech as Führer, Hitler told his audience:

> The struggle against Marxism became a central objective...I vowed to begin the fight and not to rest until this plague had finally been removed (1933).

Russia, her people — 'inferior Slavs' — and her land, had always been part of his grand plan of conquest. Ignoring the Nazi-Soviet Pact of 1939, he ordered an invasion of the Soviet Union on June 22nd 1941, by the largest army in history — five and a half million men.

On July 31 1941, Goering (Hitler's right-hand man), sent a written order to Heydrich (Deputy Chief of police) 'to make preparations for the general solution of the Jewish problem within the German sphere of influence in Europe'.

Source 1

The German invasion of Russia, June 1941.

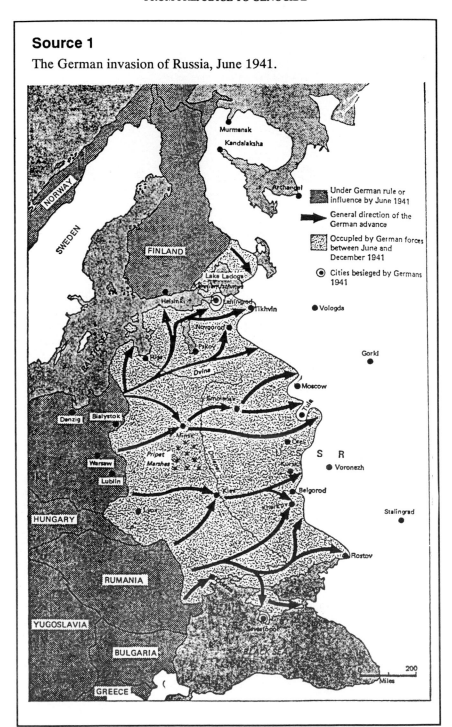

Behind the lines of the Wehrmacht, came two thousand SS, *Gestapo* and police, joined by Rumanians,Ukrainians, Latvians and Lithuanians. These men formed the *Einsatzgruppen* (killing squads), specially trained to kill all the Jewish people of the Soviet Union and Baltic States.

An *Einsatzgruppe* murder squad arrive at its place of work, the Eastern Gailician town of Drohobycz, autumn 1941.

The Germans conquered an area in which nearly three million Jewish people lived. 250,000 escaped east into unoccupied Russia, but approximately two million of those who remained were murdered, most of them within a few days of the invasion.

Source 2

The *Einsatzgruppen* would enter a village or a city and order the prominent Jewish citizens to call together all Jews for the purpose of resettlement. They were requested to hand over their valuables to the leader of the unit, and shortly before the execution to surrender their outer clothing. The men, women and children were led to a place of execution which in most cases was located next to a more deeply excavated anti-tank ditch. Then they were shot kneeling or standing, and the corpses thrown into the ditch.

(Otto Ohlendorf, speaking at his trial for War Crimes in 1946)

The most notorious of these mass killings was that of *Babi Yar*, a ravine near Kiev (see map) where, on two days in September 1941, Nazis, with the support of Ukrainian Militia men, shot and buried 33,000 Jews and an unknown number of Gypsies in one enormous grave.

Source 3

Dina Pronicheva fell into the pit but survived. She told her story after the war: 'All around and beneath her she could hear strange...sounds, groaning, choking and sobbing: many of the people were not dead yet....Then she heard people walking near her, actually on the bodies. They were Germans who had climbed down and were bending over and taking things from the dead and occasionally firing at those which showed signs of life'. (Quoted in M.Gilbert, *The Holocaust*)

142

By August 1941, eight hundred years of Jewish life and culture had been wiped out.

Wherever possible, Jews tried to resist the killers. But the forces against them were overwhelming. Sometimes the Jews succeeded, if only briefly, in halting the tide of killing. At Lubieszow, Jews armed themselves with axes, hammers, iron bars and pitchforks, to await the arrival of local Ukrainians intent upon murder as soon as the Red Army withdrew, and before the Germans had arrived. (Martin Gilbert, *The Holocaust*)

Thousands of Gypsies were also murdered by the *Einsatzgruppen*. They were labelled 'asocial' and 'racially impure'. According to Donald Kenrick and Grattan Puxon, who have researched and written about the treatment of Gypsies during the Holocaust :

Source 4

The *Einsatzgruppen* were certainly not obliged to kill Gypsies, in particular women and children, and they must have done so for a mixture of three reasons:

1. A generally sadistic and bloodthirsty attitude towards non-Germans.

2. Knowledge that the Gypsies were a legitimate object of persecution and 'could be hunted like game'.

3. Indoctrination that the Gypsies were an undesirable and dangerous people.

---

1. Comment on the reliability of Source 3.

2. Explain the meaning of 'sadistic' and 'indoctrination' as used in Source 4.

3. When else were Gypsies 'hunted like game'? (see Chapter Two p.42)

Many Ukrainians had been extremely harshly treated under Stalin's rule. In 1940, the Soviet Union invaded *Estonia, Lithuania* and *Latvia*. This helps explain why the majority of people living in the Ukraine and the Baltic States welcomed the German troops as their 'liberators' in 1941. Some were Nazi sympathisers and were happy to help murder Jews. Some formed their own local Fascist militias. There was a long tradition of antisemitism in the Baltic States.

There were also Ukrainians and Balts who chose to fight with the Russians and those who helped hide Jews. Archbishop Shepetitsky, the head of the Ukrainian Church, himself hid more than 200 Jews and instructed his relatives to do likewise, which they did.

Source 5

Anatoli Kuznetsov, from the Ukraine, remembers seeing a poster put up by the Nazis in his home town:

'Then my eye fell on something ....which made me wonder if I was seeing straight:

JEWS, POLES AND RUSSIANS ARE THE BITTEREST ENEMY OF THE UKRAINE !

It was in front of that poster that I began to wonder for the first time: What exactly was I? My mother was Ukrainian, my father Russian. So I was half Ukrainian and half Russian, which meant I was my own enemy. The more I thought about it the worse it seemed. My best friends were: Shurka Matso, who was half Jewish, and Bolik Kaminsky, who was half Polish'.

(Anatoli Kuznetsov, 1982)

The Russian Defence

Non-Jewish Russians, including some Armenians, also suffered and were murdered by the killing squads. In less than nine months, over two million Soviet prisoners-of-war had died as a result of deliberate neglect — many starving or freezing to death. Hitler had imagined that his army would defeat and occupy the Soviet Union within six months. But after initial success, (see map Source 1) the German troops were slowed down by the bitter Russian winter. 1942 saw the bloodiest fighting of the war to date, when the Germans tried to take *Stalingrad*:

Stalingrad was reduced to rubble. In bitter cold, fighting street by street, both Russians and Germans went through indescribable suffering. At last in February 1943 the remnants of an army of a third of a million men surrendered to the Russians. The Russians themselves lost more men in the Battle of Stalingrad than the United States was to lose in the whole war. (J. and G.Stokes, *Europe and the Modern World 1870-1970*)

144

Source 6

Russian resistance poster: 'Fight the German beasts. It is possible to destroy Hitler's army and it is a duty'.

1. Why did many Ukrainians and Balts welcome the German Army at first?

2. What did the Nazis hope would happen as a result of putting up posters such as the one in Source 5?. How does Anatoli's confusion suggest that they were not always successful?

3. In what way is the image of Source 6 more powerful than its words?

4. Why was the defeat of Germany at the Battle of Stalingrad so significant?

The War had become a World War in December 1941, when Japanese aircraft bombed the US naval base at Pearl Harbour, Hawaii. On December 8, both America and Britain declared war on Japan. So did Costa Rica, Haiti, Honduras,Nicaragua, El Salvador, Cuba, Guatemala, Panama and the Dominican Republic. Japan was an ally of Germany and Italy, who both declared war on the USA. China had been at war with Japan since 1937. During the Second world war, she joined the USA and Britain.

While taking on the Americans, the Nazis continued with their deadly plans for the Jews of Europe.

PART TWO: 'THE FINAL SOLUTION'

On August 1, 1941, Himmler (Head of the Gestapo and Reichsfhürer of the SS) witnessed an execution by the *Einsatzgruppen* near Minsk in Bylorussia. His face and coat were splattered with brains. He almost fainted and after this episode asked the Head of Police to find a new method of mass killing.

The method used by the *Einsatzgruppen* was 'inefficient' and a drain on precious German ammunition. Soldiers got tired of pulling triggers all day, it made their shoulders ache. Locals came to watch the killing for 'fun', and there are reports of some troops losing morale and drinking heavily in order to face their task.

Sometime during 1941, Himmler summoned Hoess (Commandant of Auschwitz) to Berlin and told him: 'that the Führer had given the order for a Final Solution of the Jewish Question'. He said a way must be found of exterminating the remaining Jews of Europe as quickly and effectively as possible. Adolf Eichman, originally head of Jewish Emigration, then Jewish 'Resettlement', was now to be directly in charge of the Destruction.

Source 7: Himmler to Hoess :

The Jews are the sworn enemy of the German people and must be eradicated. Every Jew that we can lay our hands on is to be destroyed now during the war, without exception. If we cannot now obliterate the biological basis of Jewry, the Jews will one day destroy the German people.

1. What were your reactions when reading Source 7 and about the proposed 'Final Solution'?

2. When the Nazis said 'Final Solution' ('*Endoslung*' in German), what did they actually mean?

Who gave the order?

Some historians are interested in whether or not Hitler actually gave the order for the Holocaust to begin. Most agree that it could not possibly have happened without his command and full knowledge.

Source 8

The Nazi records provide little help. Typically, Hitler and his lieutenants cloaked their most criminal activities in euphemistic (disguised) language, [and] tried...to keep their murderous plans secret...The Nazi dictator was reluctant to commit himself to paper...and preferred always to give orders orally (Michael Marrus, 1988).

Marrus also points out that:

1. Hitler received reports on the killings and

2. Himmler said the policy was determined by the Führer. It was up to Himmler to put Hitler's 'wild talk' into practice.

The question of whether Hitler and the Nazis had been planning the Holocaust for years is another issue for historians. Some point to his murderous speeches about Jews as evidence of his true intentions (see pp.64 and 123). Others suggest that the 'Final Solution' had not been part of a long-term plan. They argue that it evolved gradually after Emigration policies failed.

No serious historian believes that Hitler knew nothing of the 'Final Solution' On March 26th 1942, during a ceremony to honour officers awarded the Iron Cross, Hitler said:

> ### Source 9a
> I know exactly how far I have to go, but it is so that the whole east becomes and remains Germanic...We don't need to express our ideas about that now, and I will not speak about it. That (task) I have given to my Himmler, and he is already accomplishing it.

And the notes of a discussion between Hitler and Horthy (the Regent Ruler of Hungary) on 17th April 1943 reveal Hitler's thinking:

> ### Source 9b
> Where the Jews were left to themselves, as for instance in Poland, the most terrible misery and decay prevailed. They are just pure parasites. In Poland this state of affairs had been fundamentally cleared up. If the Jews there did not want to work, they were shot. If they could not work, they had to succumb. They had to be treated like tuberculosis bacilli, with which a healthy body may become infected. This was not cruel, if one remembered that even innocent creatures of nature, such as hares and deer, have to be killed, so that no harm is caused by them. Why should the beasts who wanted to bring us Bolshevism be spared more? (International Military Tribunal, Nuremberg, document D-736, cited in M. Gilbert, *The Holocaust.*, 1986)

1. To what extent are Sources 9a and 9b evidence of Hitler's knowledge of the Holocaust?

2. Read Source 8. Identify and explain three of the problems Michael Marrus describes.

The camps

Concentration camps had already been established, including at Auschwitz, in Poland, initially used as a prison camp for Poles suspected of subversive activities (see map Source 11). Experiments with *gassing* Jews and Soviet prisoners of war, had been tried as early as September 1941 — in Auschwitz.

In December 1941, 700 Jewish people were put in special vans at *Chelmno* in Poland and gassed by exhaust fumes channelled back into the van. The Chelmno gassings then went on daily for six months. The Commandant's boast was: *'Ein tag, ein tausand'* (One day, one thousand [killed by gassing]). More than a thousand gypsies were also murdered in gas vans at Chelmno in those first weeks.

Source 10a

Franz Schalling, a member of the German police, describes what he witnessed there in the film *Shoah* by Claude Lanzmann.

CL: Did the Jews enter the van willingly?

FS: No, they were beaten. Blows fell everywhere, and the Jews understood. They screamed. It was frightful!...

CL: Describe the gas vans.

FS: They stretched, say, from here to the window. just big trucks, like moving vans, with two rear doors.

C: What system was used? How did they kill them?

FS: With exhaust fumes. It went like this. A Pole yelled 'Gas!' then the driver got under the van to hook up the pipe that fed the gas into the van.

CL: Yes, but how?

FS: From the motor.

CL: Yes, but through what?

FS: A pipe — a tube. He fiddled around under the truck, I'm not sure how....

CL: Who were the drivers?

FS: SS men...

CL: Could you hear the sound of the motor?

FS: Yes, from the gate we could hear it turn over.

CL: Was it a loud noise?

FS: The noise of a truck engine.

CL: The van was stationary while the motor ran?

FS: That's right. Then it started moving. we opened the gate and it headed for the woods.

CL: Were the people already dead?

FS: I don't know. It was quiet, No more screams. You couldn't hear anything as they drove by.

Source 10b

Yakov Grojanowsky was a young Jewish man from the village of Izbica Kujawska in German-annexed western Poland. He was forced to help bury the bodies at Chelmno but managed to escape on 19th January 1942. He later recorded everything he had seen and done. These are two excerpts from his diary:

Wednesday 7th January 1942 The corpses were thrown one on top of another, like rubbish on a heap. We got hold of them by the feet and hair. At the edge of the ditch stood two men who threw in the bodies. In the ditch stood an additional two men who packed them in head to feet, facing downwards. The orders were issued by an SS man who must have occupied a special rank. If any space was left, a child was pushed in.

Thursday 8th January 1942 The place where we found ourselves was surrounded by armed gendarmes ready to shoot. The entire forest was patrolled by gendarmes. The tiniest false move on our part gave the gendarmes cause for the most dreadful and cruel behaviour...Two hours later the first lorry arrived full of Gypsies. I can state with one hundred per cent certainty that the executions had taken place in the forest. In the normal course of events the gas vans used to stop about one hundred metres from the mass graves. In two instances the gas vans, which were filled with Jews, stopped twenty metres form the ditch. (Testimony of Yakov Grojanowsky, Jewish Historical Institute, Warsaw, cited in M. Gilbert, *The Holocaust*, 1986).

Source 10a is part of an interview for a *documentary film*. Source 10b is taken from a diary written soon after the events described. How reliable does this make each one?

Gas was used on a much larger scale in the death camps. These were built at the end of 1941 — Birkenau (at *Auschwitz*, which became known as Birkenau-Auschwitz II, capable of housing 200,000 inmates), *Chelmno, Belzec, Majdanek, Sobibor* and *Treblinka*. Four thousand inmates including Jewish women were forced to build Auschwitz, which was made up of forty camps including Birkenau. One third died during the building. The death camps were surrounded by many smaller camps, where conditions varied. Some were labour camps (such as Auschwitz III where slave labour worked for I.G. Farben) and some were smaller killing centres.

In Western Europe, some concentration camps had small gas chambers and crematoria e.g. *Mauthausen* in Austria. *Ravensbruck* (near Berlin) became a 'women's concentration camp', though women were also taken to all other camps. The Nazis set up 'transfer camps' where people waited until the trains were ready to transport them to the 'East'. Two such transit camps were: *Drancy*, in France and *Westerbork*, in Holland.

The Nazis built a so-called model camp in the Czech town of Terezin (renamed *Theresienstadt* in German). Many famous Jews were sent there. It was designed to mislead public opinion, with a bank front, false schools, nurseries and cafes. But in reality, the conditions were terrible — and more than 30,000 Jews died there. Between 1942 and 1945, 88,191 Jews were deported from Theresienstadt to Auschwitz and other death camps.

There were more than 100 concentration camps in Europe, including the one built on Alderney in the Channel Islands after it was occupied by the Germans in June 1940. Jews, Spanish Republican and Russian prisoners-of-war were brought there and many were then worked to death.

Himmler (left) and other Nazis, inspecting the Mauthausen concentration camp.

Source 11

Major concentration camps

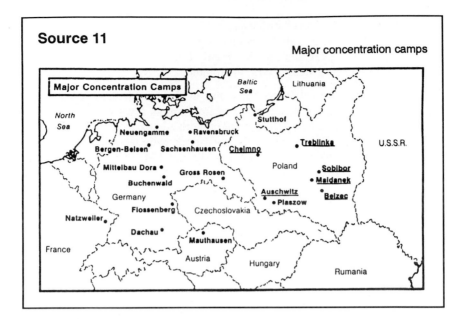

Why were the death camps all in Poland?

1. To be far away from Germany.

2. Poland was known to be a particularly antisemitic country.

3. To be near where the majority of Jewish people lived.

4. The camps were usually built in quiet, rural, isolated places.

Why do you think the above four factors were important?

The Wannsee Conference

In January 1942, a small conference of senior Nazis, headed by Heydrich, met at Wansee, a suburb of Berlin. The purpose of the meeting was to co-ordinate the 'Final Solution to the Jewish Problem'. The new policy was explained. Europe was to be searched for Jews. A list was drawn up, showing the total number of Jewish people left in each country, occupied and unoccupied, including the Jews of Britain.

Jews would be forced from the ghettos to the death camps . They were to be told that their destination was 'resettlement in the East' and that they should take all their valuables with them. Money was taken from Jewish people's bank accounts, in order to pay for the train tickets.

Source 12

L a n d	Zahl
A. Altreich	131.800
Ostmark	43.700
Ostgebiete	420.000
Generalgouvernement **(Poland)**	2.284.000
Bialystok	400.000
Protektorat Böhmen und Mähren	74.200
Estland – judenfrei –	
Lettland	3.500
Litauen	34.000
Belgien	43.000
Dänemark	5.600
Frankreich / Besetztes Gebiet	165.000
Unbesetztes Gebiet	700.000
Griechenland	69.600
Niederlande	160.800
Norwegen	1.300
B. Bulgarien	48.000
England	330.000
Finnland	2.300
Irland	4.000
Italien einschl. Sardinien	58.000
Albanien	200
Kroatien	40.000
Portugal	3.000
Rumänien einschl. Bessarabien	342.000
Schweden	8.000
Schweiz	18.000
Serbien	10.000
Slowakei	88.000
Spanien	6.000
Türkei (europ. Teil)	55.500
Ungarn	742.800
UdSSR	5.000.000
Ukraine 2.994.684	
Weißrußland aus-	
schl. Bialystok 446.484	
Zusammen: über	11.000.000

153

Deportation

Source 13

We were taken to the train station under SS guard, with the *Gestapo* standing on all sides. Our route passed through the streets of Prague and thousands of Czechs lined both sides as an expression of their sympathy for the Jews. Many men removed their hats and some of the women wept openly when they saw how cruelly the Nazis treated us, old and young, and the small children, too. Even now, no one dreamed they were sending us to Poland. We thought: Holland, Belgium, Germany — but never Poland. (M.G., quoted in I. Trunk, 1979)

Source 14

The most painful moments were the mass deportations where most of my friends were disappearing. All the people who had been deported were never heard of again. Clothing started to arrive back, marked with names, and people found their relatives' clothing. (Esther)

But the ghettos were sealed off and some never heard the rumours. It was very hard to contact other ghettos or people on the 'other side'. The extermination camps had deliberately been built in isolated places. All SS had to swear an oath of secrecy about their purpose. Many people refused to believe the rumours about the gas chambers.

In the East, the deportations usually began with wild shooting. People were driven out of their homes, beaten and shot at; doors were broken down with axes and rifle butts. Anyone trying to hide was killed on the spot. They were often held at gathering points for days, through insufferable heat, rain or snow, with no water. Or they were locked up in schools, synagogues or churches. Many died before the trains had arrived to take them away.

The order to round up Gypsies came in 1943. Some were supposed to be exempt but this order was not always observed. Gypsy communities all over Europe were arrested and deported to concentration and death camps, often with the collusion of the local authorites and churches.

Bernhard Stembach, was a German Gypsy who had left the Army (see p.135):

I returned to my family in the internees camp in Frankfurt. I did work in different areas....Even the women had to work. In the meantime I had met my wife and married. We had a child and lived there till 1943. Then it happened — we went to Auschwitz.

Thousands tried to avoid deportation :

Source 15

I can never forget something that happened then. All of us were suddenly ordered to line up immediately on the Hamburgplatz. Thousands of Jews were huddled together, guarded from all sides by German military and Jewish policemen. No one knew what was about to take place. Then a gallows was quickly raised and, right before our eyes, they hanged a young man. The Germans blared through their loudspeaker: 'This is the way everyone caught trying to escape the ghetto will end up!' (M.G. in I.Trunk, 1979)

The Nazis used the promise of food to persuade people to gather for deportation: 'That was when I saw the people who were really starving, those for whom bread and jam were a kingdom richer than life.' (M. Gray, 1972)

The deportations often split up families.

The deportation had no noticeable effect on the German war effort. Most of the soldiers used were unfit for military service at the front.

The Central prison, Lodz Ghetto. Jews were taken from there to the death camps.

1. Look at the list of the Jews of Europe, Source 12. Can you translate all the place names? Which country had the largest and which the lowest number of Jews?

2. How did the Nazis deceive Jews into believing they were not going to their deaths?

The plan was to murder, often by gas, all of the Jews — religious, assimilated, converts to Christianity, men, women, old and young.

> **Source 16**
> I think they heard the baby crying and that brought them as far as our hiding place.'Let the child go, he hasn't done anything, he's only a baby!' But the murderer's heart of stone was not moved. He replied: 'He's a baby now, but he'll grow up to be a Jewish man. That's why we have to kill him. (Hadassah, aged 16, quoted in Itzhak Tatelbaum, 1985)

Chaim (Harry) Nagelsztajn

Harry was born in Hrubieszow (near Lublin, see map p.2) Poland in 1927. His father, Shlomo, was a builder. His mother was called Mincha and he had two brothers and four sisters. There were 10,000 Jewish people living in the town in 1939:

> I went to a school where there were Jewish and Catholic boys. I also attended an evening Cheder, a Jewish school. We lived in the Jewish quarter of town and most of my friends were Jews. In the late 1930s, you could see more antisemitic graffitti, the synagogues were attacked and Jews were often beaten up, including my father'. (Harry)

After two years of Nazi occupation, the deportations began. Harry's father built a special cellar below the house. He, Mincha and five of the children went into hiding there on October 27, 1942. Harry, his sister Manya and her boyfriend Meyer decided to find somewhere else to hide:

Opposite: Back row: (left to right) Gittel, Eli, Manya. Front row: (left to right) Joshua, Yittel, Harry.

Source 17

'Will you come with me, Manya?' Meyer's voice was pleading and tense as he called her name. Helplessly Shlomo watched his daughter's struggle...If she went with Meyer, she might be safe or she might be caught; if she stayed with them, the same was true, the pain was in the choosing.

'Manya, if you're coming, we must leave immediately!' Meyer demanded.

'You go ahead,Manya,' Mincha whispered, holding her arms out to her eldest daughter...'If you go, maybe one of us will survive'. Manya and her mother clutched each other and sobbed their grief.

'I want to come too,' said Chaim....Mincha couldn't believe her ears. She wanted to scream out: 'No Chaim!'. Her world revolved around her family, and it was splintering away...She let him go. her knees buckled, she gagged, retching the emptiness inside her. 'Be strong, Chaim, and care for your sister. I love you.'

(From M.Korenblit and K.Janger, (1983) *Until We Meet Again*, Putmans and Sons, New York).

Their hiding place for the next two weeks was to be a haystack on the farm of Meyer's friend Josef Wisniewski. Josef had hollowed the haystack out enough to hide ten of them, including Meyer's parents, brothers and sisters. He brought them food and drink every night. Later, this farmer and his family were shot by the Germans for the crime of helping Jews.

After two weeks, Harry, Meyer and Manya, unable to bear their hiding place anymore, gave themselves up to the Gestapo. They had heard that workers were needed, to clear the homes of those Jewish people already deported from the Ghetto. Three months later, they were arrested and Harry was taken to Majdanek.

1. List all the reasons Manya and Harry (Source 17) would have had for a) staying with their family and b) hiding elsewhere.
2. What might have been Josef Wisniewski's motives for risking his family's life by hiding Harry and nine other Jewish people?
3. Why do you think that Harry, Meyer and Manya gave themselves up to the Nazis?
4. Source 17 was written by Manya's son and a friend about forty years after the Holocaust. What sort of evidence is it and in what way does it add to your understanding of the time? Quote from it to support your answer.

The Journey

More than 300,000 people died on these train journeys to the death camps.

Source 18

My name is David. I am a Polish Jew aged 13. I have been taken from the Warsaw ghetto, along with many other Jews...for the deportation to a so-called labour camp called Treblinka. We are lined up beside a railroad cattle car...Once we are inside, there is no room to sit. In order to make room we are forced to stand with our hands above our heads. There is no roof...Suddenly the door is slammed shut and sealed. A water bucket is tossed in for use as a disposal container for human waste...Terrible cries pierce the air...an old lady jammed near me has just died. A little boy is screaming for his mother. (Quoted in I. Tatelbaum, 1985))

Despite the rumours, people could not conceive of the 'Final Solution'. Though persecuted before, Jews had always survived as a people and the thought of a plan to murder them all was inconceivable. *'We will live through it'* was a popular saying in camps and ghettos.

Source 19

In 1944, Esther and her mother were deported from the Lodz ghetto to Auschwitz:

Although we had been under Nazi Occupation for so long and suffered all the degradation, hunger and disease, we were not prepared for what Auschwitz was ...We thought we were being sent to another place of work (Esther).

---

1. Use Sources 18 and 19. How do they help explain why it was so difficult for prisoners of the Nazis to resist their treatment?

2. Why, despite rumours, did many people not believe the truth about the death camps and what 'resettlement in the East' really meant?

Arrival

The entrance to Auschwitz.

Source 20   *Transport* by Leo Haas (survivor of Auschwitz).

Source 21

Some people arriving at the death camps did not know what sort of a place they had been brought: 'When we did arrive at Auschwitz, we said, 'Where are we?' and the people who worked at the railways said, 'You mean you don't know what this place is?' I had seen the barbed wire and people that looked very deranged...and we thought, 'That's not for us' because it looked like some sort of lunatic asylum. And then from a distance I saw someone go towards the wire and fall, I was told, 'She's touched the electric wire, she's dead now.' And it still did not sink in. They even gave us on arrival a tin of something to eat while we were being pushed towards selection and this was the most painful moment, which I have never got over...separation from my mother...' (Esther).

Esther's mother Sara.

Some appear to have heard rumours about the death camps. Before the Second World War, Viktor Frankl was a psychiatrist in Vienna. He and 1,500 other Jews were put on a train bound for 'the east'.

Source 22

Fifteen hundred persons had been travelling by train for several days and nights: there were eighty people in each coach... Suddenly a cry broke from the ranks of the anxious passengers: 'There is a sign, Auschwitz!' Everyone's heart missed a beat at that moment. Auschwitz — the very name stood for all that was horrible: gas chambers, crematoriums, massacres...
(V. Frankl, 1962)

Dr Frankl's father, mother, brother and wife were all murdered.

SS Oberstormfhürer Johann Kremer, Doctor of Medicine and Philosophy, arrived at Auschwitz on August 30, 1942. Kremer was one of the doctors responsible for conducting medical experiments on inmates (described below). He recorded his first day in a diary:

Source 23

Received strictly confidential instructions. Took the oath. Accommodation at hotel, next to the railway station, Room 26. Tropical heat...Dust and innumerable flies. Excellent food in the Home. Lunch for just half a Reichsmark — Duck Liver, stuffed tomato and salad...

Two days later Kremer noted: Was present for the first time at a special action at 3a.m. By comparison, Dante's inferno seems almost a comedy. Auschwitz is justly called an extermination camp! (Diary of Johann Paul Kremer in Kazimierz Smolen (ed), 1978)

---

1. What was the artist Leo Haas trying to convey in his picture Source 20?
2. What can we learn about the feelings of prisoners arriving at the death camps from Sources 21 and 22?
3. What sort of 'oath' do you imagine Kremer is referring to in Source 23? What does he mean by 'special action'?

Rudolf Reder recalled an incident shortly after he arrived at Belzec on August 11th 1942:

> Soon after my arrival at Belzec, one very young boy was selected from each transport...He was a fine example of health, strength and youth. We were surprised by his cheerful manner. He looked round and said quite happily, 'Has anyone ever escaped from here?'

> It was enough. One of the guards overheard him and the boy was tortured to death. He was stripped naked and hung upside down from the gallows — he hung there for three hours. he was strong and still very much alive. They took him down and lay him on the ground and pushed sand down his throat with sticks until he died. (Quoted in M.Gilbert, *The Holocaust*, 1986)

'Selection'

The new arrivals were immediately 'selected' by Nazi guards and medical examiners, deciding who would live and who would die. Almost all babies and children, particularly girls, along with most women and the old and sick, were sent straight to the gas chambers.

Some pretended to be older than they really were, or to have a useful trade. When Harry arrived at Majdanek, he told the Nazis he was 17, three years older than his actual age. He also told them he was a builder. For others, it was to be the last time they ever saw members of their family:

'Selection' on the railway platform at Auschwitz.

Source 24

An SS non-commissioned officer came to meet us, a truncheon in his hand. He gave the order; 'Men to the left! women to the right!' Eight words spoken quietly, indifferently, without emotion. Eight short, simple words. Yet that was the moment when I parted from my mother, I had not had time to think, but already I felt pressure of my father's hand. We were alone. For a part of a second I glimpsed my mother and my sisters moving away to the right. Tzipora held my mother's hand. I saw them disappear into the distance; My mother was stroking my sister's fair hair, as though to protect her, while I walked on with my father and the other men, and did not know that in that place, at that moment, I was parting from my mother and Tzipora forever. (Elie, aged 15 in I. Tatelbaum, 1985)

1. Deportees were often tortured on their way to the camps in an effort to kill their spirit and hope before they even arrived at the death camps. Why do you think the Nazis did this?

2. Discuss whether or not it is possible for us to understand how Esther and Elie might have felt about being separated from their mothers at Auschwitz.

3. What other 'useful trades' besides 'builder' do you imagine prisoners pretended to have in order to save their lives?

Responses

How did the victims behave during the selections? The historian *Isiah Trunk* has written about some of the responses:

Source 25

Husbands often broke from the ranks and ran to their families... despite the fate in store for them if they did so. Families tried to stick together at any price. Special concern was given to the children, and people tried to ease their final minutes.

Source 26

Rudolf Hoess, the Kommandant of Auschwitz, wrote his autobiography while in a Polish prison. He describes how a mother, who knew what lay ahead, managed to gather the strength to joke with her children, despite the terror in her eyes.

Some women, while undressing, would scream dreadfully, tear out their hair, and become hysterical. They were instantly taken behind the gas chambers and shot. Sometimes the victims became defiant, especially children. They refused to enter the gas chamber.... Hoess tells of a Jew, who, walking past him, hissed: 'Germany will pay a heavy penalty for the mass murder of the Jews.'....Some religious Jews would look upon their final road in terms of martyrdom. (I.Trunk, 1979)

Opposite: Jews at Auschwitz after 'selection'.

Source 27

Martin Gilbert recounts a now famous incident at Birkenau:

On October 23rd (1943), 1,750 Polish Jews from the group held at Bergen-Belsen were deported to Birkenau. There they were driven into the undressing chamber by SS Sergeant Major Josef Schillenger. A former roll-call leader in the men's camp at Birkenau, Schillenger had become feared and hated for his habit of choking Jews to death while they were eating their meagre meals. The women were ordered to undress. As they did so, the German guards, as usual, seized rings from fingers and watches from wrists. During this activity, Schillinger himself ordered one of the women to undress completely. This woman, who according to some reports was a former Warsaw dancer by the name of Horowitz, threw her shoe in Schillinger's face, seized his revolver, and shot him in the stomach. She also wounded another SS man, Sergeant Emmerich. The shooting of Schillinger served as a signal for the other women to attack the SS men at the entrance to the gas chamber. One SS man had his nose torn off, another was scalped. Schillinger died on the way to the camp hospital. The other SS men fled. Shortly afterwards the camp commandant, Rudolf Hoess, entered the chamber, accompanied by other SS men carrying machine guns and grenades. They then removed the women one by one, and shot them outside.

The revolt of the Jewish women at Birkenau was recorded by two prisoners who worked in the camp. (M. Gilbert, *The Holocaust*, 1986)

---

1. List the five responses mentioned in Sources 25 and 26 in each case, what would happen to the prisoner.

2. Does the fact that the evidence in Source 26 is taken from Hoess's autobiography make it more or less reliable? Explain your answer.

3. What do you imagine were the motives of the dancer in Source 27?

The gassings

Those destined for the gas chambers were stripped and then marched, to the sound of music, into low buildings that looked like shower-blocks, but were really gas chambers. Some were big enough to gas 2,000 people at once. At Treblinka, the Germans called the path leading to the gas chamber ; Himmelweg, or 'Road to Heaven.' (in the film *Shoah* by Claude Lanzmann)

> Before entering the gas chamber, prisoners were told to leave their clothes neatly together and above all remember where they had put them, so that they would be able to find them again quickly after their shower.

> The women went in first with their children, followed by the men, who were always fewer in number. The door would be closed and the gas immediately discharged through vents in the ceilings of the gas chambers. About one-third of the people died straight away. The remainder staggered about and began to scream and struggle for air. The screaming, however, soon changed to the death rattle and in a few minutes all lay still (Rudolph Hoess).

Hoess knew so much because there were special photographers who recorded the murder, for training purposes. In addition, the gas chambers had 'peep holes' through which the Nazis and their visitors chose to watch the gassings. Top Nazis from Berlin, officers and civilians, were invited to watch the gassing and burning of 8,000 Jews from Cracow (Poland) in 1943.

If you were making a documentary film about the Holocaust and had the job of interviewing one of the officers who chose to watch the gassings, what sort of questions would you ask them?

Certain Jewish inmates of the camps were the *Sonderkommando* or 'special work detail'. It was their job to empty the gas chambers and then to throw the corpses into pits. The majority of these *Sonderkommando* were themselves murdered after three months.

Source 28

Filip Müller was part of the Sonderkommando at Auschwitz: 'They fell out. People fell out like blocks of stone, like rocks falling out of a truck. But near the Zyklon gas there was a void...An empty space. Probably the victims realised that the gas worked strongest there. The people were battered. They struggled and fought in the darkness. They were covered in excrement, in blood, from ears and noses...children had their skulls crushed. It was awful...It was terrible to see.That was the toughest part...It was pointless to tell the truth to anyone...You couldn't save anyone there'. (Excerpt from the film *Shoah* by Claude Lanzmann)

Erich Winter was another man who was made to do this work. He had been a soldier serving in the *Luftwaffe* (the German airforce), until the Nazis discovered he was a Gypsy. He and his brother Starnoski were sent straight to Auschwitz, in their uniforms:

Source 29

'You could see on the walls...people had scratched with their fingers... I can't describe it...it was appalling.' (Quoted in BBC TV documentary, 1989, *The Forgotten Holocaust*)

1. Why do you think the Sonderkommando were usually killed after three months?

2. Read Sources 28 and 29. What problems do the two men have in describing the work they had to do? Did they have to do the work? How do you imagine they managed to carry out their job?

3. What difference to your understanding of their feelings might it make to actually see and hear them talking?

The burning

Women usually had their heads shaved before they were gassed. The hair was then sold to stuff mattresses. The dead were also plundered to help the German war effort. Gold teeth were removed for melting down, then the bodies were burned — at first in the open air and later in ovens. In the villages around Auschwitz, Poles had been removed and replaced by ethnic Germans.

Bone pieces were sold for fertiliser. Skin was sometimes used to make lampshades.

Source 30a

The oven room of crematorium III by David Olére (a painter in the Sonderkommando at Auschwitz)

Source 30b

Pigtail

When all the women in the transport
had their heads shaved
four workmen with brooms made of birch twigs
swept up
and gathered up the hair

Behind clean glass
the stiff hair lies
of those suffocated in gas chambers
there are pins and side combs
in this hair

The hair is not shot through with light
is not parted by the breeze
is not touched by any hand
or rain or lips

In huge chests
clouds of dry hair
of those suffocated
and a faded plait

a pigtail with a ribbon
pulled at school
by naughty boys.

(Poem by Tadeusz Rozewicz, Trans. Adam Czerniawski)

Source 31

Wedding rings, taken from people murdered in the death camps.

The vast quantity of inmates' belongings — clothes, suitcases and other possessions were sold or stolen by the Nazis.

1. Some historians say that the Holocaust was unlike any other event in history, not because of the numbers murdered, but because of the *industrialised* way they were killed. How does the above section illustrate the industrialised murder?

2. How might D. Olére have known what the death camp crematorium looked like so that he could draw Source 30a?

3. Why might Source 31 be a particularly disturbing picture for some people?

4. Read the poem *The Pigtail*. Do you find it more powerful than if you had read a straightforward description about mounds of hair? Explain your answer.

Those not killed on arrival

Seldom less than half, and often more than three quarters of every transport went straight to the gas chambers at Auschwitz. People who survived the first selection became reduced to numbers. Their numbers were tattooed on their arms. Harry's number was *A-19879*. Gypsies' tattoos all began with the letter 'Z' ('*Zigeuner*' is German for 'Gypsy').

A Gypsy child, a survivor of Auschwitz, with her tattoo number on her arm.

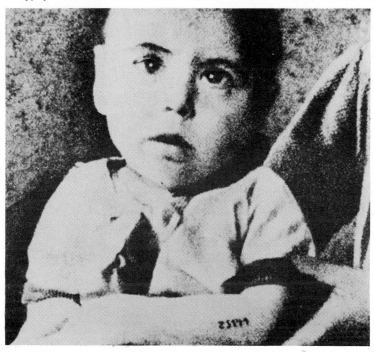

All their possessions were removed and sent back to Germany, they were shorn of all hair, disinfected and dressed in thin grey-striped trousers and jackets, with no underwear.

Humiliation, Dehumanisation and Work

Divided into work units, headed by a prisoner called a *kapo*, they worked a twelve hour day, from making haversacks and boots for the German army, to building roads. Some German firms were keen to win contracts to set up a factory in the concentration camps and take advantage of the slave-labour there. The Krupp factory, (armaments) and Siemens (an engineering firm) were built on land adjacent to Auschwitz-Birkenau. Thousands of Jewish slave-labourers were employed in the Buna works making synthetic oil and in the many coal mines of the region. Victims were forced to work for a certain period (three months on average) until they dropped dead from exhaustion. Work was harsh and gruelling. They were insulted by the guards all day, called 'Shit' and 'arsehole'; fed at starvation level; regularly beaten and tortured. Nearly all women inmates stopped menstruating.

Harry was given twenty-five lashes of the whip because he went to the toilet without permission:

> The made a lot of Jews look like kids. You couldn't stand up to them because they'd just shoot you. They made you degraded, took all your confidence away. Everybody was for themselves. You felt sympathy...but what could you do? (Harry)

Harry describes the attitude he developed towards work:

> I became one of the best workers. I was doing everything because if you wanted to survive, keep your mouth shut, do what they tell you. If they want volunteers, put your hand up....go! You just lived from day to day. I never thought I'd survive...but each day I lived, I worked hard...I wanted to tell the world what the Nazis had done to us, to my family and everyone.

People who gave up hope were called 'Musselmen' — the walking dead. Those who were ill or who weakened, were usually sent to the gas chambers.

> After three weeks work in Majdanek, laying paving stones in the wind and cold, wearing only a little jacket, I couldn't take it anymore and they put me in a barrack for the sick. I had pleurisy and typhoid and I couldn't remember a thing. I was in a coma for ten days. I remember imagining my mother was behind me, stroking my hair and speaking to me in Yiddish: 'Don't worry Chaim, you'll survive'. When I woke up all the infection had gone to my leg, I couldn't stand on it. One day the SS took me to a sort of washroom. When I saw all these old people with smashed up faces and bodies there, I knew I was going to the gas chambers. They

were all crying. I just kept saying: 'I'll go to where the rest of my family is. Why should I be the only survivor?' I didn't care whether I lived or died.

In the meantime, a couple of elderly fellows hid themselves behind some blankets in a corner of the room and the SS came in and started counting. They counted twenty-five people and ordered twenty-five uniforms to pretend that we were going out to the camp to work. Then the Germans left and the two old fellows came out from behind the blankets. A Czech doctor who had treated me before, came in and saw me there. The Secretary counted again and counted twenty-seven. So the doctor took me and this young barber and sent us back to our beds. That's how I was saved ....by another two going into the gas chambers. (Harry)

---

1. Explain the terms *dehumanisation* and *brutalisation*. How and why were concentration camp prisoners dehumanised and brutalised?

2. If you were to meet Harry, what sort of questions might you ask him about the experiences he describes above?

Source 32
This is a document found at Auschwitz which had been drawn up by a camp official. It is an estimate of the income and expenditure, per prisoner, if each prisoner is used for three months:

Expenditure
Food......................................90 Marks
Clothing and Footwear........110 Marks

Income
Labour...............................234 Marks
Ashes after cremation..............4 Marks

Net Profit   128 Marks

---

1. Explain how the Germans got 234 Marks income from the prisoners' labour.

2. What does this document tell us about the attitudes of some people at the time?

Some survivors and historians describe the death camps as: *'another planet'*. A world beyond the understanding of anyone who was not there. But others disagree and stress the importance of remembering that Auschwitz was not another planet. Instead, they say, it was our planet and part of human history.

Source 33

What we put up with, you know, it's impossible to describe. It is too awful. What I am telling you now is only the surface — the tip of the iceberg — Because what we experienced and suffered in Auschwitz, that can't be put into words. (Bernhard Stembach, German Gypsy)

Some talk about a new form of society having been created, based on mass slavery and terrible cruelty, where human life was worthless in the eyes of the Nazis. People had to make unimaginable choices:

1. The story of *Sophie's Choice* by William Styron, reveals the choice given to a Polish mother of two children. She was allowed to keep one of them with her, the other to be sent to the gas chamber.

2. *Filip Müller*, of the Auschwitz *Sonderkommando* describes the choice he had to make when a group of people from Czechoslovakia, his country entered the 'undressing room':

   The violence climaxed when they tried to force the people to undress. A few obeyed, only a handful. Suddenly, like a chorus, they all began to sing...That moved me terribly...I realised that my life had become meaningless. Why go on living? For what? So I went into the gas chamber with them, resolved to die. With them. Suddenly, some who recognised me came up to me...A small group of women approached. They looked at me and said, right there in the gas chamber...'So you want to die. But that's senseless. Your death won't give us back our lives...You must get out of here alive, you must bear witness to our suffering (excerpt from the film *Shoah* by Claude Lanzmann).

---

1. Professor Lawrence Langer has called these sort of dilemmas 'Choiceless choices'. What does he mean? Use Sophie and Filip's 'choices' to help you explain.

2. From what you have found out so far, in what way does Auschwitz sound like 'another planet'? Why do survivors like Bernhard (Source 33) find it impossible to put into words? Why do some survivors and historians disagree with Auschwitz being described as 'another planet'? What is your opinion of this debate, given the information you have?

Searching the Ashes

This note was found buried in the piles of human ashes at Auschwitz. It was written by *Salmen Gradowski*, a member of the *Sonderkommando*:

> Dear finder, search everywhere, in every inch of soil. Tens of documents are buried under it, mine and those of other persons, which will throw light on everything that was happening here....We ourselves have lost hope of being able to live to see the moment of liberation.

On the 17th of October 1962, Salmen's sixty-five page notebook was found in a small jar buried three feet below ground, near the ruins of the gas chambers:

> ...None of us were really conscious of what was happening to us...This is a horrible death and as I write these lines, I shiver at the very thought that I too will experience something like this... (extracts cited in M. Gilbert, *The Holocaust*, 1986).

What is the value of this evidence found buried in the ashes of Aushwitz?

Some became totally brutalised. People who had been lifetime friends turned on each other and Jewish *kapos* beat other prisoners. But many managed to cling to their humanity, sharing each morsel of bread, every scrap of blanket and even sacrificing their own lives for another.

Source 34

For the first time we have become aware that our language lacks words to express this offence, the demolition of a man...Nothing belongs to us any more; they have taken away our clothes, our shoes, even our hair; if we speak they will not listen to us us, and if they listen, they will not understand. They will even take away our name: if we want to keep it, we will have to find ourselves the strength to do so, to manage somehow so that behind the name, something of us, of us as us, still remains. (Primo Levi, 1958)

What did Primo Levi mean by 'the demolition of a man'?

Roll Calls *(Appel)*

The *Zehappel* lasts almost three hours. This word, meaning 'roll call', became the dread and the lifestyle of Auschwitz. Twice daily we would be lined up with lightening speed by fives in order to be counted. Lined up at 3 a.m., we would stand there for three or four hours until the official SS staff showed up to count our heads. In the evening it lasted from five to nine (Livia, age 13, quoted in I. Tatelbaum, 1985).

Medical experiments and Torture

In many of the camps, so-called 'medical experiments' were carried out, without any anaesthetics, largely to satisfy the curiosity and sadism of the doctors. The SS camp staff included 350 qualified doctors who took part. The most feared was *Dr Mengele* of Auschwitz, who carried out 'experiments' on pregnant women. He liked to cut them open and see how long it took for a foetus to die. He also enjoyed research into the effects of torture, castration, sterilisation, infection and injection with poison. He would inject dye into the eyes of brown-eyed people, to make them 'Aryan-blue.' Hundreds of Jewish and Gypsy 'patients' were murdered in this way.

Ferdinand Labaloue survived experiments into the effects of hypothermia at Dachau concentration camp. He was put in freezing water until he turned blue. Of the sixty-five in the 'experiment' group, he believes that sixty-one died during the tests. The Nazis gave him the title Prisoner of Honour for his endurance. In 1944, he escaped from Dachau, dressed as an SS officer. He now suffers from heart, lung and intestine troubles.

What explanations do you imagine the Nazis gave for their 'experiments'?

Gypsies and the Holocaust

On December 16 1942, [Himmler] issued an order for the German gypsies to be transferred to Auschwitz...Between February 26 and March 25 1943, 11,400 Gypsies from Germany and elsewhere were transported to a special Gypsy camp within Auschwitz. Here, unlike other prisoners, they were able to live together with their families, probably to facilitate the medical experiments. (Jeremy Noakes, *History Today*, 1985)

Dinah Gottliebova, a Jewish Czech artist, worked in the Auschwitz camp hospital, where Mengele ordered her to make coloured portraits of Gypsy prisoners. She painted this portrait in 1944 and, knowing that the woman would be gassed as soon as the painting was finished, took as long as she dared to complete it

Portrait of a Gypsy, Auschwitz, 1944, by Dinah Gottliebova (survivor of Auschwitz).

1. The murder of the Gypsies has been referred to as the 'Forgotten Holocaust'. What is meant by this?

2. Which country 'lost' the highest per cent of their Gypsies (see Source 35)? Can you think of reasons why the percentages vary so much?

Source 35

THE FATE OF THE GYPSIES UNDER NAZI RULE

0 miles 200
0 km 150

In 1939 there were more than 700,000 gypsies living in Europe. At least 200,000 of them were murdered by the Nazis, as part of a deliberate policy aimed at "ridding" Europe of both its gypsies and its Jews. A gypsy was defined by the Nazis as a person with at least two gypsy great-great-grandparents.

Mass murder sites where gypsies as well as Jews were slaughtered.

Camps at which gypsies were forcibly sterilized.

Concentration camps in which gypsies are known to have been murdered.

100,000 Number of gypsies in 1939, country by country.

Number of gypsies murdered between 1942 and 1945: the Serbian figure is a minimum estimate.

ESTONIA
1,000
1,000

GERMANY
20,000
15,000

HOLLAND
500
500

LATVIA
5,000
2,500

U S S R

BELGIUM
600
500

LITHUANIA
1,000
1,000

Bergen-Belsen

WESTERN U.S.S.R.
42,000
30,000

Valogne

Dusseldorf

Gross Rosen

Chelmno

Treblinka

Sobibor

Babi Yar

LUXEMBOURG
200
200

Buchenwald

Natzweiler

BOHEMIA
13,000
6,500

Majdanek

Auschwitz

Belzec

POLAND
50,000
35,000

Dachau

Nikolaev

FRANCE
40,000
15,000

AUSTRIA
11,200
6,500

HUNGARY
100,000
28,000

SLOVAKIA
80,000
1,000

Simferopol

ITALY
25,000
1,000

Zemun

RUMANIA
300,000
36,000

CROATIA
28,500
28,000

Black Sea

SERBIA
60,000
12,000

By 1939 many German and Austrian gypsies had been sent to Buchenwald and Dachau. In 1940 all surviving German gypsies were deported to Poland, and forced to live in special sections set aside for them in the Ghettoes being established for Jews. Several thousand Serbian gypsies were murdered during German "field operations" in 1941, and many Crimean and Ukrainian gypsies were killed in January 1942 at mass-murder sites intended primarily for Jews. On 16 December 1942 a Nazi decree ordered gypsies from all over Europe to be deported to Auschwitz, where 16,000 were murdered on arrival at the camp.

"In Europe, generally only Jews and Gypsies are of foreign blood". OFFICIAL GERMAN COMMENTARY ON THE NUREMBERG LAWS, 1935

© Martin Gilbert 1978

Gays and the Holocaust

Richard Plant, author of *The Pink Triangle — The Nazi War Against Homosexuals,* quotes the following figures: 'Somewhere between 5,000 and 15,000 homosexuals perished behind barbed wire fences...(they) constituted a very small minority (but)...all statistics must be regarded with caution. We do not know...how many gays were detained in a specific camp during a specific month.' Other estimates of homosexual victims are as high as 100,000. Very few surviving gay prisoners have written memoirs or come forward for interviews.

Source 36

After a homosexual arrived in camp... He was battered, kicked and slapped... According to at least one witness, homosexuals and Jews were not only given the worst beatings, but their pubic hair was shorn; others lost only their head hair... Hoess... believed that homosexuality was an illness that might spread. So they were sealed off in separate barracks and work details and ordered to visit the brothels which most camps had. Prisoners often shared the guards' violent prejudice against gay men.

The prisoners with the pink triangle never lived long. They were exterminated by the SS quickly and systematically. (Raimund Schnabel, Historian)

---

1. Why have few surviving gay prisoners written memoirs or come forward for interviews?

2. In your experience, is Hoess's view (Source 36) still heard today?

3. Why are some people homophobic (prejudiced against homosexuals)?

The last year of the war

Even after Spring 1944, when it became clear that they were losing the war, the Nazis continued to use hundreds of trains and thousands of their staff, to continue with the deportations and to keep the gas chambers in operation.

The Jews of Hungary, 1944

Hungary entered the war on the side of Germany in April 1941. But when the Hungarian leadership began seeking peace with the Allies, Germany occupied the country on March 19th 1944.

The Hungarian government under Regent (Ruler) Horthy had already introduced anti-Jewish laws in 1938, 1939 and 1941. Fascist parties there were
popular, in particular the *Arrow Cross Party*, which had half a million
members. However, Horthy and his ministers and army refused to hand over
Hungarian Jews to the Nazis. After occupation, Eichmann and two of his
staff arrived in Budapest to organise the deportation of all Hungary's Jews
to Auschwitz.

Source 37

Eva, a thirteen year old girl from Nagyvarad wrote in her diary
(smuggled out by the family's domestic help): 'I do not want to die, I
want to live even if I am the only one who can remain here, if only
they would let me live....'.At Auschwitz, Mengele snatched her from
the arms of a woman doctor who was hiding her, and sent her to her
death. (Quoted in *The Hungarian Observer*, Vol. 2 No.5, 1989)

The deportations began in April 1944 and were carried out on an unpreceden-
tedly rapid scale, made necessary because of the imminent arrival of the
Soviet Army on Hungary's eastern border. 564,507 Hungarian Jews were
murdered. During the summer of 1944, Hoess proudly reported that he was
'processing' 10,000 'units' a day.

---

1. Why do you think Eva (Source 37) knew about the Holocaust in
   1944?

2. What did Hoess actually mean when he said he was 'processing
   10,000 units' a day?

Source 38

Excerpt from Testimony buried by *Sonderkommando*, Salman Lewenthal:

Six hundred Jewish boys aged from twelve to eighteen, dressed in long striped clothes, very thin; their feet were shod in worn-out shoes or wooden clogs. The boys looked so handsome and were so well built that even those rags did not mar their beauty.

They were brought by twenty-five SS men, heavily burdened [with grenades]. When they came to the square the *Kommandoführer* gave the order for them to un[dress] in the square. The boys noticed the smoke belching from the chimney and at once guessed that they were being led to death. They began running hither and thither in the square in wild terror, tearing their hair [not knowing] how to save themselves.

The *Kommandoführer* and his helper beat the defenceless boys horribly to make them undress. His club broke, even, owing to that beating. So he brought another and continued the beating over the heads until violence became victorious.

The boys undressed, instinctively afraid of death, naked and barefooted they herded together in order to avoid the blows and did not budge from the spot. One brave boy approached the Kommandofuhrer [standing] beside us [...] and begged him to spare his life, promising he would do even the hardest work. In reply he hit him several times over the head with the thick club.

Many boys, in a wild hurry, ran towards those Jews from the *Sonderkommando*, threw their arms around the latter's necks, begging for help. Others scurried naked all over the big square in order to escape from death.

The young, clear, boyish voices resounded louder and louder with every minute when at last they passed into bitter sobbing. This dreadful lamentation was heard from very far. We stood completely aghast and as if paralysed by this mournful weeping.

With a smile of satisfaction, without a trace of compassion, looking like proud victors, the SS men stood and, dealing terrible blows, drove them into the bunker. Some boys, in spite of everything, still continued to scurry confusedly hither and thither in the square, seeking salvation. The SS men followed them, beat and belaboured them, until they had mastered the situation and at last drove them [into the bunker]. Their joy was indescribable. Did they not [have] any children ever? (Bezwinska and Czech: *Amidst a Nightmare of Crime*, quoted in M. Gilbert, *The Holocaust*, 1986)

Source 39

In the same month, Rudolf Hoess, Commandent of Auschwitz, wrote in his diary: 'Every wish for my wife and children has been fulfilled. The children have been able to live freely and naturally. My wife has had her own garden — a paradise of flowers...In my family, love of flowers and especially animals, has taken pride of place...'

Bearing in mind that Hoess was in charge of the SS in Source 38, can you explain the difference in his behaviour and attitude towards children in Sources 38 and 39?

The Perpetrators

Himmler described the SS involvement in the 'Final Solution' as 'a page of glory in our history, which has never been written and must never be written'.

Who were the tens of thousands of men and women who ran the death camps? Evidence suggests that there was no one 'type' of person who joined the SS. Some were sadists or psychopaths, others seem to have been rational, 'normal' individuals who got used to committing and witnessing atrocities.

> From the evidence in *Hitler's Army*...as well as that set out in *Those were the days* [two recently published books on the Holocaust period]...some (many? most?) German and Austrian (particularly Austrian?) policemen and soldiers enjoyed killing Jews (and Russians? and Poles?). (Colin Richmond writing in the *London Review of Books*, Feb. 13, 1992)

Many had very educated backgrounds. For example:

Source 40

Name

Hans Frank	Lawyer	Governor General of Poland; in *Einsatzgruppen*
Helmut Knuchen	Professor of Literature	Colonel, SS; Head of Security Police, Paris 1940-44
Ernst Bibersten	Protestant pastor	In *Einsatzgruppen*
Karl Brandt	Doctor	Hitler's private surgeon and conducted medical experiments in camps.

Training

The people who worked in the death camps were often the same as those who had run the euthanasia centres (see p.94). They were not all Germans. Approximately 80% of death camp staff were Ukrainian or other non-German nationals; of the Germanic staff, 40% were Austrian.

As part of their training, men in the SS were given a puppy Alsatian to train and care for and then before they could pass *their* training, they had to strangle it. The whole emphasis was on inducing a sense of mission, discipline, brutality and hatred towards the 'enemy'. The Deaths Head Units wore the badge of a skull and crossbones. They were insulted, humiliated and paraded to see floggings and torture, then punished if they showed any signs of revulsion or compassion.

Source 41

Professor Omer Bartov describes the typical German soldier (*Wehrmacht* not SS) on the Russian front:

The photographs of smiling Wehrmacht troops, each with his little camera, busily taking pictures of hanged 'partisans', or of piles of butchered Jews, this horrific *Exekutions-Tourismus*, can only be understood as the ultimate perversion of the soldiers by a terroristic system of discipline, backed by a murderous ideology, which achieved its aim of preserving cohesion at the price of destroying the individual's moral fabric and thereby making possible the extermination of countless defenceless people.

(From O. Bartov, 1991)

Responses

Franz Stangl was commandant of Treblinka death camp. In an interview with the writer Gitta Sereny in 1971, a few days before his death, he described his response to what he saw as commandant:

Source 42

Sereny: 'Would it be true to say that you got used to the liquidations?'......he thought for a moment. 'To tell the truth', he then said.....'One did become used to it'.

Sereny: 'In days? Weeks? Months?'

Stangl: 'Months. It was months before I could look one of them in the eye'.

Sereny: 'Even so,...there had to be times, perhaps at night, in the dark, when you couldn't avoid thinking about it?'

Stangl: 'In the end, the only way to deal with it was to drink. I took a large glass of brandy to bed with me each night and I drank'.

Sereny: 'Would it be true to say that you finally felt they weren't really human beings?'

Stangl: 'Cargo' he said tonelessly. 'They were cargo'

Sereny: 'There were so many children. Did they ever make you think of your children, of how you would ever feel in the position of those parents?'

Strangl: 'No...I can't say I ever thought that way....You see I rarely saw them as individuals. It was always a huge mass'.

(G. Sereny, 1974)

Source 43

And after the war when Hoess was asked if he had ever considered whether the Jews whom he had murdered had in any way deserved such a fate:

'We SS men were not supposed to think about those things; it never occurred to us ....It was something already taken for granted that the Jews were to blame for everything....It was not just newspapers like the *Stürmer* but it was everything we ever heard. Even our military and ideological training took for granted that we had to protect Germany from the Jews.... We were all so trained to obey orders without even thinking that the thought of disobeying an order would simply never have occurred to anybody'.

Choices

Did those responsible for the killings have any choice? Did any refuse? And what were the consequences for them? There are examples on record of soldiers and police choosing not to participate. The following excerpt is taken from an interview with a (German) member of the police in charge of executing Jews in the town of Hrubieszow, Poland, where Harry's parents and five brothers and sisters were shot dead:

Source 44

The Jews were unloaded inside the barracks compound behind the prison camp where the Russian prisoners of war were held and were to be shot close by to where we were. As I was absolutely opposed to this action I went and stood behind the lorry in which the Jews had been brought. I did not think I had to take part in the shooting. However Meister Kozar [the sergeant] found me standing there and ordered me to take part in the execution.....I refused because I had no desire to shoot defenceless people. I had no wish to become a murderer. I said this to Kozar and he did not press me further to carry out this order. (Quoted in E.Klee,W.Dremen and V.Riess, 1991)

Source 45

And according to *Professor Franz Six* of the *Einsatzgruppen*:

'During the war a person could at least try to have himself transferred from an Einsatzgruppen. I myself managed to do this successfully....I was not demoted as a result of my transfer.....There were without doubt cases where people who were transferred from an *Einsatzgruppe* suffered disadvantage.....Nonetheless, as far as I know, nobody was shot as a result...'. (Quoted in E. Klee *et al*, 1991).

---

1. Why do historians consider it noteworthy that some of the leading Nazis were highly educated (Source 40)?

2. What was the purpose of the SS training? How did it make officers perceive children like Harry and Esther as unworthy of life? What other long-term factor does Hoess mention when explaining how he came to see Jews as deserving to die? Do you think that we are all capable of becoming mass-murderers?

3. Read Source 41. What is the *Executions-Tourismus*? How does Bartov attempt to explain the behaviour of many German soldiers? Does this help you understand the events which culminated in the Holocaust?

4. How did the Nazis make it easier for men like Stangl to forget that concentration camp prisoners were individuals with families?

5. In your opinion, is Hoess's statement about obedience (Source 43) accurate? Refer to Sources 44 and 45 in your answer.

6. From what you have read and discovered so far, do you think the 'Final Solution' had been intended from the beginning of Nazi rule?

7. Who else besides the SS was responsible for the Holocaust? For example, the firm of I.G. Farben, who made Zyklon B gas for the gas chambers. List some of the people without whom the Holocaust would have been impossible.

8. Why are some of those responsible sometimes called 'the desk-killers'?

יוגנט שטימע

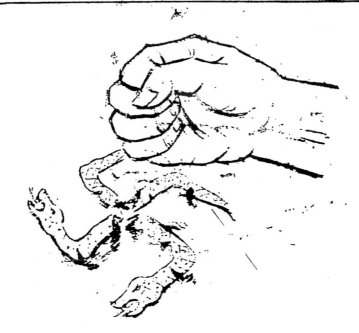

פאשיזם דאס צוזאמענדריקט אונדזער

אויך אין טיפן אונטערערד, אונטער דער נאציישער טעראָר־הערשאַפֿט, האָט די בונדישע
יוגנט געהאַט איר פרעסע — 2 צייטונגען, איינע אויף יידיש און אַ צווייטע אויף פויליש.
אויפן בילד — אַ פאַדערשטע זייט פון דער אונטערערדישער "יוגנט־שטימע".

Chapter Nine

Resistance, Collaboration, Indifference and Rescue

This chapter examines people's responses to the Holocaust. It concentrates on the victims and on other ordinary Europeans and the choices they made. There are examples of those who chose to resist by various means, those who collaborated actively with the Nazis, those who were 'bystanders' and those whose actions saved individuals from the gas chambers.

1. The difficulty of resistance

Those wanting to resist faced severe problems: collective punishment, terror and shock, hunger, illness and malnutrition, lack of weapons, isolation, insecurity and antisemitism.

a. Reprisal

> **Source 1**
> When Jews talked about the possibility of rebelling, they were aware that the Nazis would murder all the Jews in their town or ghetto. That is why a small number of Jews would not endanger that majority. An uprising was started only when the majority of Jews in the area decided that the Germans would kill all the Jews there in any event. So there was nothing to lose. (I.Tatelbaum, 1985)

For every German killed or even wounded by the resistance, dozens and even hundreds of Jews could be murdered in reprisals. So resistance was not always popular in the local area. For example, in Czechoslovakia, SS General Reinhard Heydrich was assassinated by two Czechs on 27th May

1942. As punishment, one thousand Jewish people were deported from Prague to Treblinka, Belzec and Sobibor. Then 199 Czech men and boys were murdered at Lidice. The village was burned to the ground.

1. In pairs, discuss and make a list of the choices that many Nazi victims faced.

2. Do you think Jews were right not to rebel in small numbers? What evidence is there to support this view?

b. Terror and Shock

The Nazis used the screaming of orders, ferocious dogs, whips, arbitrary shooting and public hangings to keep people in constant fear. A Polish railwayman, Franciszek Zabecki, witnessed the following scene at Treblinka station before the trains were sent into the death camp:

Source 2

One mother threw a small child wrapped in a pillow from the wagon, shouting: 'Take it, that's some money to look after it'. In no time an SS man ran up, unwrapped the pillow, seized the child by its feet and smashed its head against a wheel of the wagon. This took place in full view of the mother, who was howling with pain. (cited in M. Gilbert, *The Holocaust*, 1986)

---

c. Hunger, Illness, Malnutrition

Twenty-five per cent of inmates in concentration camps died of hunger and disease before the organised extermination began. Rations consisted of watery soup made of potato peelings and a crust of bread. Hunger and degradation weakened people's resistance.

More than one million of the Jews held in concentration camps were children, or were old, ill, insane.

d. Lack of weapons

Weapons were extremely difficult to obtain. Also, how much use were a few pistols against the tanks and machine guns of Europe's best-trained army? Many of the Nazis' prisoners did not know how to fight and at first there were no weapons in the ghettos.

Jewish resistance groups had little support from outside. There were 500,000 Jewish people in Palestine and thousands in the other communities of the free world. However, they were not always as helpful as the resistance groups wanted (See Chapter 10).

e. Isolation, Insecurity, Antisemitism

Before the Holocaust, the Nazis had done their utmost to take away the physical strength and self-respect of the Jews. They tried to destroy their organizations and completely isolate them.

It was sometimes easier for non-Jewish inmates to escape. There are 250 recorded attempts to escape from Auschwitz. It was relatively easier to escape from Auschwitz I (mainly Poles) than Birkenau-Auschwitz II (mainly Jews). The number of recorded escapees from Birkenau was thus proportionaly fewer — no more than twenty, and less than ten successful escapees.

Escape was difficult and extremely dangerous. The prisoners were debilitated, in addition to being demoralised, by hunger and ill-treatment. Their heads were shaved, their striped clothing was immediately recognizable, and their wooden clogs made silent and rapid walking impossible. They had no money and, in general, did not speak Polish, which was the local language, nor did they have contacts in the area, whose geography they did not know either....Anyone caught trying to escape was publicly hanged, often after cruel torture. (Primo Levi, 1958)

Rudolf Vrba, who escaped from Auschwitz-Birkenau in Apr. 1944.

Even when Jews managed to escape from a ghetto or camp, they could not always be sure that they would find shelter with the local population. Even people who were sympathetic towards the Jews were often afraid to help escapees.

Source 3

An entry in the Auschwitz records indicates the fate of two Gypsy escapees: 'On May 4th, 1943, Josef (Z.1904) and Franz Rozycka (Z.2035) tried to escape from a work commando. They were put in Block II bunker and shot on May 22nd'.

1. Use the above sources to write five sentences about the difficulty of resistance.

2. Why could escapees not always find shelter with the local population?

3. How can you tell that the escapees in Source 3 were Gypsies? (see p.172 if you need a clue).

f.   Disbelief and Hope

The vast majority of Jews could not, any more than any human being, believe they were about to be killed. If they heard rumours about gas chambers, many refused to believe them. Some young people could have escaped, but didn't. They preferred to remain with their families, often with old or sick parents whom they could not leave.

Source 4

The SS arranged for some of the camp inmates to send postcards home: The contents were brief and all said the same thing: they were well, were working and lacked for nothing. The card came from the mysterious place: Waldsee.

'It is impossible to describe the effect these cards had on the Jews. One heard the exclamations, 'See! They're at work! Nothing has happened to them...The postcards acted as a sleeping drug....and removed any thought of revolt or escape'. (Moshe Sandberg, a Hungarian Jew, quoted in M. Gilbert, *The Holocaust*, 1986)

---

1. Why did so many people not want to believe they or their family would be killed?

2. Why do you think the Nazis allowed inmates to send postcards home? Refer to Source 4 in your answer.

---

2. Types of resistance

Historians disagree about what exactly 'resistance' was . Was it only physical, armed action: killing Nazis and bombing German supply lines? Or should we include any action or behaviour which enabled people to survive and therefore spoil the Nazis' aims?

Disobedience took the form of: refusing to register as a Jew; refusing to wear a yellow star; refusing to live in a ghetto. In 1941 in the Vilna Ghetto, hundreds of Jews refused to go to Ponary (the extermination site) and lie down on the ground. Spiritual resistance involved continuing to worship, celebrating the Jewish festivals of Rosh Hashana and Channukah. All such worship was punishable by death.

Source 5: Jokes

These jokes told by Jews are taken from Emmanuel Ringelblum's diary, *Notes from the Warsaw Ghetto*:

Hitler came to Heaven and saw Jesus in Paradise.
'What is this Jew doing here without an armband?' he demanded.
'Let him be,' said St.Peter, 'he's the boss's son.'

A police officer came into a Jewish home and wanted to confiscate the possessions. The woman cried, pleading that she was a widow and had a child to support. The officer agreed not to take the things, on one condition: That she guess which of his eyes was the artificial one.
'The left one,' the woman guessed.
'How did you know?'
'Because the right one has a human look.'

Source 6

Attempting to stay alive was ..... resistance. Escaping, hiding or giving birth to a child in the ghetto was resistance. Praying, singing or studying..was resistance...Schools were organized, concerts were given and a library and museum were in operation. Vilna, the 'Jerusalem of Lithuania' became the 'Jerusalem of the Ghettos'. (Y.Suhl, 1975)

Despite opposition from certain political groups, a theatre group opened in the Vilna ghetto on January 18, 1942. In its first year, the theatre put on 111 performances, selling 34,804 tickets.

---

1. 'Every act — however small or ordinary that ensured survival.... was an act of resistance'. (Michael Elkins)
   Do you agree? What do you think counted as resistance in the ghettos? Refer to the above examples in your answer.

2. How might exchanging recipes, songs and jokes help a person survive?

3. Why are the jokes in Source 5 called 'gallows humour'?

4. Some people in the Vilna Ghetto objected to the theatre. They said: 'No theatre in a graveyard'. What did they mean? What arguments do you imagine the actors used in their own defence?

Jewish resistance group, Vilna 1944.

i. **Partisans and Resistance groups**

These were men and women who operated in every country occupied by the Nazis. Some groups were made up of Jews and non-Jews working together (for example in Italy, France and Russia). In Yugoslavia, many Jews joined the partisans led by Tito. There were Gypsy partisan bands in Slovakia, Italy, USSR and Yugoslavia.

In many areas, such as Poland and the Ukraine, it was unusual for Jews to

be welcomed into the partisan movement. For this reason, they tended to set up their own specifically Jewish partisan groups. Some groups were organised along political lines, led by communists, socialists, and nationalists.

Misha Gildenman (known as 'Uncle Misha') led a Jewish partisan group in Ukrainian territory. He saved hundreds of Jews. Thousands left the ghettos and joined 'family camps' in the forests.

Left: Misha Gildenman

Source 7
Zog Nit Keynmol! **(We Survive!)**

Written by Hirsh Gilk, poet of Vilna when he learned of the Jewish uprising in Warsaw (see below). This song became the hymn of the Jewish partisans. Gilk died while fighting, in 1943.

We must never lose our courage in the fight,
Though skies of lead turn days of sunshine into night.
Because the hour for which we've yearned will yet arrive, And our marching steps will thunder: we survive!

From land of palm trees to the land of distant snow,
We have come with our deep sorrow and our woe,
And everywhere our blood was innocently shed,
Our fighting spirits will again avenge our dead.

What role did songs such as this play in helping those involved in resistance? In your answer, refer to words in the song.

Resistance fighters destroyed German military stores and communications, they organised local anti-Nazi activity and attacked German troops. On July 31st 1942, four partisans, dressed as Gestapo, set fire to lists of Jewish people held at the Association of Belgian Jews Headquarters in Brussels.

Newspaper of underground movement.

ii. In the ghettos

In the ghettos, Jewish socialist Zionists and communists tended to organise the underground movements. The Bund was the socialist Jewish workers' association. It printed a daily newspaper, organized public kitchens, medical supplies and a trained militia. Couriers were often young women who posed as Poles and smuggled food and other essentials into the ghetto.

The main aim of the underground groups was survival. Their newspapers reported on the progress of the war, the mass deportation and annihilation of Jews and the defeat of the Nazis.

---

1. What was the importance of underground papers to:
    a. the resistance and
    b. the Nazis?

2. Why were *girls* often used as couriers?

As news of the Holocaust spread and once young people had witnessed the murder or deportation of most of the elderly and children from the ghettos, so their determination to resist grew. By 1943, many felt they had nothing to lose. The Jewish Combat Organisation (ZOB from its Polish initials) handed out this leaflet to workers in the Warsaw Ghetto, in March 1943 :

> Jews! The German bandits will not leave you in peace long. Gather around the standards of resistance. Take shelter, hide your women and children, and join, with whatever means you have, the fight against the Nazi butchers.

The Jewish Councils (see p.202) did not always agree with armed uprisings, if they believed the ghetto might survive. The majority of ghetto inhabitants were not involved in active resistance.

Thousands went into hiding with water and food supplies, led by the ZOB, which distributed leaflets to keep up morale, executed traitors and organised fighting units. They appealed urgently for help by radio to London, Geneva, New York and Jerusalem.

The Warsaw Ghetto Uprising

At 6 a.m. on Monday, April 19, 1943, 2,000 SS troops entered the ghetto with tanks, machine guns and trailers of ammunition. The Nazis aimed to round up all the Jewish people left there. 700 members of the ZOB units retaliated with grenades and guns, forcing the shocked Germans to retreat, with 200 of their men dead or wounded.

The Jews in the ghetto celebrated, although they knew they could not win in the end. But the resistance lasted for 42 days — until time, space, food, water and weapons ran out. Mordechai Anielewicz was 24 years old when he died commanding the uprising. In his last letter, he wrote :

Source 8

'Goodbye my dears...The dream of my life has come true...Armed Jewish resistance and revenge have become a fact. I have witnessed the marvellous and heroic stand of Jewish fighters'.

His hiding place was betrayed and he commited suicide on May 10th 1943 rather then fall into the hands of the SS. The ghetto fighters had managed to get hold of only a very small amount of pistols, grenades and explosives from the Polish underground outside the ghetto.

Source 9

Self Defence in Warsaw by Arthur Szyk.

Vladka Meed was a Jewish girl aged 17 in 1939. Born Feigele Peltel, she changed her name to the Polish 'Vladka' in order to work for the ghetto underground movement from the 'Aryan' side of the ghetto. She smuggled weapons across the wall to the ZOB during the revolt and helped escapees to hide in the homes of Christians.

Vladka's forged identity card.

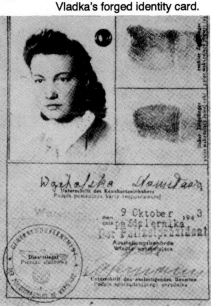

Captured fighters, Warsaw Ghetto.

The Germans set fire to the ghetto and threw gas into the ZOB Headquarters bunker. Some Jewish civilians surrendered, others commited suicide rather than fall into German hands. Seventy-five ZOB fighters escaped through the Warsaw sewers and were captured alive. 70,000 ghetto inhabitants were killed or captured.

Yet hundreds remained in the cellars and bunkers under the ruins of the ghetto. Clashes between Jewish fighters and Nazis continued till June 1944. Only one per cent of the half million people in the Ghetto survived.

The Warsaw Ghetto Uprising was the first act of organised military resistance to the Nazis and its news inspired other groups in concentration camps and ghettos to resist.

1. In what way do Sources 8 and 9 celebrate the Warsaw Ghetto Uprising?

2. Are they reliable sources, even though their authors make their feelings very clear?

3. Why do you think the Warsaw ghetto got so little help from outside?

Choiceless choices

In his novel *The Accident*, Elie Wiesel describes a group of Jews hiding in a bunker. Their lives are threatened by a crying child. The mother, Golda, and all the others turn to Shmuel, the ritual slaughterer (of animals), and say:

> 'Make him shut up. Take care of him, you whose job it is to slaughter chickens. You will be able to do it without making him suffer too much'. And Shmuel gave in to reason: the baby's life in exchange for the lives of all. He had taken the child. In the dark his groping fingers felt for the neck. And there was silence in heaven and on earth.

1. Why could this be described as a 'choiceless choice'?

2. 'And Shmuel gave in to reason'. What does the author mean?

3. Elie Wiesel was a survivor of Auschwitz. He believes that the only acceptable way of communicating about the Holocaust now is via stories. How can stories inform us about the Holocaust? What other means are there?

C. Inside the camps

Despite the conditions (see Chapter 8), there was resistance in the concentration camps, from individual acts such as the dancer's (see p. 166) to armed uprisings. The majority of inmates did not or could not actively resist, but every camp had its underground group and there are hundreds of examples of individual or group revolts.

There were armed uprisings in Auschwitz, Treblinka and Sobibor. The *Sobibor* extermination camp witnessed one of the most extraordinary stories of resistance. Led by Sasha Pecherski, a Jewish Soviet prisoner of war, this was to be a mass escape, since individual breakouts led to such fierce reprisals. The escape plan had the support of important kapos (Jews with responsibility for guarding other inmates).

On October 14th 1943, the plan was put into action. After cutting the camp's communication lines, inmates killed key SS men. The women ransacked the SS living quarters and stole weapons and axes. All 600 Jews rushed out of the camp. They were met by 200 armed Ukrainian and Polish guards. Only about sixty escapees survived, including Sasha who managed to rejoin the Soviet partisans. The Germans, outraged at the successful uprising, destroyed Sobibor death camp.

1. Why did Sasha Pecherski insist on making the Sobibor Uprising a mass escape?

2. Most history textbooks never mention these revolts. Does that matter? How does learning about resistance affect your understanding of the Holocaust?

3. Historians argue about the significance of Jewish resistance to the Holocaust. Some, for example Raul Hilberg, say it was unimportant and emphasize the fact that most people did not actively 'fight back'. Those who disagree ask: 'How in these conditions, did Jews manage to resist at all?'. Discuss.

d. Rescue from outside

Appeals sent to the free world from occupied Europe met with a varied response. Small amounts of money and supplies were smuggled into the ghettos and sometimes even into the camps. There were also attempts to enter occupied territory and save the lives of Jewish people.

One such attempt was made by *Hannah Senesch*, a Hungarian-born Jew who had emigrated to Palestine before the war. In 1943, she joined the British army and was parachuted into Nazi-occupied Yugoslavia. She aimed to get to Budapest, Hungary, where her mother and relatives lived. She was twenty-three when she was captured by the Nazis. Tortured for five months, Hannah refused to give any information. Evidence suggests that even the Nazis admired her strength, but on November 7 1944, they murdered her.

Left: Hannah Senesch.

Hannah Senesch is a heroine of modern Israel. What aspects of her story help to explain why? To some, though, she seems naïve. Why?

The Resistance in Germany

There was never a unified resistance movement in Germany. There were different groups who opposed the Nazis at certain times or on specific issues. Among these groups were: the Red Patrol in Berlin, the Socialist Front in Hanover (Social Democratic Party), student groups and individual civil servants and clergymen.

In February 1943, the Jewish husbands of two hundred non-Jewish women were rounded up at their workplaces. Day after day, the women gathered at the detention centre where their husbands were being held and shouted, 'We want our men! We want our men!' Unable to stop them, the Gestapo guards gave in and released the men. The protest was unique. So was its outcome.

Once the war began, only the armed forces could act against Hitler with any hope of success. There were a few individuals in the German army who could bring themselves to join the resistance to Hitler. Johannes von Blaskowitz, a senior General in the German Army, protested to Hitler after seeing the massacre of Polish civilians. There are reliable accounts of individual German soldiers hiding and helping individual prisoners of the Gestapo.

After Germany's defeats at Stalingrad (December 1942) and in North Africa, dissatisfaction grew. Some army officers opposed the atrocities committed by the *Einsatzgruppen* (see chapter 8).

The July Plot

On July 20, 1944, at 12.42 pm, a bomb exploded in the Conference room at Hitler's Headquarters. It was placed there by Colonel Graf von Stauffenberg, a top-ranking military officer and aristocrat. He had been badly wounded while fighting in Tunisia, losing his left eye, his right hand, and two fingers of his left hand. While recovering, he determined to kill Hitler and end the war.

Four men died instantly. Twenty others were wounded. Hitler was only slightly injured by the blast. He ordered that no mercy be shown to anyone involved in the Plot or to their friends. All the adult members of the von Stauffenberg family were executed. Between 180 and 200 people were put to death.

1. If 'some army officers' loathed the atrocities commited by the Einsatzgruppen, why did only a few join the resistance to Hitler?

2. Why do you think some historians are reluctant to call the July plotters 'Anti-Nazis'? Think about who they were and when they decided to organise and execute the Plot.

3. Design a front cover headline and short article to appear in the Nazi Party newspaper of 21st July, describing the Bomb Plot and its organisers.

3. The Jewish Councils

Judenrate (Jewish Councils), were set up by the Nazis to run the ghettos. They were ordered to collect money from the ghetto population and supply men and women for labour. They also organised the Jewish police (see p.202), hospitals, food and fuel distribution, sanitation and continuation of religious functions (birth, marriage, death ceremonies etc). And later, they had to organise Jews to be 'resettled'.

They were in an impossible position. Wanting to protect the Jewish communities, but at the same time carrying out *Gestapo* orders which aimed to destroy them. If they refused to serve on the Council, they were severely punished and, in many cases, killed. Today, there is much debate about the role of these Jewish Councils. Did they help the Nazis? Did they protect Jewish people in the ghettos? What could they have done? What should they have done?

Once in the job, Jewish Council members became the focus of jealousy and extreme anger. Some used their position to save members of their own family and secure extra food and luxuries. Some tried to save as many Jews as possible, while others could not cope with the choices they had to make. Every Jewish Council and Council leader behaved differently:

Adam Czerniakow, head of the Warsaw Judenrat, was ordered to deliver six thousand Jews daily to the Nazis, or else his wife and thirty-nine others would be shot. He managed to save a few workers, students and husbands of working wives. But the Nazis would not agree to saving the orphans of the ghetto. The orphans were deported with *Dr Janusz Korczak*, a writer, doctor and broadcaster, who was devoted to them. When the Nazis ordered the orphans to the death trains, Korczak refused his Polish friends' offer of rescue and instead led the children onto the train. He and they were all murdered in Treblinka. Unable to carry on, Czerniakow took a cyanide tablet, leaving a suicide note to his wife and colleagues:

'I am powerless...I can no longer bear all this'

The Jewish Police

These men were used by the Nazis to help run the ghettos and organise the deportations. They were usually hated by the ghetto. Martin Gray, who spent time in the Warsaw Ghetto wrote in his book, *For Those I have Loved*:

Source 10

A Jewish policeman was in Mrs Celmajster's daughter's room, tugging at the little girl, who clung to her mother.....he raised his club so I charged at him, head down, hitting him right in the face. Flattening him......I had dreamed of killing such men.....But now suddenly I felt close to him, he was a victim like myself.

Esther remembers a Jewish policeman called Jakubowicz who, in 1942, pretended not to see her, her mother, brother and neighbours when they were hiding from the Nazis, thus risking his own life and enabling them to spend two more years in the ghetto together.

---

1. What was 'clever' about the Nazis' tactic of setting up and using the Judenrate (Jewish Councils)?

2. Explain the change in Martin Gray's view of the Jewish policeman (Source 10).

3. Discuss whether, in your opinion, the Jewish Councils and Jewish police were victims or collaborators.

---

4. Collaborators

In each country occupied by the Germans, the reaction of local people varied. There were always some who welcomed the Germans and were active supporters of fascism, for example the Latvian *Thunder Cross*, the *Arrow Cross* in Hungary and the Dutch Fascist Party with 80,000 members. Lithuanian and Ukrainian national movements welcomed the Germans as liberators (from Russian Soviet power) and participated in (and sometimes initiated) the first killing of Jews e.g. in Kovno and Lvov.

Source 11

Norwegian pro-Nazi poster.

Can you work out the message of this Norweigan pro-Nazi poster?
Comment on the words and images.

Some agreed with the Nazis but did not wish to soil their hands with blood. Others did not necessarily agree with Nazi ideas, but knew they could benefit personally from working with them.

France was divided into an Occupied zone including Paris and a Southern zone ruled by a French government under Marshal Petain, hero of the First World War. Vichy France, as the Southern zone became known, set up its own concentration camp system and passed its own laws against Jewish people. By 5th September 1942, 9,872 Jews had been rounded up by French police and sent to Paris where they joined thousands of other French Jews from the occupied North. From there they were deported to Auschwitz. However, many French people, including Catholic priests, sheltered Jews and urged their people to do likewise. In Southern France, the people of *Le Chambon*, led by their Protestant minister Andre Trochme and his wife Magda, sheltered 5,000 Jewish people. After the war, two of the rescuers, Henri and and Emma Heritier, said: 'We did nothing extraordinary'. These French Protestants equated the persecution of the Jews with their own past oppression by French Catholics.

In *Yugoslavia*, the SS found willing helpers among some of the Albanian police. Kuna Cevcet, a Gypsy, remembers an incident in 1942:

Source 12

Ljatif Sucuri, an uncle of mine who was about 35 at this time, knew the Albanian chief of police, a general. When an order came through for the police to round up Gypsies, Ljatif told him that if any Gypsies were killed he would personally kill the police chief and the rest of us would burn down the houses of the Albanians. He told the police chief to inform his superiors over the telephone that there were no Gypsies at Mitrovica, and this he did. (Quoted in D.Kenrick and G. Puxon, 1972)

It was, in most cases, the local police (Dutch, French etc) who rounded up Jews for deportation and who were the key figures in the collaborationist aspect of the 'Final Solution' in Western Europe.

There were also hundreds of people who filled out all the forms needed to organise the Holocaust and approximately one hundred train drivers on the deportation routes. Very few of these went into the camp zones. Special drivers took the trains on their last few miles.

The Case of Henrik Gawkowski

Henrik Gawkowski

Source 13

Henrik used to drive trainloads of people to Treblinka: 'It was extremely distressing to him. He knew the people behind him were human, like him. The Germans gave him and the other workers vodka to drink. Without drinking, they couldn't have done it' (excerpt from the film *Shoah* by Claude Lanzmann)

---

1. What made the Judenrate leaders different from the collaborators mentioned above?

2. What do you think the motives were of the French collaborators mentioned here?

3. What prevented the Albanian chief of police (Source 12) from collaborating?

4. In small groups, think of arguments for and against the view that Henrik Gawkowski was partly responsible for the Holocaust.

5. Bystanders

What about those who did not welcome the German armies or want their nation ruled by a foreign force? Or those in Germany who were not Nazis and disliked the treatment of their Jewish neighbours? Or those who were *indifferent* to the Holocaust? Why did so many people stay silent?

Inge Deutschkron remembers the day the Nazis rounded up the Jews of Berlin. People hurried home: *'They did not want to look'*.

Villagers who live in Treblinka remember the Holocaust. One farmer used to work in his field, so near to the death camp he could hear the terrible screams and see people being murdered. He says: *'At first it was unbearable. Then you got used to it'* (in the film *Shoah* by Claude Lanzmann).

Source 14

Abraham Bomba, a survivor of Treblinka, remembers his journey to the camp:

We were in the wagon; the wagon was rolling in the direction east. A funny thing happened, like maybe its not nice to say, but I will say it. Most of the people, not only the majority, but ninety-nine percent of the Polish people when they saw the train going through...they were laughing, they had a joy, because they took the Jewish people away.' (excerpt from the film *Shoah* by Claude Lanzmann).

A significant number of rescuers were Catholics and many gave their lives or suffered imprisonment. Cardinal Angelo Roncalli, the future Pope John XXIII, from his base in neutral Istanbul, successfully urged the Bulgarian King not to allow Bulgarian Jews to be deported. The then Pope, *Pius XII*, has been criticised for not condemning the Nazis' extermination policy sooner than he did and for not urging Christians to protect or help victims of the Holocaust. However:

> 'As the German round-up of Jews began in Rome, he personally ordered the Vatican clergy to open up the sanctuaries of Vatican City to Jews in need of sactuary. Within five days, a total of 477 Jews had been given shelter within the Vatican itself, and more than 4,000 others were given sanctuary in the monasteries and convents of Rome. This was more than four times as many Jews as the Germans were able to deport from the city.' (Martin Gilbert, *The Holocaust*, 1986)

The Pope claimed that if he had criticised the mass deportations publicly, it would only antagonise the Germans and increase the suffering of the Jews.

---

1. Explain in your own words, the statements by Inge Deutschkron and the farmer living near Treblinka.

2. How does Source 14 contradict the Polish farmer?

3. What did Pope Pius XII mean when he claimed that his protest would only make the Jews suffer more? Why do you think that the bishops and priests who stayed silent during the Holocaust have received particular criticism?

4. If ordinary people did nothing to prevent the Nazis achieving their goals, can they be accused of collaborating because they stood by? What should they have done? What could they have done? What choices did they have?

---

6. Rescuers

Approximately 200,000 Jews were saved from the Holocaust by perhaps 50,000 of their fellow Europeans (figures estimated by Yad Vashem, Israel's documentation centre). Other sources estimate there were up to 500,000 saved. There are examples of these rescuers in every country. Individuals, like *Josef Wisniewski*, the Polish farmer who hid Harry, (see p.158), groups, such as the Bulgarian farmers who threatened to lie down on the railway tracks to stop Jews being deported. More Norweigan Jews were saved than deported and in the case of *Denmark*, virtually a whole nation acted as rescuers.

Figures for the numbers of Gypsy, gay, communist and other victims rescued, are harder to obtain.

Before studying examples of those who rescued victims of the Holocaust, consider the differing circumstances in each occupied country.

Local conditions influenced the rate of extermination and the methods used. For example:

- the existence of German military rule, martial law and/or an occupation regime of the utmost severity, imposing rigid restrictions on movement and communication, as well as low and even (as in Poland) debilitating ration scales;

- the co-operation of the local population;

- how much self-government the Nazis allowed;

- the level of antisemitism;

- how assimilated the Jews were.

Explain how each of these factors might have influenced the rate of extermination.

The factors which influenced whether or not certain individuals chose to be rescuers varied too. For some, it was their own values:

> We have got to live as humans and not as beasts. They were worse than beasts...These people had the right to live like other people....Jewish people are the same....all people are the same....

> I knew they were taking them and they wouldn't come back. I didn't think I could live with knowing I could have done something...
> (Quoted in P. and S.Oliner, 1988)

Others have explained their actions as due to *parental influence*:

> My parents taught me discipline, tolerance and serving other people when they needed something...My father would not judge people who lived or felt differently than he did. That point he made to us.
> (Oliner, 1988)

The person's religion and whether they had Jews as friends were also significant.

a. Eighty-five per cent of *Italian Jews* survived the Holocaust. The Italian army of occupation in Croatia refused to participate in the deportation of Jews, while the local Croat Utashi forces were actively involved, in the most cruel way. They even had concentration camps of their own for Jews, in which tens of thousands died (Loborgrad, Djakova, Stara Gradiska, Jasenovac). While many Italians did help the Nazis in their round-up of Jews, there are numerous examples of Italian peasants, maids, lawyers, doctors and civil servants who hid, fed and helped Jews to escape. For example, **Federico Sartori,** a peasant farmer living in a tiny house near Padua with his family of five, took in a family of thirteen Jewish people.

b. **Raoul Wallenberg** was a Swedish diplomat sent by his government to Budapest, Hungary on July 9, 1944 to protect the Jews living in Budapest from assault by local Hungarian fascists. When, later in the year, Jews were marched out of Budapest towards Vienna, he tried to rescue them by issuing documents to protect them. He sheltered 13,000 Jews by establishing safe houses for them under the Swedish flag and gave out 20,000 Swedish passports to Budapest Jews. He worked closely with other foreign diplomats, for example **Giorgio Perlasca,** a diplomat at the Spanish Embassy in Budapest, who saved 3,000 Jews.

Wallenberg disappeared in January 1945 and was taken prisoner by the USSR and is almost certainly dead.

c.   **Dr Gertrude Luckner**, a German Roman Catholic social worker and writer, helped save hundreds of Jews from the Nazis. She was captured, tortured and imprisoned for two years in Ravensbruck concentration camp. When the Gestapo asked her who her bosses were, she replied: 'My Christian conscience'.

d.   **Oscar Schindler** was a German from the Sudetenland in Czechoslovakia. He posed as a Nazi and was allowed to employ twelve hundred Jews at his factory in Poland by pretending they were essential to the German war effort. There he protected them from the SS, fed them well, provided medicine and even rescued three hundred women from Auschwitz, bribing Nazi officials there.

e.   **Selahattin Ulkumen** was a Turkish diplomat on the Greek island of Rhodes, occupied by the Germans in 1943. The following year, the Gestapo ordered all the Jewish community to register for 'transportation'. Selahattin Ulkumen insisted that: 'Under Turkish law, all citizens are equal'. He managed to save forty-two people from Auschwitz. But 1,651 Jews were deported from Rhodes to Auschwitz. Most were gassed.

f.   In 1942, **Anne Frank** and her family (Jews, originally from Germany) went into hiding in a secret annex above Otto Frank's workplace in Prinsengracht, Amsterdam. For two years the Franks stayed in the annex, with four other Jewish people. They were kept alive by **Miep Gies,** her husband **Jan, Mr Koophuis, Mr Kraler** and **Elli**, colleagues of Mr Frank. On August 4th 1944, the police came and arrested all those hiding in the annexe. Otto Frank was the sole survivor of the death camps. The story of Anne Frank is known throughout the world, because the diary she wrote while hiding in the annexe, was found by her father after the war.

Source 15

Miep Gies refuses to be seen as a hero for her part in hiding the Franks and their friends: I did what I felt I had to do. That's all...I stand at the end of the long, long line of good Dutch people who did what I did or more...it is an individual decision...we only did our human duty to help people who need help...my story is of very ordinary people during extraordinary times.

---

g.   **Denmark** was an occupied country. In October 1943, the Nazis decided to round up Denmark's Jews for shipment to the death camps. The entire country 'from King to fisherman' acted as an underground movement

Above: Erik Staermose, one of the heads of the Danish-Swedish Refugee Service.

Above: Signe Jansen, head nurse of the Bispebjerg Hospital, Copenhagen. She found hiding places for 2000 Jews who passed secretly through the hospital on their way to Sweden.

and ferried the eight thousand Jews to neutral Sweden, where they were safe. The Germans found only 500 Jews still in Denmark. All were sent to Theresienstadt concentration camp; 423 survived the war.

The explanation of Jorgen Knudsen, an ambulance driver, and Dr Koster, are typical of others. Knudsen said: 'What else could I do?,' and Dr Koster:

> It was the natural thing to do, I would have helped any groups of Danes being persecuted. The German picking on Jews made as much sense to me as picking on redheads.

---

1. Choose the three rescuers you find most memorable, explain why.

2. 'Those who rescued and hid victims of the Nazis were heroes'. Using some of the above examples, discuss whether or not you agree with this statement.

3. Of those who chose to rescue others, what sort of factors (e.g. religion) do you think influenced their decision? Refer to specific examples in your answer.

4. Think about the experience of hiding for two years in a cramped secret annexe with seven other people, some of whom you like and, some you don't. What aspects of daily life would you have to be extremely careful about? (The Franks' hiding place was above offices which were used every day.) What do you imagine you would miss most?

5. It is fifty years since the war ended. You are taking part in a TV programme about human behaviour during the Holocaust. Explain why you did/did not decide to help Jewish people (or anyone being hunted by the Nazis) at the time.
   (Remember the factors which affected how people acted — their religion, the influence of their parents, whether they had children, whether or not they knew Jewish people etc.)

6. After the war, Emmi Bonhoeffer, wife of Dietrich (see p.109) said: 'Resisters were stones in a torrent and the water crashed over us'. From the evidence you have read in this chapter, do you agree with her?

7. 'The opposite of love is not hate, but indifference' (Elie Wiesel). What does he mean? Do you agree?

Chapter 10

International responses to the Holocaust

This chapter looks at when and how the free (unoccupied) countries heard about the Holocaust; how they responded to the news; what and whether they could have done anything to help and what action they took.

Source 1

Every day we saw thousands and thousands of innocent people disappear up the chimmney. There they came, men, women, children, all innocent. They suddenly vanished, and the world said nothing. We felt abandoned. By the world, by humanity. (Filip Müller, *Sonderkommando*, Auschwitz. (excerpt from the film *Shoah* by Claude Lanzmann)

Filip Müller

Ils étaient en sang. Ils savaient...

Knowledge

There was a gap between what people heard and whether they actually believed it. 'People believe what they are prepared to believe' (Michael Marrus, historian). At the time, many could not comprehend the reality when they heard that whole communities of Jews were being systematically slaughtered and that people were being gassed and burned in camps specially built for the purpose.

> A dog run over by a car upsets our emotional balance and digestion: 3,000,000 Jews killed in Poland causes but a moderate uneasiness. Statistics don't bleed: it is the detail which counts. We are unable to embrace the total process with our awareness. We can only focus on little lumps of reality. (Arthur Koestler, 1944)

On 7th December 1939, Hitler signed the *Nacht und Nebel (Night and Fog) Decree*, authorising the seizure of 'persons endangering German security'. Those seized were not to be executed immediately, but were to 'vanish without a trace into the night and fog'. The German initials 'NN' — Nacht und Nebel— against a concentration camp prisoner's name meant execution.

But, despite Nazi attempts to destroy records and witnesses of the events, it was impossible to hide the enormous atrocities of the Holocaust. The Nazis often managed to keep the transport destinations secret, but the transports themselves, the mass killings and the smell of burning bodies could not be kept secret:

- Groups of anti-fascist and Jewish inmates managed to copy and hide important records of events they had witnessed;

- Some local people who worked in the camps talked 'outside' about what they saw;

- Refugees escaped to Switzerland, Turkey and Spain with stories of the slaughter;

- German soldiers back from Russia talked about what they had seen and done;

- Journalists from neutral countries wrote reports which were sent all over the world. The British press regularly carried news of Nazi persecution.

The Nazis made no attempt to hide their actions before 1939. In that year, Hitler promised to destroy all the Jews (see p.123) and *The Times* newspaper referred to 'a slow road to extermination'. *The Jewish Chronicle* printed the following telegram on 20/10/39:

Source 2

From the "Jewish Chronicle,"
October 20, 1939

Above is a reproduction of a postcard written in Yiddish which arrived in a neutral country from Berlin. It reads: "I appeal to you, help, help us. Men of Polish nationality who have been taken away return home as ashes. They are all slaughtered, young, healthy people. Do all you can to make it known; write to all countries, to all newspapers; help us, save us, take us out — our men and 15-year-old children. People, have mercy. Shout it in the streets. Quickly, quickly."

The *Einsatzgruppen* began their 'work' in June 1941 (see p 139-143) and details began reaching the West almost immediately. Certain well-publicised incidents also raised public awareness at least of the desperation of Europe's Jews. One such incident was the case of the ship *Struma*.

The *Struma* set sail from Rumania on the December 12, 1941 with 769 Jews escaping from the Nazis and the violent antisemitic persecution unleashed in Rumania in autumn 1941. The captain was Bulgarian and the flag Panamanian. The ship broke down and was stranded in the Black Sea for nine weeks with no provisions or fresh water and only one lavatory. Jewish people in Turkey supplied them with food but Turkey would not let the passengers in unless Britain agreed to allow them into Palestine. Britain refused and no-one else offered help. At one stage, Britain gave permission for children aged between eleven and sixteen to enter Palestine, but the Turkish authorities would not allow them to travel overland across Turkey. Finally, on February 24, 1942, the Turkish government cast the ship adrift (with its engine still unrepaired) in the rough water of the Black Sea. And

215

the next day, after being torpedoed by a Soviet submarine, she sank. Everyone aboard drowned except a man called David Stoliar. The case of the *Struma* received widespread publicity and created some sympathy in Britain for Jewish refugees.

The Wannsee Conference confirmed the 'Final Solution' in January 1942 (see p.152)

In March 1942, the Pope's representative in Bratislava (Czechoslovakia) Giuseppe Burzio, sent information about the fate of deported Jews. He told the Vatican that 'the deportation of 80,000 persons to Poland at the mercy of the Germans means to condemn a great part of them to certain death.' A report on the planned mass murder was smuggled out of Poland by the Bund. It reached the British government in May 1942. Referring to deportations, killings and gassings at Chelmno (Dec.1941), the report stated :'The Germans have already killed 700,000 Polish Jews'.

In August 1942, Gerhardt Riegner, representative of the World Jewish Congress in Switzerland, sent a telegram to London and Washington. He had learned the details from a German industrialist, Edouard Schulte, who had a factory near Auschwitz:

Source 3

Received alarming report that in Führer's headquarters plan discussed and under consideration according to which all Jews in countries occupied or controlled Germany numbering three and a half to four millions should after deportation and concentration in East be exterminated at one blow to resolve once for all the Jewish Question in Europe...the action reported planned for autumn methods under discussion including prussic acid...we transmit information with all reservation as exactitude cannot be confirmed...informant stated to have close connection with highest German authorities and his reports generally speaking reliable.

The British and American authorities witheld this information for three months while they investigated its reliability. Riegner felt helpless:

> 'These were the worst days of my life. [I felt] absolute despair. People didn't accept facts. People could not live with absolute evil.'

In November 1942, the US government publicised the information they had. But the press in the West tended to tone down such reports. Some feared they were false atrocity stories (as had happened in World War One) or perhaps did not consider the news very important, among all the other war news.

On December 11th, 1942 the front page of the *Jewish Chronicle* carried reports under the banner headline:

TWO MILLION JEWS SLAUGHTERED
MOST TERRIBLE MASSACRE OF ALL TIME
APPALLING HORRORS OF NAZI MASS MURDERS

Early in autumn 1942, Jan Karski, of the Polish Underground, made secret visits to the Warsaw Ghetto. When he left for London, Karski asked the Jewish representatives of the ghetto: 'What do you want me to say to the outside world?' They told him:

> Our entire people will be destroyed...Place this responsibility on the shoulders of the Allies. Let not a single leader of the United Nations be able to say that they did not know that we were being murdered in Poland and could not be helped except from the outside.

Karski was to take the following message to the Jewish leaders of America and Britain:

> Tell them to take drastic steps. Let them accept no food or drink, let them die a slow death while the world is looking on. Let them die. This may shake the conscience of the world.

Karski's descriptions of the suffering in the Warsaw Ghetto contributed to a wave of public sympathy in Britain for Jews in Nazi Europe. British Jews called for action, They were supported by some Christians, newspapers and the Polish authorities in London. On December 17, 1942, the British government joined an inter-allied declaration denouncing the murder of Jews (see below).

Liesl spent the war years in England:

> I hadn't a clue what was happening to my family. I had letters for a little while via the Red Cross. And then everything stopped. I just assumed they were having some sort of bad time and I'd see them when the war ended. I didn't know, we didn't know. But now it turns out Churchill knew very well what was going on during the war

However, the *scale*, organisation and exact meaning of Auschwitz was not really known until the escape of two young Jews (Rudolf Vrba and Alfred Wetzler) from Auschwitz in mid-1944. They aimed to warn the Jewish people of Hungary that they were next in line to be exterminated.

1. Read Source 1. What do you think Filip Müller expected or hoped the world would do?

2. 'People believe what they are prepared to believe'. What does Michael Marrus mean? Are there any events you have heard about which you find hard to believe?

3. What might readers have found hard to believe about Source 2? Why did the author of the postcard want people to 'shout it in the streets'?

4. How much did Britain know about the destruction of the Jews by December 1941? Can you think of any explanations for their treatment of the Struma and its passengers?

5. Read Source 3.

    a. In August 1942, was the plan merely 'under consideration'? List the ways in which Riegner was accurate about what was happening by this date.

    b. Select the phrase from the Source which suggests he is not sure about this information.

    c. How does he describe his source of information?

    d. Why did the authorities wait three months before publishing Riegner's information?

    e. What did the Jews of the Warsaw Ghetto ask those of Britain and America to do? What effect would this have had? Who else did they expect to take action on hearing the news about the Holocaust?

Possible Action

What *could* the free world have done to rescue or help Jews already leaving Europe, those in Occupied Europe and those in the ghettos and camps, without harming the war effort?

A distinction must be made between the time when rescue was possible, before war broke out and after 3rd September 1939, when conditions of total war meant that very few people could cross borders or get anywhere near a border. The Germans carried out almost all of the Holocaust between the summer of 1941 and the summer of 1943, while they were the absolute masters of Europe, its communications, its coastline and ports, and with the full weight of their military and secret police power. There were very few possible routes of rescue and there were immense risks and difficulties, principally capture, betrayal by local people and exhaustion.

The following strategies were suggested at the time or have been suggested since the war:

a. The Allies did make clear and precise declarations condemning the war crimes, most notably in December 1942 (see p.223). But promising only post-war retribution, not policies of rescue (see below), but Roosevelt, Churchill, Stalin and the Pope could have urged neutral governments (Spain, Sweden, Switzerland, Turkey) and the International Red Cross to press the Germans to release Jews/concentration camp inmates, thus showing the Nazis that the Allies were comitted to saving them.

   In the summer of 1944, Churchill referred to the Holocaust as: 'Probably the greatest and most horrible crime ever commited in the whole history of the world.'

b. They could have called on local populations all over Europe to stop helping the Nazis organise the round-ups and murders. Hungarian railwaymen were warned not to help deport Jews in the summer of 1944.

c. They could have set up the War Refugee Board (see below) earlier than 1944 and with more money and power.

d. The Allies have been criticised for not bombing the death camps and railway lines leading to the camps. However, it only became technically possible to bomb Auschwitz (and was only requested) in summer 1944, in connection with the Hungarian deportations which began that May. Churchill said: 'Get anything out of the Airforce you can'. But then the deportations stopped and the new call was for protective documents for the Jews still in Budapest.

e. They could have allowed more escapees into their countries by relaxing their strict immigration policies. Before the war, people applying to escape to America usually had to wait nine months, fill in a form four feet long, submit six copies of it and have a sponsor in America. Countries could have allowed *temporary* entry for people escaping Nazi Europe. The fact that America was so reluctant to allow in too many Jews, influenced the behaviour of Latin America, Canada, North Africa and Britain and her Dominions.

f. The Allies could have promised to help fund camps in Spain, Portugal, Turkey and Switzerland for refugees. Switzerland was willing to take thousands of French children if they were guaranteed a place to go after the war. America dithered for a year, by which time most of the children had been deported to their deaths.

g. More publicity could have been given to the mass murders once it was confirmed. At least Jewish communities could have been warned about the Nazis' extermination plans. Rudolf Vrba (see picture p.191), one of the escapees who told the outside world about Auschwitz, remained angry that the Jews had not been warned: 'Would anybody get me alive to Auschwitz if I had this information?' (cited in D.Wyman, 1984)

Which of the strategies listed above do you consider would have been i) the most easy and ii) the most difficult for the Allies to have chosen? Bear in mind conditions in Europe before and after the war began.

Responses

a. On receiving information about the Holocaust, governments and authorities expressed horror and indignation.

b. There was pressure from groups and individuals, but they were usually met with *indifference, disbelief,* sometimes sympathy and sometimes prejudice. For instance, President Roosevelt did not mention the Holocaust in any Press Conference until March 1944, though his wife Eleanor was more concerned and active.

Historian David S.Wyman comments that Roosevelt's 'steps to aid Europe's Jews were very limited. If he had wanted to, he could have aroused substantial public backing for a vital rescue effort by speaking out on the issue...But he had little to say about the problem...' (D. Wyman, 1984)

c. There were thousands of non-Jewish refugees too and neither the British or American governments wished to be seen as too 'pro-Jewish'. *Antisemitism* in both countries partly explains the authorities' reluctance to act. Indeed it was often the authorities who expressed hostility.

In 1941, 27,000 German and Austrian men and women, including Jews, were interned as 'enemy aliens' in camps all over Britain, most notably on the Isle of Man. 8,000 were transported to Canada and Australia. They were only released after loud protests in and out of Parliament. In the 1930s in the USA, certain residential districts and clubs did not accept Jews.

d. Officials told those who lobbied them demanding something be done, that the best way to help the Jews, was to *bring the war to a swift end.* Hundreds of thousands of Anglo-American and other Allied troops were in action in the war zones, first in Africa, then in Italy, then in northern Europe, seeking to defeat Hiltler's regime. Thousands of troops were also involved in fighting Japan in the Far East. 50,000 civilians died in Britain from bombing and 50,000 British merchant seamen drowned trying to maintain the food and supply lines.

Until the Allies were in a position to land troops in Continental Europe, there was sustained bombing of Germany. Britain's 1,000-bomber raid on Cologne was particularly welcomed in the Warsaw Ghetto.

When an air link was established to German-occupied Yugoslavia (to a partisan-held area), Jewish refugees were taken from Yugoslavia to southern Italy on a regular basis.

e.   The aftermath of the 1930s Depression brought unemployment and fear of foreigners as 'job-poachers' and people were anxious about members of their families who were away fighting.

f.   The British government was anxious not to upset the Arabs by letting too many Jews escape to Palestine. However, many ships carrying refugees reached Istanbul in 1944. All the refugees were allowed to go on to Palestine on collective British passports, irrespective of the quota.

---

1.   Read point d. above. In your opinion, should the Allies have given the Holocaust more priority than they did?

2.   Consider all the italicised words in the section a. to f. Explain how each prevented Britain and America from taking more effective action.

3.   Why is the comment by Dew in c. considered offensive?

4.   Why were refugee German and Austrians interned? And why was there a wave of protest when German Jews were interned in Britain in 1940?

Shmuel Zygielbaum

Shmuel was a Jewish trade union leader in Poland. His wife and children were murdered when the Nazis invaded and he was captured. He managed to escape from prison to London where he represented the Bund in the Polish-government-in-exile. There he gathered details, statistics and testimonies on the 'Final Solution'. He lobbied governments, spoke at meetings, begged for donations of arms for the Jewish resistance and for immigration policies to be relaxed so more refugees could leave Europe. His requests made no difference and in a final, desperate protest against what he saw as the inaction of the world and the crushing of the Warsaw Ghetto, Shmuel Zygielbaum commited suicide, aged forty eight, on May 12, 1943.

Source 4

In his last letter, Shmuel wrote:

I cannot be silent. I cannot live while the remnants of the Jewish population of whom I am a representative are perishing. My friends in the Warsaw ghetto died with weapons in their hands in the last heroic battle. It was not my destiny to die together with them, but I belong to them and their mass graves. By my death I wish to make my final protest against the passivity with which the world is looking on and permitting the extermination of the Jewish people... I bid farewell to everybody and to everything that was dear to me and that I have loved.

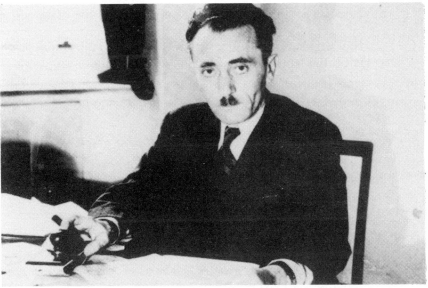

Shmuel Zygielbaum

1. What methods did Shmuel Zygielbaum use to try and motivate governments to take action?

2. Read his last letter, Source 4. Choose two statements from the letter which best explain why he chose to commit suicide.

Action taken

a. On December 17th 1942, twelve Allied governments released a United Nations statement condemning Nazi atrocities against the Jews. It spoke of:

> ### Source 5
> Hitler's oft repeated intention to exterminate the Jewish people in Europe... From all the occupied countries Jews are being transported in conditions of horror and brutality to Eastern Europe... None of those taken away are ever heard of again. The able-bodied are slowly worked to death in labour camps. The infirm are left to die of exposure and starvation or are deliberately massacred in mass executions. The number of victims of these bloody cruelties is reckoned in many hundreds of thousands of entirely innocent men, women and children... [We] condemn in the strongest possible terms this bestial policy of cold-blooded extermination... those responsible for the crimes shall not escape retribution.

After Anthony Eden read the statement to MPs, two minutes silence was observed in the House of Commons.

Two weeks later, Eden chaired a meeting of the Cabinet Committee on the Reception and Accommodation of Jewish Refugees and agreed that Britain could not admit more than 1-2,000 extra refugees. Nor did they even allow the promised 75,000 into Palestine. '....It should be borne in mind that there were already about 100,000 refugees, mainly Jews, in this country'(Herbert Morrison, Home Secretary). In 1943, the Archbishop of Canterbury urged the government to allow in more escapees and a Gallup poll suggested that 78% of those questioned supported admission for Jews threatened with death in Europe.

b. In 1938, the USA had agreed to let in 40,000 immigrants per year from Europe. By 1941, the quota was down to 10,000. In 1939, the American Congress received a proposal to admit 20,000 German Jewish children above the quota. Congress rejected the plan. Nor were they willing to let in the 70,000 Jews the Rumanian government offered to free in return for bribes.

Approximately 70,000 Jewish refugees entered the USA between 1940 and 1944. The number of applicants was always more than the number of visas available and tens of thousands of people were barred entry. In practice, the USA was so worried about negative reactions at home that 90% of its allocated places were not filled. As a result, many thousands had no way out of Nazi-occupied Europe, and they perished:

Source 6a

ADDRESS OFFICIAL COMMUNICATIONS TO
THE SECRETARY OF STATE
WASHINGTON, D. C.

Visa Form R-3

DEPARTMENT OF STATE
WASHINGTON

In reply refer to
VD 811.111 Krochmal, Jacob

July 31, 1942.

Mr. Heinrich Krochmal,
95 Lenox Road,
Brooklyn, New York.

Sir:

Reference is made to your interest in the application for a permit to enter the United States in the case of Jacob Krochmal and his family.

This case has been carefully considered by an Interdepartmental Committee, by an Interdepartmental Visa Review Committee and by the Board of Appeals in the light of the provisions of section 58.47 of the regulations covering the control of persons entering and leaving the United States pursuant to the Act of May 22, 1918, as amended. The conclusion has been reached that a favorable recommendation for the issuance of a visa may not be sent to the appropriate consular officer.

Section 58.57(g) of the aforementioned regulations provides that the Board of Appeals may not reconsider any case until after the lapse of a period of six months from the date of the previous opinion of the board in the case concerned, and section 58.57(f) provides that only the recommendation of the committees or board, without ressons therefor, shall be disclosed.

Very truly yours,

H. K. Travers
Chief, Visa Division

FOR VICTORY
BUY
UNITED
STATES
WAR
BONDS
AND
STAMPS

Letter from US Department of State, 31 July 1942.

Source 6b

THE AMERICAN COMMITTEE OF OSE, INC.

World-wide Organization for Child Care, Health and Hygiene Among Jews

FOUNDED IN 1912

24 WEST 40TH STREET   NEW YORK 18, N.Y.

HONORARY COMMITTEE
PROF. ALBERT EINSTEIN
EMANUEL LIBMAN, M.D.
MILTON ROSENAU, M.D.

BOARD OF DIRECTORS AND OFFICERS

ISRAEL WECHSLER, M.D., *Chairman,*
Board of Directors
A. J. RONGY, M.D., *Chairman,*
Executive Committee
DR. ENG. B. PREGEL, *Co-Chairman*
J. J. GOLUB, M.D., *Vice-Chairman*

D. JEDWABNIK, M.D., *Vice-Chairman*
DR. ENG. CHARLES BREYNER, *Treasurer*
L. WULMAN, M.D., *Secretary*
J. BRUTZKUS, M.D., *Counsel*
L. LAZAROWITZ, M.D., *Counsel*

MR. PIERRE D
MRS. PIERRE I
L. ROSENTHAI
M. SUDARSKI,
MR. E. WEIL

May 25, 1945.

Mr. Henry Krochmal
118 East 96th St.
Brooklyn, N.Y.

Dear Mr. Krochmal :

It is with a feeling of deepest sadness that we are transmitting to you the cable information we have received from our Swiss office that your nephew, Siegfried Nrochmal is dead since 1942, and that your nieces, Liane and Renate were deported in 1944.

The dreadful calamity which has befallen the Jewish people is of such huge proportions that the individual sorrow and bereavement must be submerged in the common grief. However, one should continue to hope in the light of recent liberation of deportees by Allied armies.

Yours most sincerely,

L. Wulman

L. Wulman, MD

Secretary

a-g

Letter to Mr Krochmal, **25 May 1945**.

Nevertheless, thousands of individuals and families were saved before the Holocaust and remain indebted to the countries who received them. 64,000 adults and 10,000 children escaped either to or through Britain. Most of the adults were domestic workers, although a significant number were professionals.

c. There was support for rescue from non-Jewish quarters. In 1943, trade union leaders asked for a lifting of immigration limits. An official of the Federal Council of Churches wrote: "This is not a Jewish affair, it is a colossal, universal degradation in which all humanity shares."

d. In Britain, organisations set up in 1943 publicized the fate of the Jews.

e. *Bermuda Conference April 19th 1943*
This was called by Britain and the USA, to discuss the fate of refugees of Nazism, not those still under Nazi control, but only those who had escaped to neutral countries. The Pyrenees was kept open for Jewish refugees. Ports in Spain and Portugal were safe havens for the tens of thousands of Jews who reached them. But neither the USA or Britain was willing to discuss exchanging German prisoners of war for refugees. The Conference authorised the movement of 21,000 refugees from Spain to North Africa but they decided that large scale saving of refugees was impossible.

On May 19th 1943, the House of Commons declared that 'to admit a large number of refugees of the Jewish religion might easily fan the smouldering fires of antisemitism which exist here into flames'.

f. After a wave of public pressure and sympathy following wider knowledge about the Holocaust, Roosevelt set up the *War Refugee Board* in January 1944. The aim of the WRB was to save the (few) remaining victims of Nazi persecution. It was an important effort, though under-staffed and under-funded. The Board sped the process of aiding refugees crossing into neutral countries and put pressure on the Red Cross to use its influence. It was responsible for the rescue of several hundred thousand, including 200,000 Hungarian Jews. In March 1944 it drafted a Presidential Statement on Nazi criminality, which was read by Roosevelt on March 24th. Millions of copies were dropped in leaflet form over occupied Europe:

Source 7
In one of the blackest crimes of all history — begun by the Nazis in the days of peace and multiplied by them a hundred times in time of war — the wholesale systematic murder of the Jews of Europe goes on unabated every hour.... All who knowingly take part in the deportation of Jews to their death in Poland or Norwegians and French to their death in Germany are all equally guilty with the executioner... Hitler is commiting these crimes against humanity in the name of the German people... hide these pursued victims, help them to get over the borders... to save them from the Nazi hangman.

But the War Refugee Board's director, John Pehle later said: 'What we did was...late and little'.

g. The Soviet Union offered security to some Jews who fled the Nazis. But they were responsible for the death of others. In the late 1930s, they refused to take Jewish refugees or to help refugee-aid projects.

After 1939, two million Jews came under Soviet control in East Poland, while others fled from the Nazis to the USSR. Many died, along with millions of Soviet citizens. The Russians also refused to divert their forces in order to launch any special attack on the concentration camps. Despite the actions of the *Einsatzgruppen* in the USSR, (see p.139-143) Soviet condemnations of Nazi atrocities did not specifically mention Jews.

h. *Neutral countries* (Spain, Sweden, Switzerland, Turkey, Portugal, the Vatican) could receive refugees and pass information on to the West. They also used diplomatic pressure to save individuals. Ships from Lisbon, Casablanca, Tangiers and Marseilles took refugees to the West after 1940. Thousands were saved in this way. But they were all vulnerable and afraid of Nazi reaction. This fear of occupation led the Swiss government to send Jewish refugees back to occupied France in 1942.

1943 was a turning point in the war. After the German defeats at Stalingrad and El Alamein, the collapse of Mussolini's regime and the Anglo-American landings at Sicily, Hitler could bully the neutrals less effectively and so they allowed in more refugees.

---

1. Read Source 5. What do the words 'bestial' and 'retribution' mean? What was the aim of this declaration?

2. What was the point of the two minute silence? Why has Eden been accused of hypocrisy?

3. Look at Source 6a. With reference to the *Response* section above, which factor a. to f., according to the letter, prevented the USA Department of State from allowing Jacob Krochmal and family to escape to America?

4. Look at Source 6b. Note the origin of the letter, the date and the change in H.Krochmal's name and address. Can you offer any explanation for his change of name? Are there any connections between Source 6a and b? What is L.Wulman trying to say in the second paragraph of Source 6b?

5. Why do you think that the Federal Council of Churches official above believed that 'all humanity' shared the 'degradation' of the Holocaust?

6. Read Source 7. What do you imagine was the aim of dropping millions of these leaflets on occupied Europe?

7. What did the War Refugee Board achieve? Do you agree with John Pehle's opinion?

Reaction of Jews in the Free World

There was and is no such thing as World Jewry. No one organisation or movement united all Jewish people. So the response to news of the Holocaust was varied. There was disbelief, uncertainty, confusion, hopelessness, outrage, caution and militant action.

Jews who lived in the free world have since been accused of not doing enough and at the time they were often criticised by those trapped in Nazi Europe. Rabbi Weissmandel of Bratislava, Czechoslovakia:

> We cannot understand how you can eat and drink, how you can rest in your beds, how you can stroll in the streets — and I am sure that you are doing all those things — while this responsibility rests on you. We have been crying for months and you have done nothing.

- Was this a fair accusation?
- How could they respond?
- Should Jewish people have been particularly responsible for 'doing something' about the Holocaust?

Along with most of the rest of the world, they were totally unprepared for the full reality of the Holocaust and had assumed there would be millions of Jewish refugees left after the war.

Even today, that reality is not as full as it might be. New evidence about the extent and details of the Holocaust is frequently revealed.

In America, the World Jewish Congress, American Jewish Joint Distribution Committee and Jewish Agency for Palestine campaigned to rescue Jews. The AJJDC alone provided more aid to European Jews than all the world governments combined. The Nazis deceived the WJC into thinking that Jews could be rescued in return for vast sums of money.

Rabbi *Stephen Wise*, President of the AJJDC, was one of the many individual Americans who was aware of events in Nazi Europe, publicised the atrocities and campaigned for action. Working with overseas Zionist organisations and anti-Nazi underground movements:

> Despite obstacles and failures, American Jews were responsible for some important achievements. Finding the mass media largely indifferent, they devised ways to spread the extermination news and create limited but crucial support among non-Jews (D.S.Wyman, 1984).

In December 1942, half a million Jewish workers in New York stopped work for ten minutes as a protest. They had debated stopping for longer, but decided against, for fear of being accused of spoiling the war effort.

In Britain, the Chief Rabbi declared a day of mourning on 13 December 1942. There were meetings, delegations to government ministers and plans made for rescue work continuing on from efforts made before the war. In Stepney, London, working class Jews marched in protest, demanding some action. But the Board of Deputies of British Jews distanced itself from any very public protest. Certain individuals took a firm stand. In 1942, the writer/publisher Victor Gollancz, wrote *Let my people go*.

In Palestine, there were half a million Jews, mostly from Eastern Europe. Many still had relatives back in Poland, Rumania, Hungary etc. At first, they could not believe accounts of the massacres. 30,000 of them joined the British Army and some heard rumours about the Holocaust while in Europe. After November 1942, protests in Palestine increased, money was raised and pressure put on the Allied governments to speed up rescue attempts.

CONCLUSION

> **Source 8**
> European Jewry was ground to death between the twin millstones of a murderous Nazi intent and a callous Allied indifference. (Henry Feingold, 1970)

> **Source 9**
> The shame and horror of our century have to do with the conduct of the European powers, the Gentile world. The central issue must not be forgotten; it is a moral issue, the issue of what the world has done and permitted to be done. To insist upon making the world uncomfortable with the memory of its guilt is a necessity...which may alone prevent a repetition of our Holocaust. (Alexander Donat in Albert Friedlander (ed), 1976)

Source 10

Above all, the story...is one of many failures, and of two successes. The failures, shared by the Allies, were those of imagination, of response, of Intelligence, of piecing together and evaluating what was known...and even at times of sympathy. The successes lay with the Nazis; in the killings themselves, and in a series of bizarre deceptions which enabled those killings to be carried out on a gigantic scale, for more than three years, almost without interruption. (Martin Gilbert, *Auschwitz and the Allies*, 1991)

1. Find out whether your local library has any record of local or national newspaper reports covering the Holocaust between 1942 and 1945.

2. Read Sources 8, 9 and 10. In what ways do they agree?

3. Which Source is the most critical of the Allies?

4. Do you agree with these historians? Write a conclusion summing up how you see the world response to the Holocaust, now that you have read this chapter.

Chapter Eleven

The End of the War —
Liberation, Reaction and Trials

This chapter looks at the end of the war, the liberation of the concentration camps and how people reacted to seeing and hearing about the full horror of the death camps. It then considers the fate of those who survived and what happened to the men and women responsible for organising the Holocaust.

The Death Marches

On November 24th 1944, Himmler ordered the destruction of the Auschwitz crematoria and gas chambers. In mid-January 1945, the Nazis began evacuating the remaining inmates by forced death marches towards the West, away from the advancing Russian troops. Thousands froze, starved or were shot on the way.

Both Esther and Harry survived these marches. Esther ended her march in Bergen-Belsen, Germany and Harry in Ebensee, Austria.

> The march lasted seven days and six nights. There were about ten thousand of us. Those who couldn't walk were just shot and left by the road. They took us to Ebensee in Austria where they built munitions factories in tunnels under the mountains to protect them against Allied bombing. The SS ran away as the Americans closed in and left just a few German guards. They tried to get us into the tunnels which they had mined, they wanted to finish us off so there wouldn't be any witnesses to what they had done...but we refused (Harry).

By the beginning of 1945, it was obvious that the Allies were winning the war. To speed up the German surrender, the Allied leaders intensified their massive air-strike on Germany. At least 500,000 German civilians had already been killed. The city of Dresden was the main centre of communications for the defence of Germany. It was chosen as the focus of the air attack. On the night of February 13th, 1945, the RAF struck the city crowded with refugees and dropped three-quarters of a million incendiary bombs, which created a fire-storm, killing over 60,000 people.

On April 30 th 1945, Hitler committed suicide. Ill, weak and aged, he blamed everyone but himself for Germany's defeat. He had gone into hiding for the last months of the war.

German surrender came on 7th May, 1945.

Below: Trummerfrauen clearing rubble in Essen, 1946.

Victorious American troops, Berlin 1945.

Liberation

In March 1945, the Soviet 60th Army, led by Marshal Koniev, liberated Auschwitz.

On April 4th 1945, the American Fourth Armoured Division reached Ohrdruf. Ohrdruf was a small camp. 3,000 Jews had been murdered there in the four days before the Americans arrived.

Lewis J.Weinstein was one of the liberators. In his autobiography, *The Odyssey of an American Jew,* he describes the reaction of General Eisenhower (Supreme Allied Commander) to the sight that greeted them:

> I saw Eisenhower go to the opposite side of the road and vomit. From a distance I saw (General) Patton bend over, holding his head with one hand and his abdomen with the other. I suggested to General Eisenhower that cables be sent immediately to President Roosevelt, Churchill, de Gaulle, urging representatives...to see for themselves.

Source 1

In his book, *Crusade in Europe*, Eisenhower wrote:

I have never felt able to describe my emotional reactions when I first came face to face with indisputable evidence of Nazi brutality....I am certain...that I have never at any other time experienced an equal sense of shock...I visited every nook and cranny of the camp because I felt it my duty to be in a position from then on to testify at first hand about these things in case there ever grew up at home the belief ...that the stories of Nazi brutality were just propaganda.

'When the US Army arrived at the gates of Ebensee, the Germans just put their rifles down....Thousands of people were jumping about and the soldiers were throwing them in the air and cheering. I was so weak, I couldn't walk'. (Harry)

1. Both Weinstein and Eisenhower refer to the importance of seeing the camps at first hand. Why?

2. Is the evidence of an influential person such as Eisenhower (Source 1) more valuable that that of an 'ordinary' person?

On April 15th 1945, the first British tanks entered Belsen. There they found thousands of unburied corpses, mostly victims of starvation. Hundreds continued to die every day after liberation.

The *Daily Mail* newspaper sent special correspondents with the Allied Armies of Liberation. One of them, Edwin Tetlow, wrote an article on April 19th, in which he said:

Source 2

The Senior Medical Officer of the British Second Army, in a sober twenty minutes' statement, told us what he had seen for himself: 'I am afraid you may think I am exaggerating,' he said, 'but I assure you I am not. It is the most horrible, frightful place I have ever seen.' Much of what the officer said cannot be printed....'We saw some enormous covered death pits. One was uncovered...'

Source 3

British serviceman Frederick Wood (later the first President of the Gypsy Council) helped liberate Belsen:

> We faced something terrible. Heaps of unburied bodies and an unbearable stench. When I saw the surviving Romanies (Gypsies), with small children among them, I was shaken...Then I went over to the ovens and found on one of the steel stretchers the half-charred body of a girl and I understood in one awful minute what had been going on there. (Quoted in D.Kenrick and G.Puxon, 1972)

1. What reasons might the *Daily Mail* have given for censoring the Senior Medical Officer's report (Source 2)? How does such censorship affect our understanding of the events?

2. The paper printed the photo of the uncovered death pit (Source 3). Do you think any aspects of the Holocaust should be kept from the public?

3. How do the photos such as Source 3 add to the dehumanisation of camp victims? Would it make a difference if we knew the names of the people?

The Guards

SS guards and SS women were usually given the task of burying the dead. Some hanged themselves, others tried to run away. Some were beaten or killed by their former prisoners.

Source 4

Edwin Tetlow describes the reactions of the S.S. at Belsen:

The SS women, the eldest of whom was only 27, were unmoved by the grisliness of their task. One even smiled as she helped to bundle the corpses into the pit. ...The male SS ...cringed and shrank, and had a dreadful fear in their eyes. They worked feverishly as if expecting at any moment to be shot by the British guards, or lynched by the crowd of prisoners looking on. When they had filled their lorry they climbed up themselves and were driven to the burial pit. All this I saw, and I do not want to see anything like it again. (*Daily Mail*, 21/4/45)

What choices did the ex-inmates and Allies have regarding what to do with the SS guards? (Use the above sources)
Do you think there was any 'correct' way of dealing with them?

Film-maker *Sidney Bernstein* was attached to the British Army as it helped liberate Western Europe in 1945. On the April 22, he visited Belsen concentration camp:

Source 5

That night he.... drank an entire bottle of whisky. It had, friends remembered, no effect on him at all.

Next day, he started preparing for a film on the Nazi concentration camps....intended primarily for showing within Germany, with an English version for distribution around the world....He wanted Germans to see for themselves, in such a way that they could never refute it, what had been happening on German soil....He said: 'Cameramen should photograph any material which will show the connection between German industry and concentration camps....German generals should be taken through Dachau and photographed, local mayors should be at the areas where bodies were being buried....Wherever possible, the name and address of every person who appeared on screen should be recorded' (Caroline Moorehead, 1984)

Bernstein asked Alfred Hitchcock to edit the material. They produced a one hour film, but the British authorities decided not to show it, in the interests of restoring good relations with Germany. It remained unseen, stored in the Imperial War Museum for forty years, until 1985, when it was screened on British television.

Local Germans

The liberating armies in Germany often forced local people to witness for themselves what had been happening in the camps.

Source 6 a

Walter Farr, a journalist with the British First Army, said that Germans living near the camps told him that they 'had no idea such things were being done'. But civilians, out for a walk with their girls, used to go near the 'extermination centre', point out the prisoners, and crack jokes at them....'Resistance Movement members were tortured to make them give way to their comrades...The townsfolk heard the cries from the torture cells'. (Quoted in *Lest We Forget*, Daily Mail, 1945)

And Martha Gellhorn, an American journalist wrote:

Source 6 b

We have all talked to many Germans since the early days of entering this country with the Army. I remember the very beginning when white sheets of surrender hung from every window and no one was a Nazi, and oddly enough vast numbers of Germans were half Jewish and everyone had hidden a Communist, and all were agreed that Hitler was a monster'.

People of the village of Burgsteinfurt were forced to watch films of the atrocities of Belsen and Buchenwald, May 1945.

1. Why did Sidney Bernstein (Source 5) want the names and addresses of every person appearing in his film to be recorded? Why did he instruct the camera crew to show the connection between German industry and the camps?
2. Present the arguments for and against showing his film in 1946 and in 1985.
3. According to Sources 6 a and b, how did German citizens react to seeing the concentration camps?
4. Which is the most reliable source? Explain your answer.
5. What is Martha Gellhorn's opinion of the Germans she talked to in Source 6b?

The reaction in Britain

In the House of Commons, April 19, 1945, the Prime Minister, Winston Churchill said:

> No words can express the horror which is felt by His Majesty's Government and their principal Allies at the proofs of these frightful crimes now daily coming into view...A solemn warning has been prepared... designed to bring home the responsibilty not only to the men at the top...but to the actual people who have done this foul work with their own hands.

Source 7
Mrs Joyce P., a member of the British Military Police in Germany after the war:

It was horrifying, but I'm glad in a way that I was there to see it, because I might have met someone else who was there and I wouldn't have believed it because it was so horrifying, you couldn't believe it. You can maybe picture 30,000 people in St.James' Park [Newcastle United's football ground] but 6,000,000.... it's just mindboggling. A lot of people were just not interested here, they said: 'Well, that's war.'... (related in interview with the author, August 1990)

---

1. In your opinion, was anyone else responsible for the Holocaust besides 'the men at the top' and 'the actual people who have done the foul work with their own hands'?
2. Can you explain why some people in Britain were 'not interested' when they heard about the Holocaust (Source 7)?

Hiroshima

The Second World War did not finish in Europe. It was brought to an end by the dropping of two nuclear bombs on Japan (Germany's ally). On August 6, 1945, an American plane dropped an atomic bomb on the city of Hiroshima. 80,000 people were killed and a further 58,890 died of the effects over the following 40 years. On August 9, 40,000 people died when a second atomic bomb was dropped on Nagasaki. On August 10, 1945, the Japanese government surrendered unconditionally.

1. Some people call the mass bombing of Dresden by the Allies a 'war crime', because so many thousands of civilians were killed. What is your opinion?

2. In 1990, Major Charles Sweeney, Captain of the American plane which dropped the atom bomb on Nagasaki, was asked whether he felt like apologising to the descendants of his victims. He said: 'Apologise? No.... The Japanese had done terrible things in China and South East Asia..... By ending the war in this way, we were saving millions of lives — Japanese as well as American'. What did he mean? Discuss the moral issues surrounding what happened at Hiroshima and Nagasaki.

The Dead

Six million Jews were murdered in the Holocaust. With the recent opening up of Russian archives it is clear that as many as two million of them were massacred by the *Einsatzgruppen* and at:

Auschwitz	2,000,000 maximum
Sobibor	500,000
Chelmno	350,000
Treblinka	850,000 maximum
Belzec	600,000
Majdanek	250,000
Trostenets	250,000
Stutthof	60,000
Theresienstadt	33,000
Jasenovac	30,000

Source 8

The extermination of the Jews

Country	Previous number of Jews	Losses Lowest estimate	Losses Highest estimate
1 Poland	3,300,000	2,350,000	2,900,000 = 88%
2 USSR	2,100,000	700,000	1,000,000 = 48%
3 Romania	850,000	200,000	420,000 = 49%
4 Czechoslovakia	360,000	233,000	300,000 = 83%
5 Germany	240,000	160,000	200,000 = 83%
6 Hungary	403,000	180,000	200,000 = 50%
7 Lithuania	155,000	—	135,000 = 87%
8 France	300,000	60,000	130,000 = 43%
9 Holland	150,000	104,000	120,000 = 80%
10 Latvia	95,000	—	85,000 = 89%
11 Yugoslavia	75,000	55,000	65,000 = 87%
12 Greece	75,000	57,000	60,000 = 80%
13 Austria	60,000	—	40,000 = 67%
14 Belgium	100,000	25,000	40,000 = 40%
15 Italy	75,000	8,500	15,000 = 26%
16 Bulgaria	50,000	—	7,000 = 14%
17 Denmark	—	(less than 100)	— —
18 Luxemburg	—	3,000	3,000 —
19 Norway	—	700	1,000 —
Total		4,194,200	app. 5,721,000 = 68%

The extermination of the Jews

Thousands of Jewish communities were destroyed. Estimates of Gypsies murdered in massacres and in the death camps range from 200,000 to over 1,000,000 — at least 70% of all the Gypsies in Nazi-controlled territory.

In addition to Holocaust victims, three million non-Jewish Poles, three million Soviet prisoners-of-war and thousands of gays and people with disabilities were killed in Europe's concentration camps. 110,000 people of twenty eight nationalities, including British, Spanish and Indonesian were killed or perished at Mauthausen.

Look at Source 8. List or discuss some of the factors which might have influenced the huge variation in the percentages of Jews murdered in the countries of Europe.

Belsen, 1946. Weeping over a mass grave.

Survivors' reactions

The war had changed the lives of millions of people and taken beloved friends and relatives. Most survivors of the Holocaust were left with no home, community or family. The majority were young, lacked education or professional qualifications. They were ill and without money or support.

Some suffered nervous breakdowns after the war and others, unable to face life, commited suicide. As late as 1947, Gypsy survivors were afraid to return to their homes in Germany. Pre-Nazi laws were still in effect which would have put them back in detention centres if they could not show documents proving German birth.

Can you think of any other problems survivors would have faced, besides those mentioned here (e.g. language)?

The search for relatives

The agony of not knowing whether family and friends had survived often went on for years. This is just one of the letters received by the Schlesinger family who had escaped from Vienna to England before the war:

Source 9

JEWISH   REFUGEES   COMMITTEE

Telephone : MUSeum 6811
Cables : "Refugees, Westcent, London"

In your reply please quote
the reference given below

BLOOMSBURY   HOUSE
BLOOMSBURY   STREET
LONDON,   W.C.I.

TRA/CH/A 7590/1

Mrs. S. Schlesinger,
Bryn Estyn,
Hendy Rd.,
Mold/Flinsshire.   23rd August 1946.

Dear Mrs.Schlesinger,

                With reference to the enquiry you submitted
to the Search Bureau for the whereabouts of your cousin, we very
much regret having to inform you that a report has now been received,
stating that Ella Fischer nee Hertzka, born 12.3.89, was deported
from Malines to an unknown destination with convoy XX/1026, on the
19th of April 1943, and nothing was heard of her since.

                We are very sorry that we have no more comforing
news for you but we wish to assure you that further enquiries are
being made and should any informatiom come to hand at a later date
we shall communicate with you at once.

                            Yours sincerely,

                    TRACING DEPARTMENT

1.   What difficulties would the tracing organisations in Source 9 have
     had in doing their work?

2.   What did being 'deported' mean?

Some survivors, like Esther and Harry, came to live in England.

Esther — survived the Holocaust. So did her brother Peretz, but no-one else
from her family. She was liberated in Belsen concentration camp, too ill to
remember the day the British troops arrived.

Source 10
When I came to, people were going mad. There was murder in
everybody's hearts and probably there was some murder in my heart
too. Despite the fact that I knew where my mother did go, I had to keep
on believing that somehow it wasn't true... I prayed with all my might,
I don't know to who, probably just to myself...'Please let me not be
damaged for the whole of my life. Let me retain some love for people.
Otherwise the wanting to survive wouldn't have been worth it'.
(Esther)

Esther's family — grandparents, aunts, uncles, cousins and parents. Photograph taken before Esther was born. The only survivor of this group was her brother Peretz (front row, far-right, sitting on their mother's knee). Esther's father is standing, far right.

What does Esther mean by 'Let me not be damaged for the whole of my life' (Source 10)? Why do you imagine this would be very difficult for her and all the other survivors?

Esther went from Belsen to Sweden in 1945. In April 1947, she came to England to be with her brother, Peretz. He was brought with other youngsters from Theresienstadt concentration camp.

For the first year after arriving in England, I lived with an elderly Jewish couple who helped bring me over here. They treated me well but could not really

Left: Esther in Sweden, 1945.

244

Above: Werner's mother Mathilde.
Photograph taken in Gurs
concentration camp, 1942.
Below: Werner, photograph taken on
the day of his engagement to Lena
Alvarez in 1946.

understand me. I longed to resume some kind of education, hoped to do nursing, but to no avail. There was no-one around prepared to give me my keep while I tried to replace my lost years.

Werner — survived the War, in England. His sister Ilse had emigrated to America in 1938. In 1940 his parents were deported to Gurs, Bas Pyrenees in Occupied France, where his father Eugene died of cholera. Werner's mother Mathilde was deported to Auschwitz in June 1944. After the war the German authorities issued a document stating that she was presumed to have died on the way to, or in Auschwitz.

Look at the picture of Mathilde Mayer. What differences strike you about her face here and in Chapter One (see p.5)

Werner lived in Manchester with a Mrs Fletcher. He became a trainee in an electrical components factory.

Liesl — survived the War, in England. Her father Willy and brother Heini did not survive the Holocaust.

Source 11

There were constant Red Cross lists read out of people who'd come back and then we heard that my mother had survived. She was incredibly ill...she was already in the mortuary at Mauthausen. When we met again, our relationship had changed. I left as a little girl who had a Mummy; I met a very different mother...I mean, how to proceed with a mother who had survived Auschwitz? I felt guilty that I was alive and the others had died. (Liesl)

What do you imagine Liesl meant by 'I met a very different mother' (Source 11)?

Liesl began her A Levels in 1945. In 1947 she went to study at Leeds University but in the same year returned to Czechoslovakia to be with her mother. She worked for the World Jewish Congress in Prague :

'We tried to live in Czechoslovakia again, but there was nobody alive that I grew up with. Out of a Jewish population of 60,000 in my town, I think I was the only one under 20 to have survived'.

They left after the Communist government came to power in 1948 and came back to London.

Liesl's mother Friedl, after the war.

Harry — survived the Holocaust. His parents, Shlomo and Mincha and five brothers and sisters, Ely, Gittel, Joshua, Letty and Pola were shot by the Nazis. He had last heard of his sister Manya in Auschwitz. He assumed that she too had been murdered.

Harry chose not to return to Poland after the war. He wanted to go to Palestine, but was not allowed in by the British authorities there. Instead, he went to Italy but could not bear being in a Displaced Persons Camp, so he joined the Polish Army and came to England in 1946.

Going 'Home'

Hundreds of Jews chose to return to the towns and villages of their birth. In some cases, they were able to start their lives again and were welcomed back. But many found their homes occupied, their possessions gone and only hostile neighbours. Some were murdered on their return.

Liesl.

Below: Harry (second from the left back row) with the Polish Army in Italy.

In 1946 in Kielce, Poland, forty three survivors were killed in a *pogrom* started by rumours based on the ancient blood libel myth. (see p.18). In 1948, there were similar pogroms in the USSR.

Palestine

Two out of three survivors went to Palestine after the war. Many of them had not been Zionists before, but either they had nowhere else to go, or the Holocaust made them feel that they were stateless and would only be safe in a Jewish homeland.

Source 12

The decision to come to Israel had not been a simple one. I had taken a big step in order to start a new life for myself. Now at last I was here. Here the 'yellow star' was a symbol of hope and freedom, and here every Jew could walk with his head held high. Each and every one of us knew what Hell was....But we had survived and here at last was our Promised Land (Agnes, quoted in I.Tatelbaum, 1985).

But the situation in Palestine (now Israel) was, and still is, extremely complicated. Jewish people had always lived there, and for many Jews living in other countries, the idea of 'returning' to the Land of Israel was central to their Judaism. (See Chapter 1 p.9). However, the vast majority of the population there were Arabs.

In 1917, the British government gave its support to the idea of a Jewish national homeland in Palestine, provided it did not prejudice the rights of non-Jews there. During the First World War, Arabs were encouraged to fight with the British against Turkey in return for a promise of eventual independence. At the time, the Turks controlled Palestine but when they were defeated in 1918, Iraq, Transjordan, Palestine and Syria were taken over by Britain and France as mandated territories. Arab nationalism ensured that Palestine was the last remaining mandate by the end of 1946. All the others became autonomous countries.

Jewish settlers in Palestine — many escaping pogroms in Russia (see p.30-32) — bought land from absentee Arab landlords. While some Jews and Arabs worked together, most communities were divided, with separate Jewish and Arab organisations. Most Arabs bitterly resented the arrival of so many Jews.

Violence erupted in 1920, 1929 and 1935-6 between Jews and Arabs and against the British authorities. Each accused the British of favouring the other. By 1937, Jews in Palestine numbered about 400,000. The Mufti of Jerusalem, an Arab leader, supported Hitler and approved of the Holocaust.

During the war, the British restricted the number of Jewish refugees fleeing Nazi Europe and trying to enter Palestine, for fear of Arab reactions. After the war, many survivors of the Holocaust were refused entry. Jewish terrorist groups set about forcing the British to change their policy and leave.

In November 1947, the fifty-seven countries of the United Nations were asked to vote on whether or not they supported a division of Palestine into two states — one Jewish and one Arab. The Arabs had refused to negotiate any division, saying that the Jewish claim to Palestine was not valid. They saw the partition of their country as an outrage and an example of Western countries imposing their wishes on the Middle East. The Arabs did not see why they should sacrifice land in order to reduce the guilt felt by European Christian countries who were responsible for the Holocaust.

After weeks of frenzied diplomacy, the U.N. voted thirty three for the partition of Palestine, thirteen against with ten abstentions. There followed five and a half months of tension and violence and in May 1948 the British army left Palestine.

An independent state of Israel was declared on May 15, 1948. On that same day the armies of Lebanon, Syria, Egypt and TransJordan invaded the new Jewish state. The war ended on January 6, 1949, with victory for the Israelis. During the fighting, thousands of Arabs fled or were forced from their homes in Israel. By April 1950, there were 900,000 refugees in Jordan, Gaza, the Lebanon and Syria. Thus began the 'Palestinian Exile'. Thousands of Palestinians are still refugees today. Since 1948, four more 'Arab-Israeli' wars have been fought.

In December 1987, Palestinians living in the West Bank and Gaza began the 'intifadah' (uprising) against Israeli rule and in support of the creation of a separate Palestinian state.

Some Jewish Israelis believe that their government should hand back the Occupied Territories of the West Bank and Gaza Strip, (occupied by Israel during the 1967 War) in order to create an independent state for the Palestinians. Other Israelis refuse to call the territories 'occupied' and believe they belong to Israel and the Jewish people, referring back to Biblical times. The Israeli writer Amos Oz describes the situation as:

Source 13

A tragedy....a clash between total justice and total justice...We are here because we can exist nowhere but here as a nation, as a Jewish state. The Arabs are here — because Palestine is the homeland of the Palestinians.

---

1. Why was going to Palestine so important for some Holocaust survivors (see Source 12)?

2. What was the role of the British in Palestine in the early twentieth century?

3. Why did many Arabs in Palestine object to the arrival of Jewish immigrants both before and after the Second World War?

4. Find out about the UN vote of November 1947 on the division of Palestine. Why do you think a majority of countries voted for the creation of a Jewish state?

5. Most Palestinians supported Iraq in the Gulf War of 1990-1991. Why? What has happened to the Palestinians in the West Bank and Gaza since the end of that war? What has happened to the peace talks started in autumn 1991? Did the election of a Labour Government in Israel in June 1992 make any difference?

6. Read Source 13. What are the two 'total justices' Amos Oz refers to? Do you agree with him? Find out about the possible solutions to the Israel/Palestinian conflict.

Displaced Persons Camps

DP camps were created in Germany by the Allies to cope with those who had survived the war and were now refugees. Former SS officers who concealed their identities managed to get into some of the camps, along with Jewish and Gypsy survivors. Inmates were often fed at near starvation levels and kept in by barbed wire and guards.

Bergen-Belsen became a DP camp, with schools and workshops. The last person left in September 1950, five years and five months after liberation. Babies were born in these camps, often to women who could not look after them.

Trials and Executions

Many Nazis, including Adolf Eichmann, fled from Europe to the Middle East, South America, the USA, or wherever they felt they could hide or live unnoticed. Others hanged themselves. Many thousands resumed their former lives in German society.

Some survivors could not wait for the courts to bring to trial and punish the men and women responsible for the Holocaust. Individual Nazis were traced and murdered by Jews and Gypsies, who in turn could be put to death or imprisoned for their action. A Jewish organisation called DIN (meaning 'Justice' in Hebrew) killed sixteen top SS men.

In 1943, the United Nations Commission for the Investigation of War Criminals (representing seventeen countries) agreed that they would pursue War Criminals and began to gather information and evidence.

After the war, the USA, USSR, France and the UK controlled Germany. They decided that each would be empowered to hold trials. They were faced with several moral dilemmas:

1. Whether to single out individuals for responsibility or blame all the German people for a 'crime against humanity'. There was some support for the latter, even from certain Germans:

Source 14

Justice will be done. Mankind will have its revenge....And the Nazis shall suffer as they have made others suffer, and those who aren't Nazis shall suffer too! For they are all responsible, they are all guilty, except a few, except a tiny minority who chose exile and the struggle for a just cause. (Peter Schwiefert, in C. Lanzmann (ed), 1976)

---

2. Whether to execute known leaders without giving them a trial.

3. Whether it was possible for the convicted to receive a fair trial at the hands of their victors.

They soon decided it was not to be a trial of all the Germans. But it was impossible to know the exact number or identity of those directly responsible. There were those who planned the 'Final Solution' — leaders of Nazi Germany, heads of the Nazi Party, the *Gestapo* and SS. There were those who carried it out — hundreds of thousands of members of the *Gestapo*, SS, *Einsatzgruppen*, police, army and bureaucracy.

---

1. If you were to ask Peter Schwiefert (Source 14) to justify his allegation that 'they are all guilty', what do think he would say? How would you respond to him?

2. Imagine your group was responsible for planning the War Crimes Trials. Organise a discussion covering points 1, 2 and 3 above and any others you consider to be important.

The first War Crimes Trials began on September 17, 1945 at Luneberg, Germany. On trial were forty five of the staff of Belsen concentration camp. Mrs Joyce P. was a member of the British Military Police and acted as a wardress at the Belsen Trials, guarding the women prisoners. The trials lasted eight weeks. Irma Greese had been leader of the women's Waffen SS at Belsen and assistant to Kramer 'The Beast of Belsen'.

Source 15
Greese was twenty three at the time of the trial. The same age as Joyce, who remembers: 'Irma was always immaculate, with her boots well-polished. She was also very arrogant, but she could smile and look very nice. She'd been in the Hitler Youth and it just took her over. They didn't do a lot of denying, there wasn't much point... None of them ever said they were sorry. They said they were obeying orders.'

Belsen Trials, 17 September 1945. Irma Greese is No. 9.

The three women in the picture opposite were sentenced to hang. 'They did not react when the verdict was read out' (Joyce P. in interview with the author, August 1990).

If you had been Joyce, responsible for guarding Irma Greese, what might your feelings towards her have been? What sort of questions would you like to have asked her?

The Nuremberg Trials

The most famous War Crimes Trials were held at Nuremberg, site of Hitler's huge annual rallies and of the infamous Nuremberg Laws.(see p.81) In October 1945, an International Military Tribunal accused twenty four leading Nazis of:

i.   Crimes against peace — carrying out wars of aggression (without the occupation of such countries as Holland and France, the Holocaust could not have occured on such a scale);

ii. War Crimes — ill-treatment of Prisoners-of-War and civilians;

iii. Crimes against humanity — extreme brutality against whole groups of people (this was a new crime in international law);

iv. Conspiracy — plotting together to commit the other three crimes.

---

1.   What exactly are 'crimes against humanity'?

2.   Some people say that the atrocities of the extermination camps were not acts of war, but criminal acts commited under cover of war. Do you agree?

Hitler, Himmler and Goebbels had already commited suicide.

Source 16

'The wrongs which we seek to condemn and punish have been so calculated, so malignant and devastating, that civilsation cannot tolerate their being ignored because it cannot survive their being repeated'. (Justice Robert Jackson, Chief American Counsel)

The Nuremberg Trials began on 20th November 1945. They lasted ten months and ten days. The tribunal included representatives from the USSR, the USA, the UK and France. The prisoners were defended by German lawyers. Hundreds of witnesses were heard. There were 17,000 pages of testimony and 3,000 tons of documents as evidence — much of it written by Nazis. The collapse of Germany was so swift that masses of top-secret

Nuremberg Trials

Nazi papers had been preserved. There were 5,000 photos of ghettos, deportations, concentration camps, crematoria and mass graves.

Despite former SS General Otto Ohlendorf saying that in the killing campaigns: 'There was no difference between Gypsies and Jews', not one Gypsy was called to give evidence.

Source 17

Witnesses
for the
prosecution

Source 18

American journalist Martha Gellhorn described the court as: Quiet... and cold... There was no anger and no hate... This tribunal was gathered to judge'. Most prisoners claimed they were only obeying orders and that they were not individually responsible for the Holocaust. Several observers have commented on how impassive the men seemed for most of the trial.

Source 19

Hoess, without the quiver of an eyelash, reported concisely and factually, on his 'processing' some 2-3 million Jews and other victims through the gas chambers, crematoria and concentration camp. His appearance and manner were those of a man who would everywhere be considered, in government and business an unusually competent and reliable administrator... he never uttered a word that might offend, he spoke of mass murder in the terms of a technician, without any gruesome details. (An Allied journalist)

Source 20

I commanded Auschwitz until 1st December 1943, and estimate that at least 2,500,000 victims were executed and exterminated there by gassing and burning, and at least another half million succumbed to starvation and disease... the remainder having been selected and used for slave labour in the concentration camp industries... We executed about 400,000 Hungarian Jews alone at Auschwitz in the summer of 1944. (Hoess)

Source 21

On day nine of the trial, a film of the camps at the time of liberation was shown in court. An American psychiatrist noted the reaction of the prisoners:

Schacht objects... turns away... Fritsche looks pale and sits aghast as it starts with scenes of prisoners burned alive in a barn... Keitel wipes brow, takes off headphones... Hess glares at the screen... Funk covers his eyes, looks as if he is in agony... Goering... not watching most of the time... Funk now in tears... Speer looks very sad... as human skin lampshade is shown, Streicher says, 'I don't believe that'.

Source 22

Defence Lawyer: Did you ever participate in the annihilation of the Jews?

Hans Frank (Governor of Poland): I say yes... because having lived through five months of the trial, and particularly after having heard the testimony of the witness Hoess, my conscience does not allow me to throw the responsibility solely on these small people. I have never installed an extermination camp for Jews or supported the existence of such camps; but if Adolf Hitler has laid that dreadful responsibility on his people, then it is mine too... A thousand years will pass and this guilty side of Germany will still not be erased.

---

1. What sort of Nazi documents would have been produced as evidence during the Trials?

2. What is the cartoonist (Source 17) trying to say?

3. Martha Gellhorn (Source 18) describes the men on trial as 'impassive'. What does she mean? Does the evidence of Hoess (Source 20) and Hans Frank (Source 22) support or conradict this description? What about the photograph of the defendants?

4. How seriously should the judges have taken the claim: 'We were only obeying orders'?

5. How would you describe the reaction of the defendants in Source 21? Do you think that some leading Nazis might have been genuinely shocked at what they saw on the film?

6. Read Source 22. Hans Frank was Governor of Poland (see Chapter 7 p.127) during the Holocaust years. What sort of responsibility for the Holocaust did he have? What sort of guilt does he admit to in this source?

The verdict

The verdict on the twenty one defendants took forty seven minutes to read, on 1st October 1946. Twelve were sentenced to death by hanging, three to life imprisonment, four to lesser prison sentences and three were acquitted:

```
     DEFENDANTS AND SENTENCES OF NUREMBERG TRIALS

Wilhelm Frick - Designer of Nuremberg Laws; death by hanging

Herman Goering - President of the Reichstag, Chief of the Luftwaffe;
                 death by hanging (Goering committed suicide.)

Joachim von Ribbentrop - Nazi Foreign Minister; death by hanging

Field Marshal Wilhelm Keitel - Chief of Der Fuehrer's Command Staff;
                 death by hanging

Dr. Ernst Kaltenbrunner - Chief of the Gestapo; death by hanging

Alfred Rosenberg - Reich Minister for the Eastern Territories; death
                 by hanging

Hans Frank - Governor of Poland; death by hanging

Julius Streicher - Professional propagandist and racial antagonist;
                 death by hanging

Fritz Saukel - Chief of Nazi slave labor; death by hanging

Gen. Alfred Jodl - Chief of Operations of Nazi Supreme Command; death
                 by hanging

Arthur Seyss-Inquart - Governor of the Netherlands; death by hanging

Rudolf Hess - Hitler's Deputy, Chief of the Nazi Party; life imprisonment

Walther Funk - Head of the Reichsbank (receiver of articles from
                 extermination camps; life imprisonment)

Admiral Erich Raeder - Commander-in-Chief of Hitler's Navy; life
                 imprisonment

Baldur von Schirach - Chief of Hitler Youth; twenty years' imprisonment

Albert Speer - Economic Coordinator of Hitler's War Effort; twenty
                 years' imprisonment

Baron Konstantin von Neurath - Hitler's Foreign Minister, "Protector"
                 of Bohemia and Moravia; fifteen years'
                 imprisonment

Admiral Karl Doenitz - Successor to Raeder as Commander-in-Chief of the
                 Navy under Hitler, successor to Hitler as Head
                 of State; ten years' imprisonment

Martin Bormann - Hitler's Depty, (sentenced in absentia); death by
                 hanging

Hans Fritzsche - Propagandist; not guilty*

Hjalmar Schacht - Financial expert; not guilty*

Franz von Papen - Diplomat; not guilty*
*Later tried by German civil court and drew long sentences but actually
served little time.
```

One of those sentenced to death was Julius *Streicher*, the man responsible for *Der Stürmer*. (see p.89-91). Between August 1941 and September 1944, twenty six articles, twelve of them written by him, demanded the annihilation of the Jews of Europe. At Nuremberg, the judge concluded:

Source 23

Streicher's incitement to murder and extermination at the time when Jews in the East were being killed under the most horrible conditions clearly constitutes persecution on political and racial grounds....and [therefore] a Crime against Humanity.

Reactions

Source 24

Kenneth East, (ex-Royal Air Force) writing in 1990:

[We] regarded the War Crimes Trials as the minimum acceptable punishment of the gang of unspeakable criminals who had brought down such untold havoc and misery upon us all.....they were so manifestly guilty ...they must be dealt with as common murderers....even if there had been no antisemitism it would have been no less necessary to conduct War Crimes Trials.

Source 25

And at the time, reactions varied: Mrs Hallard, a tobacconist of Camberwell Green: 'There should not have been a trial — they should all have been hanged right away'.

Source 26

Mrs. Kathleen Shannon, a business woman: 'I think we have missed a great opportunity to show that we are more civilised than the Germans. We could have kept them in detention and given them an opprtunity to work out their salvation or forever remain prisoners'. (Both quoted in a London newspaper, 1946)

1. Do you find yourself in agreement with Kenneth East, Mrs Hallard or Mrs Shannon?

2. What was the aim of punishing those responsible for the Holocaust? Do you think the Allies achieved their aims? Read the verdicts again.

3. Read Source 23 on the role played by Julius Streicher in the Holocaust. Do you agree with the judge? In your opinion, should the writings, activities and even membership of neo-Nazi groups such as the National Front in Britain or the Ku Klux Klan in America be called criminal?

After Nuremberg

The trials continued. High government officials, including cabinet members, diplomats, ambassadors, military leaders, SS, police officers, members of the *Einsatzgruppen*, doctors and judges were tried.

Source 27

Jim Callaghan, former Prime Minister of Britain:

In January 1946, as a young MP and not yet demobbed from the Navy, I went on a British delegation to Russia. While we were in Kiev, we spent a day attending a war-crimes trial. The evidence on that day concerned the rounding-up and murder of Jewish chidren. A Nazi SS Obersturmbahnführer was being questioned. He was asked whether it was not his duty to protest against the inhuman slaughter of such children. I shall never forget his reply:

'As a National Socialist', he said, 'I could not but approve of their deaths'. (Quoted in the *Jewish Chronicle*, 13/11/87)

Those industrialists who supplied the death camps with the equipment necessary to implement the Holocaust, were considered guilty. *I.G.Farben* was the world's biggest industrial organisation and made, among other things, the deadly Zyklon B gas used in the death camps. It also worked 25,000 people to death in the camps. Heads of the firm received prison sentences. All were free by 1951. Bruno Tesch, whose firm (*Degesch und Degussa*) delivered a huge proportion of the Zyklon B to Auschwitz, was sentenced to death by the British.

5,025 people were convicted between 1945 and 1949 in the American, British and French zones and more in the Russian zones, though numbers are hard to establish. Many others were tried elsewhere in Europe. From 1946, trials were also held against Japanese war criminals.

In July 1948, it was decided that trials in the British zone should stop, in the interests of: i. The future development of Germany; ii. disposing of the past; iii. concentrating on the education of the young. However, other countries continued to try those accused of War Crimes comitted on their territory. By 1969, 80,000 Germans had been investigated and 6,000 convicted.

Eichmann

Adolf Eichmann was in charge of organising the deportation of Jews from all over Europe: 'More, perhaps, than any other official...he made the Holocaust work' (Ian Black, *Guardian* 5/5/90). In 1945 he was captured but he escaped to Argentina. In 1960, an Israeli agent, Zvika Malclin, traced and captured him. In April 1961 an Israeli court put him on trial for: 'Crimes against the Jewish people and against humanity'. He was hanged on May 31, 1962.

Eichmann on trial in Jerusalem 1961, inside a bullet-proof glass cage.

Source 28
Poem

All there is to know about Adolf Eichmann

EYES..Medium

HAIR..Medium

WEIGHT..Medium

HEIGHT..Medium

DISTINGUISHING FEATURES.......None

NUMBER OF FINGERS....................Ten

NUMBER OF TOES............................Ten

INTELLIGENCE...........................Medium

What did you expect?

Talons?

Green saliva?

Oversize incisors?

Madness?

(Leonard Cohen, *Flowers for Hitler*)

De-Nazification

The Allies tried to rid Germany of twelve years of Nazi rule. Universities, schools, courts, the media — all the institutions and organisations which had been dominated by Nazism were investigated. They broke the Nazi Party structure and introduced new textbooks and anti-Nazi journalists were put in place of Nazi-sympathisers.

But how could they change attitudes or ensure that no pro- Nazi remained in a position of influence? Thousands of officials in West Germany were ex-Nazis, fewer in East Germany. By May 1951, ninety two per cent of dismissed teachers were reinstated. Three-fifths of all top police officers and 800 judges who had hanged people for 'grumbling' and other fabricated 'crimes' under Nazi rule, were still in place.

Ex-Nazis in Britain

Since the war, Britain and the USA have been criticised for doing little to stop Nazi sympathisers and collaborators from entering Britain, the USA and Canada. Referring mainly to men from the Baltic States (Lithuania, Latvia and Estonia), critics say that these men were useful during the Cold War because they could supply information against the USSR and were very anti-Soviet. Britain had begun by repatriating them but became reluctant to continue after bloody reprisals against them by the Soviets. So they were often not screened properly on entering Britain. In 1990, documents were released from American vaults which revealed details of 'Operation Rat-lines'. This was the codename for the organised smuggling of thousands of Nazi war criminals to safety in the west, by members of the Vatican and the intelligence services of France, Italy and Britain. Men such as *Ante Ravelic*, the fanatical leader of the Utashi puppet government installed by the Nazis in Yugoslavia in 1941, were able to escape to South America. Ravelic is alleged to have been responsible for at least 500,000 murders.

During the 1950s and 1960s, the British government refused to extradite men wanted in the USSR on charges of mass murder during the war.

The USSR was criticised for its lack of openness regarding events after the war. For example, *Raoul Wallenberg*, the Swedish diplomat who rescued thousands of Hungarian Jews (see p.209) was captured by the Russians and has never been heard of again. Thousands of Soviet documents relating to the Holocaust became available in 1992.

Since 1979, in what was West Germany, forty two men have been sentenced to death and scores of trials were held in the former East Germany, Australia, Holland, France, Canada, the USA and Russia. In 1990 fifty three people said to have served in the *Einsatzgruppen* were known to be living in Britain. In order to prosecute them, the British law had to be changed to allow a British citizen to be tried for crimes commited abroad while citizens of another country. The House of Commons voted to change the law, but the House of Lords voted 207 to 74 against, on June 4, 1990. The law was finally passed in 1991. 92 alleged Nazi war criminals living in Britain were under investigation in 1992.

1. Does the reaction of the SS officer in Source 27 surprise you? Explain your answer.

2. What do you imagine were some of the problems of de-Nazification? Think about each institution separately: universities, schools, courts and the media.

3. Present the arguments for and against Britain's decision to end trials of suspected Nazi War Criminals in 1948 (see above).

4. What point is Leonard Cohen trying to make in Source 28? Is it useful to know what Eichmann looked like (see photo on page 261).

5. Do you think that men and women suspected of Nazi War Crimes should be put on trial in the 1990s?

Chapter Twelve

Then and now

Since 1945, there have been thousands of books, films, newspaper articles, poems, paintings, sculptures and conferences about the Holocaust. It continues to affect the lives of millions of people — not only those directly involved, but their children and grandchildren and people living far from where it happened and who were not even born at the time.

For the few survivors, their experiences appear to have dominated their lives. Elie Wiesel: 'For the survivors, death is not the problem. We learned to live with the death. The problem is to adjust to life'. Scars are physical as well

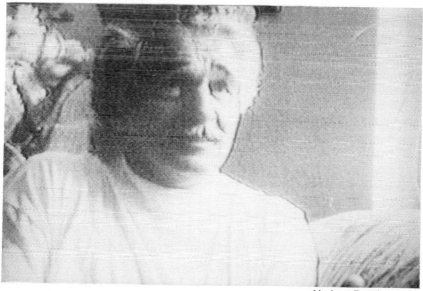

Herbert Dambromski

as mental. Some walk with difficulty because of severe frostbite in the camps: one German Gypsy, Herbert Dambromski was so badly beaten on the head while in a concentration camp, that he is permanently deaf.

The Holocaust reminds us of what human beings are capable of. As Rabbi Hugo Gryn, from Berehovo, Czechoslovakia, a survivor of Auschwitz, now living in London, observes: 'God did not put the Jews into Auschwitz, man did'.

Modern Germany

Source 1
Axel von den Bussche was a German Army officer during the war and he became a member of the resistance to Hitler:'He's left us Germans with an undigestible part of our lives... which may be forgotten, can hardly be forgiven and is still not understood'.

Source 2
Bernt Engelmann, once a political prisoner in Dachau, writing in 1988: 'There was no national shame, no remorse. Most of the Nazis, apart from the top war criminals, went straight back into office in the Federal Government. Most kept their ill-gotten money, stolen from Jewish businesses and homes, or from slave labour in their factories.'

He feels there is more shame among the younger generations. Hundreds of schools and communities have traced the history of local Jewish people who 'disappeared' in the 1930s. Ironically the *documents* relating to births, marriages and lives of German Jews tend to have been very well preserved.

All over West Germany, memorials were held on the 50th anniversary of *Kristallnacht*, November 9, 1988. Many synagogues have been made into Jewish Museums. For example in Affaltrach, near Heilbrom, where there had been a Jewish community since the 17th century. At its opening, the mayor, Otto Widmaier, said:

Source 3
There is no longer a Jewish community that could make use of a restored synagogue in our district. That is an awesome truth we must neither suppress nor forget.... The youth of today are not responsible for what happened then, but they are responsible for what history will make of it. We must learn from our history what man is capable of doing, and, from that lesson, achieve the strength to over-come...prejudice and hatred in future.

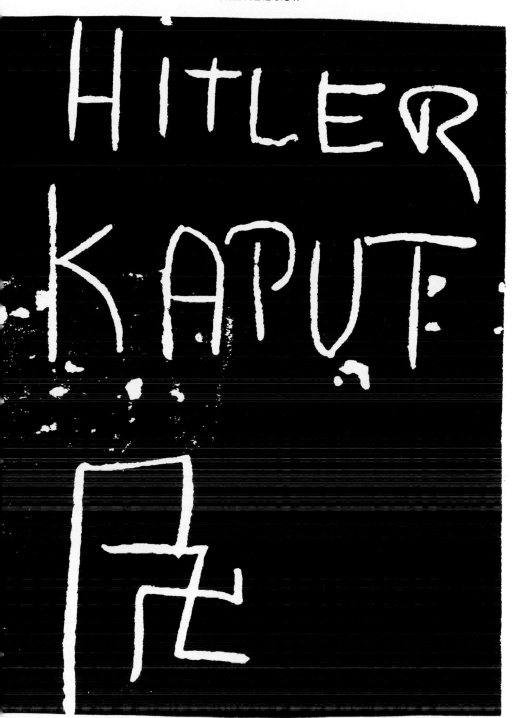

'Hitler is finished'

Niklas Frank, son of Hans Frank (Hitler's lawyer and Governer-General of Poland during the Holocaust, see p.127 and p.257) wrote about his father in 1985:

Source 4

I have to decide, was my father in the first place my father or a criminal?   And I think there was no choice...he was a criminal...He was a coward, that I hate most and he knew all about his crimes and he went on with them...I feel guilty to be a member of the German people because we don't want to live with this past...therefore I am ashamed. (Quoted in 'Sins of the Father', programme in *The Human Factor* series, ITV 1989)

The reaction of many Germans to Frank's book was hostile. His brother denounced him as a liar. But Niklas' daughter Francesca also says she feels guilty:

Source 5

I feel guilt as a German...The culture of mine is the same as the culture which produced my grandfather...My grandfather influenced my father, however much he rebelled against it, some ways of life must still be in him and some of those have come down to me so I've got bits of my grandfather's thinking in me. (Quoted in 'Sins of the Father')

The German State has paid compensation to Jewish survivors for their suffering, but only to very few Gypsies and none at all to gay people who were incarcerated in camps.

There are approximately 40,000 Jewish people in Germany today. Fritz, a German Jew born after 1945 says.:

'With my head I belong here in Germany...I am successful, respected and feel safe...But the heart remains unquiet...nervous, often even fearful. With my heart I am not German and never will be'. (Quoted in Peter Sichrovsky, 1986)

Other German Jews disagree about how much Germany has changed.

I agree with my father: nothing has changed....To become de-Nazified all they had to do was to say 'Good morning' instead of 'Heil Hitler' when they picked up their breakfast rolls at the bakery. (Mario)

I can't keep on saying, like the other Jews here, that nothing has changed and that the Germans are still swine. The people here have also been changed by the war, and today we are living here in one of the world's greatest democracies. (Tuvi, quoted in Sichrovsky, 1986)

Jews in Poland today.

In communist East Germany, as it then was, the government refused to acknowledge that some of its people could have been responsible for the Holocaust. They blamed it on 'fascist West Germany'. Some of East Germany's leaders were active anti-Nazis during the Hitler period, but hundreds of ex-Nazis live and work there and antisemitism continued after the war. In 1990, the East German government issued a statement which included the following:

Source 6

Immeasurable suffering was inflicted on the peoples of the world by Germans during the time of National Socialism. Nationalism and racial madness led to genocide, particularly of the Jews in all European countries, of the people of the Soviet Union, the Polish people and the Gypsy people......We ask the Jews of the world to forgive us. We ask the people of Israel to forgive us for the hypocrisy and hostility of official East German policies towards Israel and for the persecution and degradation of Jewish citizens also after 1945 in our country.

---

1. Read the words of Axel von den Bussche, Bernt Engelman, Otto Widmair and Niklas and Francesca Frank. What do they tell you about the varied responses of Germans to the Nazi/Holocaust period?

2. Can you explain Francesca's feelings of guilt (Source 5)? Can you understand those feelings?

3. Read the excerpts taken from the stories of Fritz, Mario and Tuvi. They are all children of people who survived the Holocaust and then chose to stay in or return to Germany. Discuss the reasons why their parents might have taken that decision.

4. Read Source 6. What information does it give you about the attitude of the (then) East German government towards the Nazi/Holocaust period up to 1990?

Revisionism

Today, there are people who deny that the Holocaust ever happened. They are called revisionists because they try to revise (rewrite) history. Most are neo-Nazis who believe that Nazism would be attractive if only they could get rid of its unfortunate association with the death camps. Most people choose to ignore them, but their work has provoked outrage.

Source 7

After the war, I didn't think about it.
I've been through a lot since then.
I guess if I was Jewish, I couldn't walk away from it.
Last week I read in the paper how some people was sayin'
Maybe it was just a few Germans,
Maybe everybody exaggerated what went on there.

I never wrote to a paper before, but I wrote then.
I says, 'If you'd have been there to smell it,
you'd have knowed it happened.

(A farmer from Appalachia, USA who served as an American G.I. in the Second World War, quoted in Julie Heifetz, 1985)

In his last book, *The Drowned and the Saved*, the Italian novelist and Auschwitz survivor Primo Levi imagines members of the SS taunting their Jewish victims: 'However this war may end, we have won the war against you; none of you will be left to bear witness, but even if someone were to survive, the world would not believe him. There will perhaps be suspicions, discussions, research by historians, but there will be no certainties, because we will destroy the evidence together with you. And even if some proof should remain and some of you survive, people will say that the events you describe are too monstrous to be believed: they will say that they are exaggerations of Allied propaganda and will believe us, who will deny everything, and not you.'

1. If you had to prove to a Revisionist that the Holocaust did happen, what evidence would you use?
2. Should we give publicity to Revisionists by writing about them? Is that taking them too seriously? How would you react to anyone who tried to deny that the First World War had ever happened?
3. What provoked the farmer in Source 7 to write to his local newspaper?
4. Read the Primo Levi extract above. Do you feel that the Holocaust is too monstrous to be believed?

Source 8

'Oppression does not stand on the doorstep with a toothbrush moustache and a swastika armband. It creeps up insidiously, step by step....'
(Lord Chief Justice of Great Britain, Lord Lane, 1989)

Source 9

We must be listened to... It happened, therefore it can happen again...and it can happen everywhere... it is not very probable that all the factors will occur again simultaneously... but violence... is there before our eyes... It is therefore necessary to sharpen our senses, distrust the prophets... those who speak and write 'beautiful words' unsupported by intelligent reasons...there is no need for wars and violence... After the defeat, the silent Nazi diaspora has taught the art of persecution and torture to the military and political men of a dozen countries, on the shores of the Mediterranean, the Atlantic and the Pacific. Many new tyrants have kept in their drawer Adolf Hitler's *Mein Kampf*... it can still come in handy. (Primo Levi, 1986)

---

1. Explain what Lord Lane is saying in Source 8.

2. In what way does Primo Levi in Source 9 agree with him? Quote from the Source to support your answer.

3. Which 'new tyrants' (in the last thirty years) might Primo Levi have in mind?

Above: Wang Weilin stands in front of four tanks. He pleaded for an end to the killing and was pulled away by bystanders. Tianenman Square, Beijing, China, June 1989.

The suffering of the Jews was not worse than the suffering of American Indians or Australian Aborigines when they were hunted down and murdered. Genocide had happened before. But the Holocaust was different. The motives and methods of its perpetrators were unique — the planned total annihilation of a people, wherever they lived, using mechanised mass slaughter.

> They invented very little and they did not invent the portrait of the Jew, which was taken over lock, stock and barrel from writings going back to the tenth century....They had to become inventive with the ' Final Solution'. That was their great invention and that is what made this entire process different from all others that had preceded that event. (Raul Hilberg, US Historian)

A Khmer Rouge rally under Pol Pot (1975–79) they were responsible for the murder of more than one million Cambodians.

Many aspects of Nazism live on. Antisemitism, racism, prejudice, brutality, terror, dictatorship and mass murder continue. As do indifference, collaboration and resistance.

In 1949, the United Nations agreed on a Genocide Convention, which was inspired by the Holocaust. It defined Genocide as:

> any..... acts committed with intent to destroy, in whole, or in part, a national, ethnic, racial or religious group.... Persons committing genocide... shall be punished... whether they are rulers, public officials or private individuals.

It has not been possible to rid the world of genocide or brutality.

East Timor

There is genocide happening as this book goes to print, on the Indonesian island of East Timor, (see map). It was invaded in December 1975 by the Indonesian army and: 'in the first few years after the invasion as many as 200,000 of a population of about 600,000 East Timorese died. Many died of disease or starvation but thousands were extrajudicially executed. Hundreds of others have 'disappeared' and remain unaccounted for, most assumed to be dead' (*Amnesty International,* July 1992).

In its reports, Amnesty describes continuing 'gross and systematic violations of human rights'. And the destruction is more than physical. The East Timorese culture is being destroyed as well.

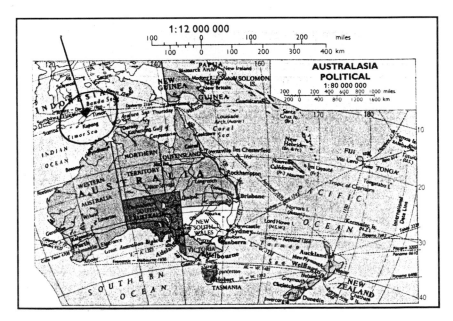

274

Indonesia wants the land and resources of East Timor. There is a Timorese guerrilla movement, helped by local members of the Catholic Church, struggling to win independence. But most people feel like this man:

> We are literally against the wall. They are armed and we are unarmed. What can we do? Those who are able to resist, do so, but they are in the forests. (Quoted in *'Cold Blood: The Massacre of East Timor'*, York-shire TV, 1992)

The UN has condemned Indonesia, but the Timorese people have been left to their fate by world governments. The USA supplied the majority of Indonesia's weapons, including aircraft, during the invasion of 1975.

> I must say that all the major powers, but particularly the United States, Great Britain, France and to a lesser extent Australia are guilty, are co-responsible for the tragedy in East Timor since 1975 because of the amount of weapons they have provided Indonesia, enabling them to continue the war there, but also because of their silence over the human tragedy in East Timor. That has been their major responsibility. And that has to do only with economic interest, trade and industrial investment. Nothing else. (José Ramos Horta, East Timor diplomat)

One of the East Timorese people, speaking on YTV's documentary asked why the UN had decided to help liberate Kuwait when Sadam Hussein's army invaded it, but was not willing to do the same for East Timor when it was invaded by Indonesia. Can you answer this question?

The Western media rarely mentions what is happening in East Timor. Atrocities in Europe tend to receive more attention.

'Ethnic cleansing'

On 29th July 1992, representatives of 40 Western countries met in Geneva to discuss the refugee crisis which followed months of fighting in the former Yugoslav republics.

There were 2.5 million homeless people from Bosnia alone:

'The vast majority of refugees were brutally forced out of their homes by those damnable practices known as 'Ethnic Cleansing''. (Sandako Ogata, chief of the United Nations High Commission for Refugees)

275

"Ethnic Cleansing' is the euphemism for the practice of kicking out minority populations, which has been indulged in by all sides in the conflict in Bosnia Herzegovina' wrote Andrew Marshall in *The Independent* on 29th July. However, most reports and eyewitness accounts describe the Serbian troops' treatment of Muslims.

Janez Javsa, Defence Minister of Slovenia, described it as: 'an attempt at genocide against the Muslims'. (July 27, 1992, *The Independent*)

Bosnia was part of what was Yugoslavia and until summer 1992, its population consisted of 44% Muslims, 31% Serbs and 17% Croats. Despite a history of inter-ethnic conflict, including massacres during the second World War, many Muslims, Serbs and Croats lived in the same towns, streets and apartment blocks together and friendships and marriages between the ethnic groups were common.

The Serbs and Croats are accused of trying to extend their states at the expense of Bosnia-Herzegovina and its Muslim population (see map). This has been achieved by attacking villages and towns where a majority of Muslims lived.

'They are being burned out of their homes', reported journalist Maggie O'Kane on the BBC (29th July 1992). Other accounts describe how Muslims were rounded up and forced to sign away all their property to the Serbs, before being forced to leave. The men were put into sealed trains or buses organised by the military and held at Serb-run detention — or concentration — camps where they were reported to be being held in the open air and fed once a day. According to the Bosnian government, there were 57 such camps. They claimed that 93,390 Muslim and Croatian men were detained by the end of July and there were reports of 'disappearances', torture and murders. Live evidence of these camps was broadcast on 6 August 1992.

By August 1992, outside efforts to help or intervene included the following: ceasefires negotiated by the EEC; a UN peace-keeping force; economic sanctions against Serbia; no Serbian teams allowed at the Olympic games; troops, including British soldiers sent to protect humanitarian aid.

Certain countries received refugees from Bosnia: Croatia 334,000; Serbia 210,000; Germany 200,000; Slovenia 60,000; Hungary 50,000; Austria 50,000; Sweden 44,167; Macedonia 29,000; Switzerland 17,573; Italy 7,000; Turkey 7,000; Netherlands 6,300; Norway 2,331; Denmark 1,637; CIS 1,500; France 1,108; Britain 1,100; Finland 982; Belgium 870; Spain 120; Greece 7. (Source: *The Independent,* July 29, 1992)

Frenze and Frederike Schaller live near Nuremberg in Germany. On hearing about the refugee crisis, they offered to take in a family from Bosnia:

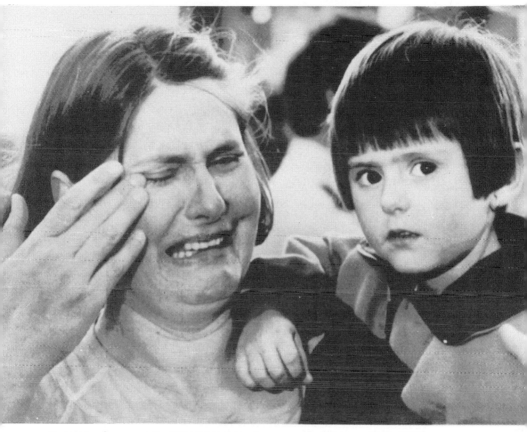

Bosnian refugees at the Schlabruegge refugee camp, Germany (July 1992).

'It was very important to give a room and hope *at once*. We shouldn't be afraid of the problem that *might* happen. We should help *first'* (Franz Schaller, speaking on Channel Four, *The World This Week*, August 1, 1992)

Meanwhile, the practice of 'ethnic cleansing' continued and the fighting escalated. On August 3, Philip Sherwell wrote:

Land-hungry Serbs are poised to drive 250,000 people from their homes in the last Muslim outpost in Northern Bosnia in an act of mass 'ethnic cleansing. (*Daily Telegraph*)

Events in Bosnia today, and in other parts of Yugoslavia, can certainly be classified as war crimes but above all they are a warning against the complacency of those who grew up after the second world war believing that the crimes committed in the name of Hitler and Stalin could never again be seen in Europe. (Tim Judah, *The Times*, 29th July 1992)

1. What are the causes of the fighting in the former Yugoslavia?

2. At the emergency Conference in Geneva, Germany and Austria urged all European countries to take more Bosnian refugees. This request was refused at the time. What were the arguments for and against?

3. What could the average British (or any country's) citizen *do* to affect the situation in the former Yugoslavia?

4. Certain politicians believed that the UN should use military force to try and stop the fighting. What do you think?

5. Why is 'ethnic cleansing' considered such a repulsive term?

6. The policy of 'ethnic cleansing' has been compared to the Nazi Holocaust. Why? What are the similarities and differences between the genocide in 1941-45 and today?

Stalin was responsible for the murder of millions of people because he suspected their views, class or nationality. In Ireland people are killed because they are Catholic or because they are Protestant. In many countries, gays and lesbians are physically attacked because of their sexuality. There was the Terror of China's Cultural Revolution in the 1960s. Pinochet of Chile (1973-1990) was responsible for the murder and torture of thousands of people. In March 1988, 5,000 Kurds were massacred by Iraqi mustard and nerve gas at Halabja in Northern Iraq. Black South Africans are still not allowed to vote in their own country.

Antisemitism

Although the majority of British Jews feel secure and a part of British society, swastikas have been painted on synagogues and Jewish children sometimes attacked on their way to school. In the countries of the former Soviet Union, thousands of Jews do not feel safe and many have left. In Carpentras, France, a Jewish cemetery was desecrated in May 1990 and a man's body dragged from its grave and impaled on the railings. Throughout Eastern Europe, newly won freedom has brought a revival of Jewish identity among the small communities, but it has also activated antisemitism. Ku Klux Klan and neo-Nazi groups in the USA declare: 'Men, women and children, without exception, who are of non-Aryan blood shall be terminated or expelled'.

All these activities are the work of a number of small organisations. But their support is growing, particularly in France and Germany. In 1992 there were approximately 150,000 members of Le Pen's *Front Nationale* and 70,000 members of German neo-Nazi groups. They watch Nazi propaganda films,

SS memorial rally, Halbe, Germany 17 November 1991. Photo: Rolf Walter.

celebrate Hitlers's birthday, talk about murdering Jews and organise harassment and violence against Germany's black and Turkish residents. There were 2,074 racial attacks in Germany in 1991, eight times more than in 1990 (according to government figures). In April 1992, the German far right Republikaner Party, led by former Waffen SS officer *Franz Schönhuber*, won 11% of the vote in regional elections. In August 1992, neo-Nazis and their supporters fire-bombed Rumanian refugees and Vietnamese guest-workers out of a hostel in Rostock, in eastern Germany. 14,000 antifascists demonstrated against them on 29 August.

1. Why do you think antisemitism remains so much part of modern societies?
2. Jewish people in Britain disagree over how to react to attacks on graves. Some say that 'making a fuss' only gives publicity to the neo-Nazi groups and makes them seem more important than they really are. Others say that keeping quiet is dangerous. Discuss both points of view.

Racism

Black and Asian people have been living in Britain for hundreds of years. The majority are British citizens, but many do not feel a sense of belonging because of the extent of racism here. Attacks on British black and Asian people are far more frequent than on British Jews. And black people suffer more institutional racism — in the Army, the police force, education and housing. According to Home Office figures (1992), there is a racist attack every thirty minutes in Britain.

In London's East End, there are areas where British Asians need protection to leave their homes, for fear of physical attack. Children are stoned and dog excrement pushed through letter boxes.

Ethnic minority communities in the East End of London are fighting back against these attacks. Shah Munim, a Community worker who helps racially harassed families, said: 'people my age will not sit back as the older generation did. We have grown up speaking English and knowing how the system works. So we will use it to our own ends....I can't see any real improvement occuring until the Government takes the issue seriously and co-ordinates the actions of the police and councils. (Quoted in *The Sunday Correspondent,* Oct 1, 1989)

Some people think that race relations have improved in Britain, particularly in the fashion, music and sports world, involving young people. Garth Crooks, Chair of the Professional Footballers Association, believes:

> In football, it's definitely better... In 1992 you have probably four or five black players in every major club. That has flushed out a lot of people's racism, they can be confronted by it and have to deal with it, but there's still a long way to go... Politicians have got to take stock in preventing this cancer [racism and Neo-Nazism] that's moving through Europe... and not allow commerce to take priority over civil rights... Otherwise you're going to have terrible consequences.' (Garth Crooks, speaking on Reportage, BBC TV, 1992)

1. Do you believe that racism and antisemitism are a permanent part of our society? Do you think they are increasing or decreasing?

2. Read the words of Shah Munim above. Do you know what the government, police and councils do to stop racism? What more could be done by them? What else can a society do about racism/racist attitudes (e.g. in schools, football grounds)?

3. What does Garth Crooks mean by saying that politicians must not allow 'commerce to take priority over civil rights'?

Gypsies

The six million Gypsies of Europe continue to be treated as second class citizens in almost every country. They have become scapegoats for the economic and political problems of Eastern Europe, in particular Hungary, Poland, Czechoslovakia and Rumania. Laws restricting Travellers are less harsh than in the Middle Ages (see Chapter 2) but attitudes have not changed much.

There are approximately 10,000 travelling families in Britain and the majority would like to settle permanently in one place. In 1959 the Roadside Act made stopping on the roadside verges illegal. An Act in 1968 requested — but did not demand, that local Authorities provide adequate sites for Gypsies living in their area. But many have still not done as requested, so about 4,000 Gypsy families still have no legal stopping place and are breaking the law wherever they stop. Many, though not all, sites are inadequate: underneath motorways or on old tips. Securing good health and educational facilities is often a serious problem. Many Travellers would prefer that their children were educated together with non-Gypsy children in order to reduce tensions and prejudice.

They claim the nationality and use the language of wherever they live but also keep their own identity and language (Romany). There are Gypsy organisations, songs, poets, artists and writers. But contact between Travellers and non-Travellers remains rare and is usually hostile.

William Nicholson is a Gypsy and the warden of Lyncmouth official Gypsy camp in Northumberland. His wife Jane believes that part of the problem is: 'people see us from the outside not from the inside. I don't know of any Gypsy family whose children have been taken off them because of neglect'.

We're getting more and more downgraded in this country and it's supposed to be the free country of the world. I think all Councils should be made to treat us equal with other people. Unless you're on a site, you're not allowed to stop....So they're slowly forcing us off the road. We've got to live the way they want us to live. Not the way we want to live. (William)

---

1. Do you know whether your local Council has provided a site for Gypsies/Travellers to live in? If so, what sort of site is it? With what facilities? What should Councils provide for Travellers?

2. Imagine you were a Traveller and you were asked by a local resident to explain your lifestyle and why you have the right to live the way you want to live.

3. Why does there continue to be prejudice against Gypsies and Travellers throughout Europe?

Obedience

Henry Metemann, ex-Hitler Youth:

'I followed the crowds, I obeyed commands and I have learned in my later life that by doing that, I have made a horrible mistake'.

This unquestioning obedience fascinates psychiatrists. Dr Alice Miller, a Swiss psychoanalyst, believes that the strict and cruel upbringing experienced by Hitler and millions of other Germans helps explain their later obedience and sadism. Stanley Milgram, an American psychologist, also believed that the Germans had a character flaw which led them to be more obedient than the average American and thus made them more likely to fall for a leader like Hitler.

In the 1960s, he set up an experiment to test people's willingness to take orders. He paid one thousand American volunteers to take part in an exercise which required them to give electric shocks to an (unseen) man. They had to question their subject and, whenever he answered incorrectly, increase the voltage of the shock applied — although in reality, they had no control over the voltage: only the meter showed higher readings. Unknown to the volunteers, the hidden man answering the questions was an actor, who faked screams and the begging for help. 65% of them continued to apply the shocks up to 450 volts. All had been given a forty volt shock at the start of the experiment to demonstrate the pain they would be inflicting. Milgram was amazed at the results:

Source 10

I found so much obedience, I hardly saw the need for taking the experiment to Germany....I would say, on the basis of having observed a thousand people in the experiment....that if a system of death camps were set up in the US of the sort we had seen in Nazi Germany, we would be able to find sufficient personnel for those camps in any medium-sized American town.

---

1. Are you surprised by the results of Milgram's experiment — that 65% of volunteers applied electric shocks up to what they thought was 450 volts?

2. Can you explain why they did so?

3. Do you imagine the results would be the same in your country? What if you had been one of the volunteers applying the electric shocks?

4. Read Source 10. Do you agree with Milgram's conclusions? Does his experiment contribute to our understanding of the Holocaust?

Werner, Esther, Liesl and Harry

All four still live in Britain today.

Werner

He married Lena Alvarez in 1946 and became a teacher and eventually deputy Head at King David High School, Manchester. Talking about the Holocaust in 1990, he said:

> We are here now. The Holocaust is largely a Christian problem. I hate the word Holocaust.....it means a burnt offering and no-one offered anything. It has affected my views about everything...I am going to go on fighting prejudice, discrimination and hatred in Britain as long as I have the energy to do so. Anybody who uses the word 'the' in my view is a villain. What I mean by this is, if anybody says 'the Jews', 'the Catholics', 'the gays', he is going down Hitler's street. You are who you are, not because of your race, or because of your religion, but because you are you. The sin of Nazi Germany was the dehumanisation, making people into vermin. Once you've created the idea of vermin then you've made the conditions for some people to react as some Germans did.

Werner

He also described his feelings on going back to Germany, as: 'equivalent to my visiting a cemetery. My greatest pleasure in going to Germany is to talk to young people who are trying to understand what they cannot come to grips with in their own history'.

1. What does Werner mean by : 'The Holocaust is largely a Christian problem'? Looking back at Chapter One might help you answer the question.

2. Why is he so opposed to the word 'the'?'

3. Why, for him, was dehumanisation the sin of Nazi Germany?

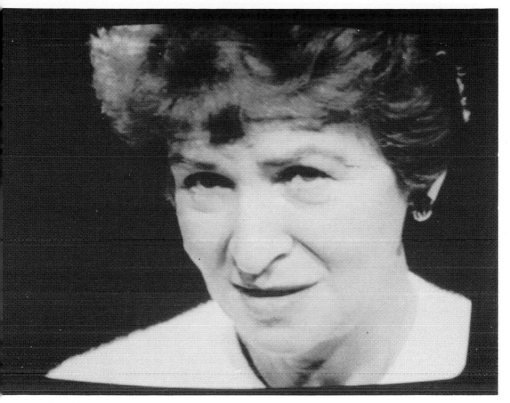

Esther

In 1948, Esther joined the New Yiddish Theatre in Stoke Newington, in the east end of London and after marriage to Stasiek Brunstein (who is a painter and also a survivor of the Holocaust) and the birth of two daughters, she worked in various offices and trained as Medical Receptionist. In 1990, she described one effect of her experiences:

> I was very scared when giving birth to my first child. I just did not believe I could produce a healthy child, because I could just see all the other babies. I had actually seen, in the summer of 1942, new-born babies being thrown down in a sheet from the top window of the hospital onto a truck. So giving birth was very important. It was also the victory. We have survived......

About Germany, she said:

> I would find it very hard to go to Germany. I don't hate *en masse*, I can't do it because it was done to me, but I feel very uneasy to meet any German who is just five years older than myself because he probably was a member of the Hitler Youth. About young Germans I have hope, because without hope, what else is there?

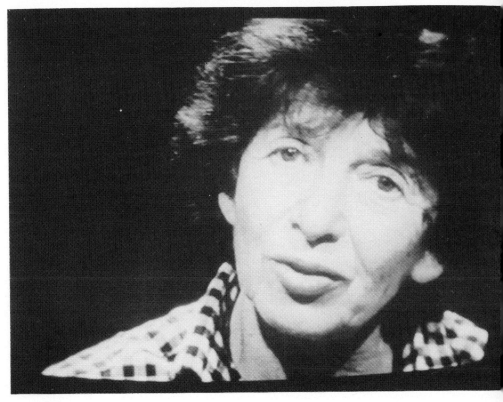

Liesl

---

1. Why was giving birth such an important event for Esther?

2. What does she mean by: 'I can't hate *en masse*'?

Liesl

Liesl married Jack Silverstone in 1949 and had two sons. She did voluntary work for years and then became a School Counsellor in Brixton, London (1966-1984). She divorced in 1971 and for the last ten years has worked as tutor on Counselling courses, founder and tutor on the Person-Centred Art Therapy course, Art Therapist, Counsellor and Supervisor.

In 1990, she described the long-term effects of what had happened to her and her family:

> It wasn't until 1979 that I started to cry and grieve and to rage. And that was a sort of liberation, setting myself free from the energy I used suppressing all that material. And in the wake of that I began to realise how that journey of mine on that train had affected me since. (see p.125)

For example in my relationship with men.....My father, I was his little girl, he loved me very much. So for me the formula of love was....you really trust someone and get very, very close and then they send you away. And you never see them again. And I think I made sure not to put myself through that again. And in the choice of relationships I had, I made sure I had people where there was a distance....because of the fear of being abandoned.

I'm a sort of banner-bearer for my family. I'm here to do them honour. I don't want to live my life with systems and strategies due to Hitler....that would be like a posthumous victory for him.

And about the reunification of Germany she says:

The selfish bit of me says I'm old, I won't see the outcome. Another bit of me is shit-scared of what might happen again, knowing full well that there are rascist movements on both sides of the dismantled wall....I am in terror of a unified Germany.

---

1. How has Liesl's experience of the Holocaust affected her relationships since? Explain in your own words.

2. What does she mean by 'That would be like a posthumous victory for Hitler'?

Harry

Harry has lived in Newcastle-upon-Tyne since 1946. In 1951 he married Cecilia and they have four children. He was a builder until he retired in 1989. In 1982, Harry's life changed with a phone call which came out of the blue. The caller was an American, Michael Korenblit, who announced that he was Harry's nephew and that Harry's sister Manya was alive and living in America. The last time they had been together was in 1943 in the ghetto when Harry was taken away to Majdanek (see p.158). He knew she had been in Auschwitz and assumed she was dead. Harry collapsed on hearing this news. Within a week, Manya and her husband Meyer (who had organised their hiding in the haystack, see p.158) arrived in Newcastle.

Manya had discovered the amazing news that Harry was still alive when she visited a cousin in Israel, who told her he'd had a letter from Harry in 1946. The cousin vaguely remembered where Harry was living and, with the help of the British Embassy, Manya's son had traced him. In 1990, Harry described the effect of this reunion:

I did not believe there was a God in this world, because seeing what I saw with my own eyes what they've done to little children, smashed their heads on the stones... I lost faith in everything. But when I found my sister, I started believing in God again. I started going to synagogue

Harry

again and it's a completely different life I've got now. We never talk much about the camps — I don't like to talk about it... I still have nightmares about the family and imagine that Germans are chasing me.

And his feelings about Germany:

I'm never going back there. I'll be bitter the rest of my life....What they've done to my family and myself....I'll never forget them, I'll never forgive them.

1. Why do you think Harry describes his reunion with Manya almost as a religious experience?

2. Can you understand his feelings about Germany? How does he differ from Esther in this respect?

Conclusion

Is it possible to understand the Holocaust?

For some survivors, it was an experience beyond description:

> 'The language to describe the Holocaust does not exist. The more I study, the less I understand' (Elie Wiesel).

Source 11

Perhaps one cannot, what is more one must not, understand what happened, because to understand is almost to justify....No normal human being will ever be able to identify with Hitler, Himmler, Goebbels, Eichmann and endless others. This dismays us and at the same time gives us a sense of relief; because perhaps it is desirable that their words (and also, unfortunately their deeds) cannot be comprehensible to us. They are non-human words and deeds.... There is no rationality in the Nazi Hatred.... it is a poison fruit sprung from the deadly trunk of Fascism.....We cannot understand it, but we can and must understand from where it springs and we must be on our guard.... Everybody must know or remember that when Hitler and Mussolini spoke in public, they were believed, applauded, admired, adored like gods.... We must remember that the faithful followers.... were not born torturers, were not (with a few exceptions) monsters: they were ordinary men. (Primo Levi, 1958)

For Esther, one of the lessons of the Holocaust is: 'the hope that young people will not be indifferent bystanders'.

When faced with violence and antisemitism or racism, the individual has (difficult) choices. Mr Rainford, an Englishman who took in Vera Gissing when she escaped from Nazi Europe, explained his action, saying: 'I knew I couldn't save the world, but I knew I could save one human being'.

And one of the people who rescued Jews in Occupied Europe explained: 'I knew they were taking them and they wouldn't come back. I didn't think I could live with that knowing I could have done something'.

Some people believe that education is the key to ensuring that society develops the sensitivity Primo Levi asks for.

Source 15

A Head of an American high school sends this letter to his teachers on the first day of school:

Dear Teacher

I am a survivor of a concentration camp. My eyes saw what no man should witness:

Gas chambers built by learned engineers.

Children poisoned by educated physicians.

Infants killed by trained nurses.

Women and babies shot and burned by high school and college graduates.

So, I am suspicious of education.

My request is: Help your students become human. Your efforts must never produce learned monsters, skilled psychopaths, educated Eichmanns.

Reading, writing, arithmetic are important only if they serve to make our children more human.

1. 'In every part of the world, wherever you begin by denying the fundamental liberties of mankind and equality among people. You move towards the concentration camp system' (Primo Levi) .

   What are fundamental liberties? Do you feel that you have the 'fundamental liberties of mankind' in your society?

2. Think of some of the people who have suffered persecution and still do — Jews, Armenians, Gypsies, Kurds and blacks. Are there any similarities in either the origins or nature of the persecution? What are the differences?

3. Read Source 11. Do you agree with Primo Levi that 'no normal human being will ever be able to identify with Hitler'? Why does he not want us to fully understand the Holocaust? What does he urge us to remember?

4. What does Esther mean by 'indifferent bystander' (see above)? Can you think of a time when you were an indifferent bystander? Did you feel you had a choice about how to react at the time? Can you think of a time when you were *not* an indifferent bystander? How did you feel at the time or afterwards?

6. What sort of school is the American Headteacher who wrote Source 12 trying to create? How could this be achieved? What, for example, can a school do about bullying?

7. Think again about all the factors which made the Holocaust possible. See Appendix 1 p.297 after you have thought of your own list. Is there anything individuals, organisations or governments could have done to prevent or get rid of those factors?

8. The words 'Nazi' and 'Fascist' are often misused today. Give an example of the misuse of the word 'Nazi'. What exactly do the two words mean?

9. Having studied the Holocaust, what has been the most memorable aspect of the events and people associated with it? Is there any one person whose story or character you remember especially vividly? Are there any questions you would like to ask about any aspect of the Holocaust?

10. Would you say the Holocaust has anything to teach us today, either in relation to your own day-to-day life or in national and international terms?

Glossary

Antisemitism	hostility towards or racism against Jews
Bolshevik	a Russian communist (Leninist) in the early 20th century
Bund	'Union'; its full name was 'General Jewish Workers' union of Lithuania, Poland and Russia'. Founded in 1897. A socialist organisation which rejected Zionism
Capitalism	an economic and political system where industry, trade etc are owned by private individuals or groups
Chanukah	the Hebrew word for 'dedication'. It is a Jewish festival — the 'Feast of Lights' — commemorating the rededication of the Temple after it had been desecrated in the second century BCE
Collaborator	some one who worked with or helped the Nazis
Communism	an economic and political system based on the sharing of all work and property by the whole community
Cossack	a group of people of Southern Russia, noted as horsemen from early times. Involved in 19th century *pogroms* against Jews
Dehumanisation	to brutalise or take away the human qualities of a person or people
Einsatzgruppen	mobile killing units of SS that followed the German Army into Poland and the Soviet Union
Emancipation	the act of setting free from slavery and from restrictions in 18th century Europe
Enlightenment	a period in the 18th century of more open thinking especially about religion and philosophy; to become free from prejudice and superstition

Ethnic	relating to a particular group of people who have the same language or cultural origins
Fascism	(the word comes from *fasces,* the ancient Roman symbol of state power). A form of extreme right-wing dictatorship. It is usually associated with aggressive nationalism and racism.
Final solution	the Nazi term for their plan to murder every Jew in Europe
Genocide	a systematic attempt to destroy a racial group or nation
Gestapo	Nazi secret police
Hebrew	the ancient Jewish language used in the Old Testament and now the official language of Israel
Holocaust	complete destruction of people or animals by fire. Some people do not use the word Holocaust because it has connotations of 'burnt offering' or 'sacrifice'. Instead they use the Hebrew words *Shoah* or *Churban* ('ruin, destruction, desolation')
Kapo	concentration camp inmates who were selected by the Nazis to oversee other inmates
Nationalist	one who works for the unity, independence, interests or domination of a nation
Partisan	a member of a military force, but not part of a regular army, fighting for the liberation of her or his country
Persecution	persistent ill-treatment or harassment
Philistines	one of the ancient inhabitants of South West Palestine, enemies of the Israelites
Race	all human beings are biologically of the same race, but the word is used to differentiate ethnic groups and also in terms like 'racial discrimination'
Racism	the belief that one 'racial group' is inferior to another and the practices of the dominant group to maintain the inferior position of the dominated group. Often defined as a combination of power, prejudice and discrimination.
Refugee	someone who has left his or her homeland because of fear of persecution. Persons lacking the protection of their own country
Pogrom	organised massacre (of Jews)
Propaganda	opinions promoted in a biased or false way

Resistance	secret organisation in an enemy or occupied country, working for liberation
Romany	language and culture of Gypsies
Rosh Hashana	Hebrew for 'Head of the Year'. It is the Jewish New Year, to commemorate the creation of the world. 1992 was the year 5752 in the Jewish calendar
SA	*Sturmabteilung*, Storm Troopers. Organised to protect Nazi rallies and to terrorise those not sympathetic to the Nazis
Scapegoat	a person or people blamed or punished for things done by others
Socialism	a system based on public ownership of the means of production and distribution
Sonderkommando	death camp inmates assigned to take bodies from the gas chambers to the crematorium
SS	*Schutzstaffel*, protection squad. Established in 1925 as Nazi protection squads, included the *Gestapo*. Squads that ran the Nazi concentration and death camps; and squads that fought with the German Army
Star of David	the Shield of David became a Jewish symbol after the 17th century. It is occasionally found in early synagogues, but also on Roman pavements and in Christian churches. David was the King of the Jews in 1000 BCE
Talmud	the book of traditional Jewish laws
Totalitarian	a political system based on the absolute power of a single party or dictator
Wehrmacht	the German Army
Yiddish	a language based on German, Hebrew and Balto-Slavic languages, spoken by the majority of Jews in Eastern Europe before the Second World War
Yom Kippur	the Jewish Day of Atonement. A fast day, to confess sins and ask forgiveness. Ten days after *Rosh Hashana*, this is the holiest day in the Jewish year
Zionism	a movement originally aimed at re-establishing a Jewish state in Palestine. Zion is one of the hills of Jerusalem on which the city of David was built and which became the centre of Jewish life and worship

Appendix 1

Factors which enabled the Holocaust to happen

Pre-conditions eg. Brutality, racism, genocide, war, revolution.

3000 years of anti-Semitism, particularly in Christian Europe.

Hitler-Dictator

Treaty of Versailles

Economic depression

Silence, lack of protest, lack of participation

Propaganda

Obedience

Indifference

Small steps to genocide

Self-preservation

Power of Nazis

Dogma

Social Darwinism

Technology and Communication

Ability to mobilise

Elimination of opposition

Anti-communism

Appeasement

Apathy

'Not our problem'

Role of Churches

Dehumanisation, brutalisation

Bureaucracy — distancing

Death camps in Poland

Collaboration

Idea of non-citizens

Appendix 2

Examples of National Curriculum Application

Chapter	Concepts	Attainment Targets			Dimensions	Cross-curricular Themes	Links with other subjects
		Knowledge and understanding of history	Interpretation of history	The use of historical sources			
One The Jews of Europe from BCE to 1918	Migration Antisemitism Diaspora Scapegoat	Origins of Judaism German Nationalism	Historians' analysis of antisemitism	Old Testament Oral testimony Contemporary pictures	Multi-ethnic Europe and Middle East Recognising stereotypes and racism	Medieval Economy Effects of industrialisation on society	Geography RE Government/ Church power Jewish culture
Two The Gypsies of Europe 1400–1928	Traveller Tolerance vs Acceptance Power	Stereotypes and persecution of Gypsies Difficulty of resistance	Problem of relying on mainly non-Gypsy sources	Photos Laws Maps	Examining own attitudes towards Gypsies Diversity of Gypsy communities	Lifestyles Varied responses to arrival of Gypsies	Gypsy culture RE Role of songs and stories
Five The Nazis in power	Totalitarianism Indoctrination Propaganda Terror	Control of education, law, church Development of antisemitism Attack on blacks, gays, people with disabilities	Contemporary explanations of the Nazi era	Nazi text books Accounts of Nazi supporters and opponents	Role of education and youth movements Role of fear Division of labour Jews who felt totally German Jesse Owens	Understanding democracy and totalitarianism Removal of citizenship Attitudes towards disability Nazi takeover of trade unions	Maths Media Studies Sociology Art PE

All chapters between them, encourage the skills of oracy, group work, information handling, study skills, communication, numeracy, literacy, drama, empathy, IT, problem-solving, mapwork, making links, graphics, critical thinking, review and assimilation of information.

Chapter	Concepts	Attainment Targets			Dimensions	Cross-curricular Themes	Links with other subjects
		Knowledge and understanding of history	*Interpretation of history*	*The use of historical sources*			
Eight: Organising Genocide — the Holocaust	Holocaust Genocide Dehumanisation Obedience Brutalisation	Development of the 'Final Solution' Experiences of deportation and camps Role of nations other than Germany	Debate about whether Hitler planned the Holocaust from 1933 Extent of documentation of the Holocaust	Survivors testimony 'Faction' Diaries Poetry Drawings Interviews	'Choiceless Choices' Role of Nationalism within the Soviet Union Enforced separation of families Behaviour of perpetrators	Medical experiments Industrialisation of murder Role of businesses in the Holocaust (making gas chambers etc)	English Psychology Science Geography
Nine: Resistance, Collaboration, Indifference and Rescue	Resistance Collaboration Indifference Rescuers	The difficulty of resistance Types of resistance	Debate over importance of resistance Role of Jewish Councils	Jokes Posters Newspapers Novels	Question of whether e.g. train drivers were responsible in any way for the Holocaust Men and women in the resistance	Motivation of ordinary Europeans who became rescuers	Music English RE
Twelve: Then and Now	Guilt Revisionists Uniqueness/ Universality of the Holocaust	Effects of the Holocaust Links with modern persecution, racism	Historians' and writers' assessment of the Holocaust	Photos Documentary Politicians' speeches	Attitudes towards Gypsies, Jews, refugees today Milgram experiements — obedience Religious faith	Question of Europe/USA responsibility e.g. export of weapons War Crimes Trials today	Social Studies Politics Psychology Economics

List of works cited and consulted

Bartov, O. (1991). *Hitler's Army: Soldiers, Nazis and War in the Third Reich.* OUP.

Bein, A. (1959). *Modern Antisemitism and its effects on the Jewish Question.* (translation).

Ben-Sasson, H. H. (ed.) (1985). *A History of the Jewish People,* Harvard University Press.

Buller, E. Amy (1943). *Darkness Over Germany.*

Bullock, A. (1991). *Hitler and Stalin: Parallel Lives.* Harper Collins.

Chorover, S. (1979). *From Genesis to Genocide.* MIT., USA.

Clébert, J. (1961). *The Gypsies,* Penguin.

Davidowicz, L. (1976). *A Holocaust Reader.* Beacon Press, USA.

Davidowicz, L. (1975). *The War against the Jews 1933-45.* Penguin.

Foingold, H. (1970). *The Politics of Rescue: The Roosevelt Administration and the Holocaust 1939-1945.* The Holocaust Library, NY.

Fisch, H. (1970). *The Dual Image.* The World Jewish Library.

Frankl, V. (1962). *Man's Search for Meaning.* Beacon Press, USA.

Friedlander, A. (ed.) (1976). *Out of the Whirlwind —A reader of Holocaust Literature.* Schocken Books, USA.

Generations of memories: voices of Jewish women (1989). The Women's Press.

Gilbert, M. (ed.) (1964). *Britain and Germany between the Wars.* Longman.

Gilbert, M (ed.) (1965). *Plough my own furrow. The Life of Lord Allen of Hurtwood.* Longman.

Gilbert, M. (1986). *The Holocaust —the Jewish Tragedy.* Fontana/Collins.

Gilbert, M. (1988). *Atlas of the Holocaust.* Pergamon Press.

Gilbert, M. (1989). *Second World War.* Weidenfeld and Nicolson.

Gilbert, M. (1991). *Auschwitz and the allies.* Mandarin.

Gilbert, M. (1992). *The Holocaust —maps and photographs.* Anti-Defamation League, USA.

Gray, M. (1972). *For those I have loved.* NY, Little Brown and Co.

Grossman, M. (1970). *With a Camera in the Ghetto.* Ghetto Fighters' House and Hakibbutz Hameuchad Publishing House, Israel.

Grunberger, R. (1971). *A Social History of the Third Reich.* Penguin.

Heger, H. (1972). *The Men with the Pink Triangle.* GMP Publishers Ltd.

Heifetz, J. (1985). *Oral History and the Holocaust.* Pergamon.

Johnson, M. and Stern Strom, M. (1989). *Facing History and Ourselves: Elements of Time, Holocaust Testimonies.* Facing History and Ourselves, USA.

Kenrick, D. and Puxon, G. (1972). *The destiny of Europe's Gypsies.* Heinemann.

Kershaw, I. (1985). *Popular opinion and public dissent in Nazi Germany.* OUP.

Klee, E., Dremen, W., Reiss, V. translated by Deborah Burnstone (1991). *Those were the days: The Holocaust through the eyes of the Perpetrators and Bystanders.* Hamish Hamilton.

Koonz, C. (1988). *Mothers in the Fatherland — Women, the Family and Nazi Politics.* Methuen.

Kuznetsov, A. (1982). *Babi Yar.* Penguin.

Lanzmann, C. (ed.) (1976). *The Bird has no Wings — Letters of Peter Schwiefert.* Search Press.

Levi, P. (1958). *If This is a Man* and (1963). *The Truce,* Abacus Books.

Levi, P. (1986). *The Drowned and the Saved.* Abacus Books.

Liégeois, J. (1987). *Gypsies and Travellers.* Council of Europe.

Litvinoff. B. (1988). *The Burning Bush —Antisemitism and World History,* Fontana/Collins.

Loebl, H. (1989). *The Holocaust —1800 years in the making.* (unpublished).

Marrus, M. (1988). *The Holocaust in History.* Weidenfeld and Nicolson.

Meed, V. (1979). *On Both Sides of the Wall.* Ghetto Fighters' House, Israel.

Moorehead, C. (1984). *Sidney Bernstein — a biography.* Jonathan Cape.

Mosse, G. (ed.) (1990). *Nazi Culture.* Shocken Kuperard, NY.

Oliner, P. and S. (1988). *The Altruistic personality, Rescuers of Jews in Nazi Europe,* Free Press. USA.

Plant, R. (1987). *The Pink Triangle — The Nazi War Against Homosexuals.* Mainstream Publishing.

Prager, D. and Telushkin, J. (1983). *Why the Jews? The reason for antisemitism.* Simon Schuster.

Pridham and Noakes (1988). *Nazism 1919-1945 Vol.3, Foreign Policy, War and racial extermination.* University of Exeter.

Sereny, G. (1974). *Into that Darkness.* Andre Deutsch.

Sichrovsky, P. (1986). *Strangers in their own land — Young Jews in Germany and Austria today,* I.B. Tauris.

Smolen, K. (ed.) (1978). *KL Auschwitz seen by the SS.* 2nd edition, Oswiecim, Poland.

Stembach, B. (1986). *Da Wolten Wir Frei Sein —Eine Sinti- familie erzahlte.* (We only wanted to be free — a gypsy family tells its story), M. Krausnick (ed.) Beltz und Gelberg, Germany.

Stern Strom, M. and Parsons, W. S. (1982). *Facing History and Ourselves —Holocaust and Human Behaviour.* Intentional Educations, Inc. USA.

Suhl, Y. (1975). *They Fought Back — The Story of the Jewish Resistance in Nazi Europe.* Schocken Books, USA.

Tatelbaum, I. B. (1985). *Through Our Eyes — Children Witness the Holocaust.* I.B.T. Publishing, USA.

Trunk, I. (1979). *Jewish Responses to Nazi Persecution.* Stein and Day, USA.

Wasserstein, B. (1979). *Britain and the Jews of Europe 1939- 45.* Institute of Jewish Affairs and OUP.

Wiesl, E. (1974). *Night, Dawn, The Accident   Three Tales.* (translated from the French). Robson Books.

Wyman, D. (1984). *The Abandonment of the Jews — America and the Holocaust 1941-1945.* Pantheon Books, USA.

Recommended further reading

All the sources cited are recommended (see above). The following is by no means a comprehensive list:

Where Shall We Go? (1991) a 56-minute video co-devised by Nick Hudson and Carrie Supple. Esther, Harry, Liesl and Werner describe their experiences and the continuing effect of the Holocaust on their lives, in response to questions asked by school students. Produced by and available from Swingbridge Video, Norden House, 41 Stowell St, Newcastle NE1 4YB

From Bitter Earth — Artists of the Holocaust. (1988). 65 minutes. Available from Shooting Stars Film and Video distribution, 225a Brecknock Rd, London N19 5AA

Adler, David A. (1989). *We Remember the Holocaust.* New York: Henry Holt and Company

Arad, Y. (1987). *Documents on the Holocaust.* Franklin Watts, USA

Auschwitz — Yesterday's Racism; an ILEA teachers' pack (1983). Harcourt Brace Jovanovich

Bauer, Y. (1980). *The Holocaust in historical perspective.* University of Washington Press.

Bauman, Janina (1987) *Winter in the Morning.* Pan Books Ltd

Bayfield, Tony (1981). *Churban — the murder of the Jews of Europe.* Michael Goulston Educational Foundation, London

Bessel, R. (ed) (1987) *Life in the Third Reich.* OUP

British Library National Sound Archive (1993) *Holocaust Life Stories* — a National Curriculum teaching pack (and audiotapes and notes). National Sound Archive (see Useful Addresses).

Cesarani, David (1992). *Justice Delayed.* Heinemann

Fox, John (Ed.) (1992). *The British Journal of Holocaust Education.* London: Frank Cass

Frank, Anne (1952). *The Diary of a Young Girl.* Pan Books

Anne Frank — an information pack. (1986) Available from Tower Hamlets Arts Project, 178 Whitechapel Rd. London E1 1BJ

Anne Frank Journal available from Anne Frank Educational Trust (see address overleaf).

Hilberg, R. (1961). *The Destruction of the European Jews.* W.H. Allen

Keneally, Thomas (1982). *Schindler's Ark.* Coronet Books

Kushner, Tony (1989). *The Persistence of Prejudice: Anti-Semitism in British society during the Second World War.* Manchester University Press

Kushner, T. and Lunn, K. eds. (1989). *Traditions of Intolerance —historical perspectives on facism and race discources in Britain.* Manchester University Press

Landau, Ronnie (1992). *The Jewish Holocaust: a Universal Experience.* London: I.B. Tauris

Peukert, D. (1989) *Inside Nazi Germany.* Penguin

Richter, Hans Peter (1961). *Friedrich.* Puffin Books

Supple, Carrie (1992). The teaching of the Nazi Holocaust in North Tyneside, Newcastle and Northumberland secondary schools (a report). Available from Alan Heinzman, Education Dept, Stephenson St, North Shields, NE30 1QA

Yahil, L. (1991). *The Holocaust.* Oxford University Press

Useful Addresses

The Spiro Institute for the Study of Jewish History and Culture, Westfield College, Kidderpore Ave, London NW3

Jewish Education Bureau, 8 Westcombe Ave, Leeds, LS8 2BS

The Wiener Library, 4 Devonshire Place, London W1

Holocaust Education Trust, BCM Box 7892, London WC1N 3XX

Minority Rights Group, 379 Brixton Rd. London SW9 7DE

Jewish Programme Materials Project, 741 High Rd, London N12

Romano Institute, 61 Blenheim Crescent, London W11 2EG

Runnymede Trust, 11 Princelet St, London E1 6QH

Anne Frank Educational Trust, Garden Floor, 43 Portland Place, London W1N 3AG

Oxfam Education, 274 Banbury Rd, Oxford OX2 7DZ

National Sound Archive, 29 Exhibition Road, London SW7 2AS

Searchlight, 37b New Cavendish Street, London W1M 8JR

Commission for Racial Equality, 10-12 Allington Street, London SW1E 5EH

Amnesty International, 99 Rosebery Avenue, London EC1R 4RE

Institute of Race Relations, 2-6 Leeke Street, London W1 9HS

Facing History and Ourselves, 16 Hurd Road, Brookline, Mass, 02146-6919, USA

Joint Council for the Welfare of Immigrants, 115 Old Street, London EC1

Refugee Support Centre, King George's House, Stockwell, London SW9

The Sternberg Centre, 80 East End Road, London N3 2SY

Picture credits

The author and publisher would like to thank the following for permission to reproduce photographs, maps and pictures. Every effort has been made to trace and acknowledge copyright but in some cases we have been unsuccessful. The publishers apologise for any accidental infringement and welcome information that would redress the situation.

311

INDEX